ISBN 978-1-5277-6660-0
PIBN 10193933

1 MONTH OF
FREE
READING

at
www.ForgottenBooks.com

By purchasing this book you are eligible for one month membership to ForgottenBooks.com, giving you unlimited access to our entire collection of over 700,000 titles via our web site and mobile apps.

To claim your free month visit:

www.forgottenbooks.com/free193933

English
Français
Deutsche
Italiano
Español
Português

www.forgottenbooks.com

Mythology Photography **Fiction**
Fishing Christianity **Art** Cooking
Essays Buddhism Freemasonry
Medicine **Biology** Music **Ancient
Egypt** Evolution Carpentry Physics
Dance Geology **Mathematics** Fitness
Shakespeare **Folklore** Yoga Marketing
Confidence Immortality Biographies
Poetry **Psychology** Witchcraft
Electronics Chemistry History **Law**
Accounting **Philosophy** Anthropology
Alchemy Drama Quantum Mechanics
Atheism Sexual Health **Ancient History**
Entrepreneurship Languages Sport
Paleontology Needlework Islam
Metaphysics Investment Archaeology
Parenting Statistics Criminology
Motivational

THOMAS ADDIS EMMET, M.D.

THE JOURNAL

OF THE

AMERICAN IRISH
HISTORICAL SOCIETY

JOHN G. COYLE, M.D.
EDMUND M GUIRE.
VINCENT J. O'REILLY,

WEST 39TH STREET
NEW YORK, N.Y.
PUBLISHED BY THE SOCIETY
1919

From a Photograph by Anna Frances [...]

THOMAS ADDIS EMMET, M.D.

THE JOURNAL

OF THE

AMERICAN IRISH HISTORICAL SOCIETY

JOHN G. COYLE, M.D.,
EDMUND J. McGUIRE,
VINCENT J. O'REILLY,
} EDITORIAL COMMITTEE

VOLUME XVIII

35 WEST 39TH STREET

NEW YORK, N.Y.

PUBLISHED BY THE SOCIETY

1919

HISTORICAL PAPERS.

NECROLOGY.

American Irish Historical Society.

THOMAS ADDIS EMMET, M. D.

A Personal Tribute

BY THE REVEREND JOHN CAVANAUGH, C. S. C., D. D.

There is a charm that eludes analysis in studying the family history of a great man. To trace far back the thin streams beginning, perhaps, in obscure, far-away springs and trickling down through time by devious ways to meet their confluence in him, is an adventure that piques curiosity in both writer and reader. You always know a man better when you have got a close view of "the rock from which he was hewn and the cave from which he was digged." If Tennyson could truly boast "I am a part of all whom I have met" what shall be said of those mystic influences exhaling from great ancestry,—especially when they were of a brilliance to attract the eye of the whole world, of a splendor to fill even strangers with pride in our common humanity, and tinctured with such heroism and romance as the world can never forget. It is hard, indeed, to turn away from the fascinating subject of the Emmet family—from young Robert, "so intelligent, so generous, so brave, so everything that we are apt to like in a young man," so lofty and intrepid in facing condemnation by a judge and a political system that the world has never ceased to condemn since, the hero of every boy of Irish blood for many generations, a figure with an irresistible appeal to all who are sensible to pathos and romance and eloquence and sublime courage. It is even harder for the scholar to resist the temptation to exegete the life and the labors and especially the seemingly inspired utterances and writings of Robert's great brother, Thomas Addis Emmet, who was the chief philosopher of the glorious but ill-fated movement of which Robert was the man of action. The late Doctor Emmet always maintained, in his talks with me, that his grandfather was the greater of the two brothers in everything except the infinite pathos of a young man's death. And even those of us who can still be moved to tears and thrills by the eloquence of that unforgettable speech from the dock are constrained to admit that in scholarship, in vision, and in statesmanship the name of Thomas Addis Emmet has not yet received due appreciation from historical sobriety. It is hard, I say, to

9

turn away from these great names, and yet precisely because they are so great and because the world knows them so well (largely through the reverential devotion of the subject of this sketch) we must for the present resist the temptation.

Even Doctor John Patten Emmet and Mary Tucker, the parents of the late Thomas Addis Emmet, must be passed over with a mere salute; for them, too, the subject of these pages has pictured in words of such filial eloquence as the world will long delight to read. Their influence was naturally the strongest of all in his early days. From them he inherited directly the aristocratic complexion of his mind, his love of ideals, and the power to keep his face always uplifted to the stars while maintaining his hold on the solidities and the prosaic duties of life. Alluring as this subject is it has no particular place in this story.

When the late Thomas Addis Emmet began his work as a young physician he was appointed to the staff of the Emigrant Refuge Hospital on Ward's Island. It was an exacting and laborious position under the best of conditions, and for a young man with his fine conscientiousness and his sympathetic sense of the needs of the poor people who trusted in him, it had a heroic side. He never missed his regular visits to them even when every consideration of prudence and simple common sense would not only have justified, but dictated the omission. More than once, for example, when the ordinary means of transportation over the water were not available, in the depth of winter, with sharp winds screeching and broken ice menacing and the mercury crouching in the bulb, he went to the hospital in a row-boat rather than miss his visit to these poor patients. More than once, too, he narrowly escaped with his life, and I have seldom heard more harrowing stories than those which deal with the experiences and perils of these trips. It was characteristic of him to do this thing in his youth and to look back on it with serene satisfaction in his old age. I believe he was prouder of this early fidelity to duty than of the most brilliant triumphs of a later day; and indeed it was to the heroic discipline derived from these experiences and the addiction to incessant labor that went with them that he ascribed the powers and energies that made his life great.

Then came his providential meeting with Doctor J. Marion Sims who was just then one of the most dazzling figures in the medical world. He had succeeded in arousing great enthusiasm for the new Women's Hospital and naturally those who had been so generous in helping to upbuild it expected large returns in service. Probably no more difficult situation could have been selected for a young physician with only five years' experience, and yet the hospital was hardly open before Doctor Sims departed for Europe leaving Emmet in what was supposed to be temporary charge, but in reality with the entire responsibility for administering and developing the new hospital and for keeping those large promises to the world that had been made by the illustrious Doctor Sims in good faith and with an earnest purpose of fulfillment. Nearly sixty-five years afterwards he spoke to me with something like awe of the difficulties and the successes of that work in a new and almost untried field. "I was only twenty-six years of age at the time" he said "and if I had saved 2 or 3 per cent of the cases that came to me it would have been all I had a right to expect. As a matter of fact I saved 95 per cent." Then followed one of those beautiful moments of self-revelation when he lifted the veils from his soul and gave you a glimpse of heights and depths that the world never suspected. "I have always believed," he said in such a moment, "that God sent me into the world to do a special work. I have always felt I was only an instrument and that what others considered instinctive judgments and intuition and genius were direct inspirations from God. Instead of being puffed up by this incredibly great success I was humbled and brought to my knees." This exquisite humility and strong sense of the supernatural accompanied him throughout his life and made him a fascinating figure amid the bustle and worldly absorption of life in modern New York.

Of his work as the greatest of American gynecologists during all the years of his professional life I am not the man to speak. At great banquets held in his honor distinguished colleagues (their own names household words in many countries) paid enthusiastic tribute from time to time to their acknowledged leader. Before Emmet's time American medical men were known only as students and not as teachers in the great professional schools of Europe. It was his privilege to be the first American voice heard uplifted in teaching on the other side of the sea. His text-books, translated into many languages, became the scriptures of authentic doctrine on all questions dealing with his specialty, and he enjoys the dazzling distinction of being the founder (as I believe), and certainly the chief developer of the science of plastic surgery. The technician has long since done him full justice for this work, but surely a plain man may say his word in exaltation of the noble worker who has laid the women of the world under greater obligation than any other scientific man who ever lived. Hardly had he taken up his work in the Women's Hospital when patients began to flock to him from places as remote as India, and from that time until his professional life ended great multitudes of the afflicted and the despairing made a path to his door. It was not merely the deftness of his hand nor the cunning of his genius that crowned him with such great success. It was some such sense of universal priesthood in medicine as the Holy Father feels in religious work for the entire world. Money he must have, of course, to keep the great institution going efficiently, and from those who could give money in return for his wizardry and devotion he took his fee; but the great title to his service was the human need, and no poor woman ever had less than perfect ministration at his hands merely because she was without means. If men who deserve monuments alwaye got them in this hustling and advertising world there would bs lifted up in honor of Emmet a monument almost as high as the monument to Washington in the Capital of our country. Some day I hope that monument will find its place in the great City of New York to which his name lent such distinction, and when it comes it ought to come out of the grateful hearts and memories of American women.

Genius, being dynamic and not static in essence, always functions; and it seems to make little difference what particular engine is available at the moment. When Doctor Emmet, having passed the scriptural three score years and ten, retired from the active practice of his profession he plunged with all his natural intensity and enthusiasm into the work of writing. All his life long he had been in odd moments poignantly interested in the drama of Irish history in which his forebears had played such leading rôles. It was the call of the blood in the first place, and it was also a good man's indignation at the triumph of cruel domination and unjust exploitation of one people by another, that drove him with desperate enthusiasm to serve the Irish cause. All the energies of his vigorous nature, all the resources of his accumulated fortune, all the passionate impulses of his superb fighting temper went ungrudgingly into the work. His name made him the link between the ancient memories and the modern dreams. He was of the royal priesthood of political Ireland. He was the bard of her ancient glories and the prophet of her triumphs in the days to come. The scattered children of the Gael who enjoyed in this noble republic the liberty for which centuries of deprivation had made them ahunger and athirst looked up to Doctor Emmet as a clansman of feudal Ireland looked up to his chief. He was not alone, of course, in this noble distinction, but he held a special and peculiar place for family reasons, and his inspiring preachments carried with them not only the force of their own eloquence but a connotation which no other personality could command. By the leaders of the Irish cause "at Home" he was trusted and honored and deferred to, so that for many years he stood as a natural interpreter of one group of Irish-blooded men to another. Of apostolic journeyings and strategic councils he endured many, and to the end of his days there was no limit to his labors except the waning of his powers and energies. And as the great King Brian, in his extreme age when he was too feeble to fight or even to ride his horse into the fray, was borne by strong and worshipping arms among his impatient soldiers, the cross uplifted in his hand and his voice raised in encouragement and counsel, so the wasted and almost wraith-like figure of the venerable Doctor Emmet was a trumpet call and a flag for grave and earnest men to hear and follow.

His most permanent service to the cause, of course, is to be found in the books he wrote, the story of his illustrious family (as well as his autobiography) and his far-flung studies into the effect of English rule on Ireland's destiny. His familiar acquaintance with the best that has been thought and written about the old land was merely another form of the operation of the genius he had earlier manifested in scientific work.

In 1867 Doctor Emmet became a Catholic. His life, hitherto, had been so engrossed in benevolent professional work that in spite of the constant inspiration of his home and the radiant example of his noble Catholic wife he had never seriously confronted the question of religious thought as a science. One day he accompanied his wife to a little church and heard an exposition of the Catholic claims. It was characteristic of him that he walked straight to the priest after the sermon and demanded to be received into the church. Of course he was put off till he should receive full instruction and this decision he accepted not without some human grumbling, for all his life long he had been accustomed to deciding things quickly and carrying them out immediately. He had been fully convinced by the preacher that the claim to infallible teaching by the church was valid and everything else followed as a matter of course. In his case the business of instruction was quickly and surely accomplished, for the things which to the ordinary mind might seem obscure and questionable at once became clear and lightsome in his crystal thought.

From that time on his religious faith and his religious duties were as much a part of his existence as the breath of his body. He never afterwards experienced religious doubt, though he had little of what is called emotional fervor except a passionate devotion—characteristically Irish—to his rosary. One day in his very old age he discussed with me a religious scruple. "I hear a great deal about the love of God, and I fear I haven't any of it at all." He had seen so much of the external expression of religious feeling and enthusiasm in voice and nerves and manner that his own profound sense of the constant presence of God and his saint-like fidelity to every form of pious duty did not appear to him as worthy to be called love of God. When the simple explanation was forthcoming he gave up his scruple on the instant and fell back like a tired child on his pillow and was once more in perfect peace. That was the nearest he ever came to wavering.

Naturally so beautiful a nature and so strong a soul was rich in prismatic virtues. It would not have been at all surprising if his long career as a highly specialized surgeon had blunted his perception of the beautiful virtue of the modesty of the body, yet it was distinctly the contrary development that took place. One of the most delicate tributes I have ever heard paid to this—so at least it seems in our day—frail and ethereal virtue fell from his lips; it was such a tribute as could never be devised by human speech on the spur of the moment, but must inevitably be the fruit of a long life of chaste living and spotless thought.

Something of this beautiful quality constantly showed itself in his daily relationships. Nothing could exceed the mingled tenderness and manliness of his friendships with men. A mind richly stored with the spoils of thought and reading, and a long life of experience and observation and genius that cut deep and unerringly into reflection as his scalpel did in surgery,—this rare man was a choice and exquisite spirit in conversation. He seemed to have remembered everything, to have forgotten nothing. He spoke in measured and deliberate phrases with staccato distinctiveness both of thought and language. In his talk and in his thinking he combined (as all true art working in whatever medium always combines) the masculine principle of strength with the feminine principle of grace. In a multitude of ways he gave you the impression of an exuberant generosity, that was legitimately his by reason of his Irish inheritance and his early southern environment. But around all these things, and above and below and behind all these things, you got the impression of a very charming personality in which the keenness of a strong mind was delicately blended with the sympathetic tenderness of a noble nature. During the period of his gradual obscuration before his death he preserved his faculties in astonishing strength and clearness. A few old friends found their way in the private elevator up to the top of the tall building which now stands on the spot where once his hospital lifted itself up as the mecca of the miserable. Sometimes when his strength permitted in the later years he received you with an affecting touch of state and dignity, dressed in formal garb and seated in a big chair surrounded by his books. Most of the time, alas, during the last decade you found him propped up in his bed, but always steadily and cheerfully at work with his cherished manuscripts. There elect souls, faithful retainers,[1] were wont to find him, to see his face light up in a guileless smile, to catch the curious flavor of his unique humor and to trace in a hundred delicate shadings of thought and sentiment and spirit within a single hour all of the great spiritual and mental qualities that have made the Emmet family so brilliant in history. One night in particular comes back to me in memory now. The American Irish Historical Society in 1916 had prepared a great dinner in his honor. The scintillant Mr. J. I. C. Clarke presided, Chauncey Olcott warbled sweet and tender Irish songs, distinguished scholars and writers

---

[1] One of the most faithful was Miss Anna Frances Levins, who always seemed to me a figure symbolic of Erin, ministering to the great patriot. Few gave Dr. Emmet such unfailing devotion as this loyal spirit or mourned him with more genuine grief.

were assembled from far and near to pay tribute.   At the tables in front of them were gathered beautiful women and brilliant men.   At that same moment a similar dinner was being held in honor of Doctor Emmet in San Francisco.   A wire had been cleared through the entire distance from New York to the City of the Golden Gate, and each diner in each banquet hall was provided with a telephone receiver which enabled him to hear all that was said at both gatherings, separated as they were by four thousand miles.   To me was accorded the honor, probably because I was at the time president of the University of Notre Dame which had conferred the Laetare Medal on Doctor Emmet, of paying the personal tribute.   Doctor Emmet himself, though set down on the program as the guest of honor was of necessity absent, being confined to his bed not only by the infirmities of age (which would have been overcome for this occasion), but by a severe attack of shingles which inflicted the most exasperating discomfort; and yet though absent in the body he seemed all-pervasively present, so harmonious was the assemblage in its reverential worship of the aged patriot.   When my address was concluded the faithful Doctor Ford, his physician, spirited me away to Doctor Emmet's bedside for a moment's chat, while the festivities went on.   The wire between New York and San Francisco was still active and it was literally true that the continent of America over its whole breadth was at that moment musical with Irish song and eloquence.   Doctor Emmet lamented his enforced absence and then added with whimsical humility "I will have to be more careful of my soul than ever now for the old devil will be after me more and more on account of all this praise and honor."

Another day he summoned me all the way from Notre Dame, Indiana, on what he said was a hurried and urgent errand.   When I reached his bedside I discovered that he wanted to arrange the details of his funeral, though his death did not actually take place till some years afterwards.   His sons were called into the room and the old patriarch announced the arrangements on which he had decided.   The funeral must be held in St. Patrick's Cathedral.   Cardinal Farley would officiate.   If he were prevented it must be Bishop Cusack, then of Albany.   The other officers of the requiem mass were duly selected and I was named to preach the sermon.   The pall bearers were chosen and among them was one whom the venerable man believed, no doubt mistakenly, to have done him grave wrong. There was mingled mischief and Christian forgiveness in the way Doctor Emmet planned to heap coals of fire upon this good man's head. Again the curious humor: "Wouldn't I like to get a look at him out of the corner of my eye when he carries me into the church." When the time finally came Doctor Emmet was not buried from St. Patrick's Cathedral, for reasons which I never understood. Cardinal Farley did not officiate, for he had preceded Doctor Emmet to the grave. Nor did Bishop Cusack because he, too, had passed into eternity. Neither the officers of the mass nor the pall bearers were those chosen by Doctor Emmet, and I did not preach the sermon because I was in the California woods when Emmet died and did not hear of his death till after the funeral. Somehow it did not strike me as singular that all these directions went astray. It seemed symbolic of the period of obscuration in everything except spiritual and mental beauty that had fallen on his life in the final years.

But nothing could change or weaken the dauntless spirit of this glorious old man. When he made his will he included this wonderful passage embodying a thought I had often heard expressed in our chats:

From my Faith in God and ultimate Justice, the stronger is my belief in Restitution to be revoked by individual action, but inevitable for the punishment of a Nation. The Irish People have suffered from persecution to an extent never before inflicted upon any other race, and through many centuries have borne the burden in preparation for her own future government. Yet the atonement has not been reached, possibly yet due for the want of unity among themselves as a people, and for having ceased the use of their native language, God's special designation for them to indicate their Nationality. God has done more for Ireland than for any other favored territory of the same extent, and nowhere has man done so little. Intellectually, God has favored the Irish People as individuals, and scattered over the world at large, no other race has done more for the development and happiness of other people. Comparatively, England is in the decrepitude of old age, and living on the wealth of other peoples, while Ireland, after her regeneration will have yet to gain the vigor of youth, and in Justice England must some time become an Irish Province. This belief is a family inheritance. Let the student of Irish history study "The Decree" written during the American Revolution by Christopher Temple Emmet, the first of the family to question the Acts of England towards Ireland. With this belief there prophesied,—that a change is near at hand, I made this additional provision to my will and wish when it is probated that . this provision should be published as my last words to the Irish People, to.

whose welfare I have devoted the study and work of a lifetime. After my death I direct that my body be temporarily placed in my vault at White Plains until my Executor is able to arrange for a suitable place for my burial in the Glasneven Catholic Cemetery in Dublin, Ireland. As I grow older, my desire becomes stronger to rest finally in the land from which my family came. I direct my Executor to set aside the sum of Twenty-five Thousand (25,000) Dollars and to expend the same in making such arrangements as he may deem necessary and fitting for such interment, including the erection of a suitable monument to my memory to be made from stone, preferably gneiss, on account of the moist climate of Ireland, from my native land, said monument to be placed by the side of my remains in the Glasneven Catholic Cemetery.

Is this final wish of Doctor Emmet ever to be granted? Perhaps the hour is not far distant when some Irish artisan—to be forever distinguished in history as a person as memorable as that other who (in an hour perhaps not too remote) will take his stand on a broken arch of London Bridge to sketch the ruins of St. Paul's—will carve upon a slab of expectant and grateful Irish granite the epitaph of Robert Emmet. Perhaps the venerated dust of Robert Emmet may be gathered from this obscure resting place to be inurned underneath that stone,—for Doctor Emmet told me once of a tradition that there was one Irish family that knew the secret of Robert Emmet's burial place and handed it down with sacramental fidelity from generation to generation till the day shall come when the secret may be divulged and the sacred dust gathered for memorial honors and reverential burial. That would be a suitable hour for the home-coming of him who may in a certain sense be called the last of the Emmets, who embodied in his life work their genius, their noble nature, and their passionate devotion to Ireland, who kept alive the fires of remembrance on the altars of the old-fashioned Irish patriotism. May the Irish sod, if so be, show a richer green above his grave, and may the blessing of Patrick, Brigid and Colum-Cille rest on his sweet memory!

TWENTY-FIRST ANNUAL MEETING OF THE AMERI-
CAN IRISH HISTORICAL SOCIETY, HELD AT THE
ROOMS OF THE SOCIETY, 35 WEST 39th STREET,
NEW YORK CITY, ON JANUARY 4TH, 1919.

The Meeting was called to order by President-General J. I.
C. Clarke.   Members from many States were present, including
a large number from Massachusetts.

Voted that the roll call be dispensed with.

Voted that the reading of the minutes of the twentieth annual
meeting be dispensed with.

Mr. CLARKE: Gentlemen, I have a report to make and I take
great pleasure in reading it to you.

REPORT OF PRESIDENT-GENERAL.

The year which has gone by—one of widely devastating war
abroad and of gigantic war effort here in which the valor, the
energy, 'the devotion, the brain-power, the muscle-power, the
money-power of the nation wonderfully conjoined,—has ended in
a peace bringing victory to our cause—the cause of humanity.
America may well congratulate herself on the result.   That the
armistice of November 11 will lead to a definite peace early in
this year is the firm belief of the best judges.   Such a peace as
may bring the right readjustment to lands and peoples and make
for steady progress of civilization is the ideal toward which we
are striving.   The two-million soldiers in training in this country
are already in process of discharge from army and navy camps.
The wounded soldiers from the front in France are returning home,
a glorious if pathetic stream.   Soon the American fighters themselves—two million of them—will be pouring back, while the
nation rearranges its civil life to suit the altered circumstances.
There is full faith that it can be done now as it was done at the
close of the Civil War in 1865.   We have, therefore, every hope
that the present year will be one of great home activity, the
resumption of individual effort taking place in the light of the
patriotism awakened by the war and, therefore, with a new sense
of historical values in the relation of events to their causes and
effects.   It is reasonably certain too that a new era of prosperity

will accompany this task of taking up anew the processes of civil life and workaday achievements.   In all this one finds cause for satisfaction.

Upon what more inviting basis could we look forward to the immediate future of our Society?   In the awakened and stimulated historical sense the Irish race in America has every right to share, and undoubtedly will do so.   And if our Society be rightly guided and administered to the full strength of its intellectuality, the result should be great in largely increased numbers, live and widespread interest in its work, and that solidification of assets which will mean continued, secure and faithful existence.

One great reason for this hope and trust lies in the fact that the call of America made vital and actual a superb movement of the Irish race in America in support of the war as well as a distinguished, a glorious participation in the actual fighting.   While it will not be possible for some time in dealing with the great record thus made to assign definitely to our people their exact share in the tremendous enterprise on behalf of human freedom, the American Irish Historical Society should work conscientiously to bring the great task to a close in a couple of years.   With our membership in forty-six states, taking advantage of the war tabulations by the general government as well as those of the states, joining assiduously in the work of other bodies with like objects, the work may be successfully accomplished.   I commend this task with all possible emphasis to the Society.   It will be the test of our worthiness, this writing of the new and splendid Irish Chapter in American History.   It should result in a compilation of the history of the deeds of the brave in the ranks as among the officers.   It should give as exact as possible a statement of numbers.   It should possess such a mass of collected lists of participants as to be a treasure house of names and locations of participants.   And not only on the military or fighting side, but among the men of our race who have wrought to great ends on the civil and constructive side.   The story for instance of our fellow-member, John D. Ryan's taking over at the call of President Wilson the tangled, wasteful and inefficient aviation construction, and with swift strokes reducing it to order and concentrated effort and directing it to massed production is surely a theme for our best pens.   And so in many other departments.   We want and should have them all.

Our true place in American life, our true level in American history must be stated without exaggeration and upon all the attainable facts. We have done much for the remoter past. Let us not lose step with the mighty present. From no finer result of historic acumen and tireless effort could we turn to the new task than from the volume very shortly to be published, showing beyond doubt the share of the Irish race in the War of the American Revolution,—the work of the historiographer of the Society, Mr. Michael J. O'Brien. It will challenge high authorities and prove its case. It will, I believe, be the final, unassailable word on its subject-matter. The opportunity to deal to-day with the great facts of yesterday is upon us. May we be worthy of it.

The report of our Secretary-General, Mr. Edward H. Daly, deals naturally with the facts within the immediate reach of the Society, and little is to be added to them. The opening of the rooms of the Society, giving it a dignified home and housing the books of the splendid John D. Crimmins' Library, as well as its own books, is a matter of the highest note. It is open daily and at the free service of members. It is presided over by the Assistant-Secretary, Miss Mary C. Donelin, who will assist all visitors, and all our members are cordially invited. It has involved an added expense, but, it is believed that when its advantages are appreciated, and our members rise as they should that the additional expense will be readily absorbed. The constant imperative calls by the government for the Liberty Loans, the number of calls by the great ministering benevolences— the Red Cross, the Knights of Columbus, the Y. M. C. A., the Salvation Army and the scores of funds covering a multitude of sharply appealing charities—all these told us that our activities in fund-collecting should be kept within bounds.

Now the lid is off. The Society makes bold to say that the Endowment Fund should be increased with all the energy possible. We have always been proud that despite our small yearly dues, the Society has never been in debt: that its Endowment Fund still stands to its credit. We have not increased our membership in the past year, but that we have held our own is quite a record in times like the year 1918.

Such a loss to the Society as that sustained in the death within two weeks past of Mr. R. C. O'Connor, of the California Chapter, our beloved Vice-President-General, is hard to replace. A scholar, a man of refined thought and expression, a dignified man, a being of genial soul and hospitable habit, and an enthusiast in the work of the Society, our thanks are due to the Nominating Committee in finding in Mr. Robert P. Troy of the same Chapter, a worthy successor to Mr. O'Connor.

That they have not seen fit to relieve me of the office I hold, and from which I have wished to retire for a couple of years past, I accept in the spirit they have stated it, namely that in this moment it is not advisable to make a change, and that hereafter the lists will be open wide as they should be.

It is a happy thing that Mr. Edward H. Daly whose affairs forbid his continuance in the Secretary-Generalship, to which he has devoted many tireless years, should consent to remain on our Executive Council. I thank him and all the officers and members for warm support through these trying times, and I close this report with the hope that we shall from to-day rise to the level of our opportunities.

Respectfully submitted,
Joseph I. C. Clarke,
President-General.

Mr. Clarke: The next order of business is the Secretary-General's report.

REPORT OF THE SECRETARY-GENERAL.

To the Executive Council of the American Irish Historical Society.

1. *Headquarters of the Society.* In March of 1918 the Executive Council hired rooms at 35 West 39th Street, Manhattan, New York City, at a rental of one hundred dollars per month for one year for headquarters of the Society, and installed a secretary-stenographer at a salary of one hundred dollars per month. This step in the direction of making our library useful to our members was deemed advisable to be taken then by the terms of the generous bequest by Hon. John D. Crimmins of his books on Irish history, literature and art "provided the said Society is prepared to receive the gift."

Considering that this implied a wish on the part of the donor that his books should be advailable for public use, the Council resolved to execute its plan for an administrative office with a paid secretary who would carry on there the routine work formerly divided between the Secretary and Treasurer's offices, and which the Historiographer and Editors of the Society's JOURNAL could occupy. Against the cost of these headquarters may be set off the allowance of fifty dollars per month formerly paid the Secretary-General for rent and clerk hire, and charges for stenographer, storage of Society's property and rent of rooms for meeting of the Executive Council. Mr. J. I. C. Clarke is occupying a portion of the rooms at a satisfactory monthly rental.

2. *Gifts to the Society.* The bequest in the will of Hon. John D. Crimmins of his library of Irish history, literature and art was the most important gift the Society has received during its existence. The collection has been received by the Society. A legacy of one thousand dollars cash was also left to the Society by his will. A resolution was adopted by the Council as follows:

At a meeting of the Executive Council of the American Irish Historical Society held at the rooms of the Society, 35 West 39th Street, Manhattan, New York City, May 3, 1918:

Present: President-General Clarke, presiding, Messrs. Barrett, Daly, O'Neill, Judge Lee, Miss Levins and Dr. Coyle.

Being a quorum on motion of Edward H. Daly, duly seconded, the following resolution was adopted:

WHEREAS, The American Irish Historical Society has duly accepted the bequest of the late John D. Crimmins of New York, namely his collection of books of Irish history, literature and art, as tendered by Mr. Crimmins' executors, and has taken possession of the same.

Be it Resolved, That the Executive Council make grateful expression of its debt to the memory of John D. Crimmins, its one time President, its valued, generous member and constant friend. In his gift of those books so dear to him and collected with love and care during long years, he rightly felt assured that they would find in our Society, caretakers and appreciators as zealous as himself. For the manner in which the bequest was made active with little or no delay, we sincerely thank the Executors—Messrs. Morgan J. O'Brien, Thomas Crimmins and Cyril Crimmins—and note with pleasure that the sum of money which Mr. Crimmins bequeathed to the Society will be paid over by them at the earliest moment of settlement of the estate.

Resolved, That the Executive Council in pledging itself to the care and housing of Mr. Crimmins' books recalls a certain proviso of his will, and it is the sense of this Council, that should this Society fail to maintain said collection, the Society will bear in mind the wish of Mr. Crimmins, expressed in his will, that the collection be kept together in the Catholic University of America at Washington, D. C.

Since the last report of the Secretary the following books have been received and acknowledgment made to the donors:

California, University of.
Publications in History, "The Name California," Vol. 4, No. 4.
"The Formation of the State of Oklahoma" (1803–1906), Vol. VI.
Publications in Zoology, "The Subspecies of the Mountain Chickadee."
"The Ethics of Co-operation," James H. Tufts.
"Educator Journal," Vol. XVIII, No. 8.

Free Public Library of Jersey City.
"27th Annual Report of the Board of Trustees."

Library of Congress.
"Handbook of Manuscripts."
"Report of the Librarian."
"Check List of Collections of Personal Papers."
"Check List of the Literature and Other Material on the European War."
"Supplementary List of Publications, since January, 1917."

Maher, Stephen J.
"The Sister of a Certain Soldier."

Minnesota Historical Society.
"Minnesota History Bulletin," Vol. 2, Nos. 4, 5, 6 and 7.

Missouri, State Historical Society.
"The Missouri Historical Review," Vol. XII, 2, 3, 4; Vol. XIII, 1.

Newport Historical Society.
"Bulletin No. 24."
"The Romance of Newport."
"The Coddington Portrait."
"Higher Education and Business Standards."
"Creating Capital."
"Bulletin No. 25."
"Bulletin No. 26."
"Bulletin, Oct. 1918."

Society, Sons of the Revolution in the State of California.
"The Liberty Bell."

Stern, Leon.
"Address of Charles L. Brown upon County Donegal."

Texas State Historical Association, The.
"The Southwestern Historical Quarterly," Vol. XXI, 3, 4; Vol. XXII, 1, 2.

War, Pamphlets Concerning.
"A Declaration of Interdependence," the Library of War Literature.
Lichnowsky, Prince.
"My Mission to London, 1912–1914."
Muhlon, Dr.
"Revelations by an Ex-Director of Krupp's."
Smith, Rev. Sir Geo. Adam.
"Syria and the Holy Land."

Oliver, F. S.
"The Irish Question."
"Summary of Constitutional Reforms for India."
Grey, Viscount.
"The League of Nations."
Rockefeller, John D., Jr.
"Brotherhood of Men and Nations."
Kahn, Otto H.
"When the Tide Turned."
Hill, G. F., M. A.
"The Commemorative Medal in the Service of Germany.
McCurdy, Chas. A., M. P.
"A Clean Peace."
Dixon, Prof. W. Macneile.
"Reports on British Prison-Camps in India and Burma."
Washington University State Historical Society.
"The Washington Historical Quarterly," Vol. IX, No. 1, 2, 3, 4.
Wisconsin, State Historical Society of.
"The Wisconsin Magazine of History," Vol. 1, No. 4; Vol. 11, No. 1, 2.
Purchased by Society.
Hackett, Francis.
"Ireland."

3. *Meetings of the Executive Council.* The Executive Council held four meetings at the rooms of the Society since the last annual meeting of the Society.

4. *Membership.* The total membership of the Society is now 1,318, consisting of 5 honorary, 113 life and 1,200 annual members. Forty-three members were elected since the Secretary's last annual report; 25 resignations and 40 deaths were reported to the Secretary during the same period, showing a net loss in membership of 22. This condition is normal by reason of the lack of interest in history while great events are occurring.

5. *Other Activities.* The successful dinner held on January 5, 1918, at the Waldorf-Astoria, at which the note of patriotism and service was sounded throughout, was the only public exercise held during 1918. The omission of the Field Day in the autumn was due to the anxious times now happily past.

Appreciation is due for the competent services of Miss Mary C. Donelin, the secretary in charge of the rooms of the Society.

Respectfully submitted,
EDWARD H. DALY,
Secretary-General.

January 4, 1919.

Mr. CLARKE: I want to say a word and express our thanks for Mr. Daly's services. We can't let him depart from this office, even if he becomes a member of the Executive Council, without expressing in some way our high appreciation of his services.

Mr. DALY: I want to thank the Society for keeping me in office for seven years and to say that it has been an education and a pleasure.

Mr. CLARKE: The next order of business is the Treasurer-General's report.

AMERICAN IRISH HISTORICAL SOCIETY.

FOUNDATION FUND.

DECEMBER 31, 1918.

Balance as shown by last report..............			$719.13
Subscriptions received since last report:			

1918

Jan. 2	Stephen Farrelly...................	$100.00		
Feb. 13	Louis D. Conley..................	100.00		
			$200.00	
	Received from other sources:			
	Transfer from General Fund..............	1,000.00		
	Interest bank balances...................	46.71		
	Total receipts.......................		1,246.71	
	Balance on deposit with Metropolitan			
	Trust Co., Fifth Avenue Branch........		$1,965.84	

ANNUAL REPORT OF THE TREASURER-GENERAL.

FOR THE YEAR ENDING DECEMBER 31, 1918.

Balance on hand at December 31, 1917, date of last report..................................	$2,372.32
Received since date of last report................	4,861.56
Total.................................	$7,233.88
Disbursed since date of last report..............	5,048.51
Balance of cash in hands of Treasurer-General.......	$2,185.37

ASSETS OF THE SOCIETY.

SECURITIES AND CASH of the Society in Treasurer-General's hands December 31, 1918:

Three New York City 4 per cent corporate stock for $1,000 each—due 1936, 1955, 1959.........		$2,988.06
Two New York City 4½ per cent corporate stock for $1,000 each—due 1960, 1962...............		2,004.36
U. S. Liberty bonds 3½ per cent of 1917.............		3,000.00
U. S. Liberty bonds 4 per cent of 1917–11..........		2,500.00
Furniture and fixtures..........................		945.00
Cash on hand—all funds—in:		
Metropolitan Trust Co., Fifth Avenue Branch.......................	$2,096.87	
Emigrants Industrial Savings Bank..	88.50	
		2,185.37
		$13,622.79

SUMMARY OF RECEIPTS AND DISBURSEMENTS FOR THE YEAR 1918.

RECEIPTS.

Balance on hand December 31, 1917.................		$2,372.32
Received since date of last report:		
Subscription to Foundation Fund...............	$200.00	
Life Membership fees—5 members..............	250.00	
Membership fees—old members.................	3,535.71	
Annual fees—21 new members......... $105.00		
Illinois Chapter—20 new members....... 100.00		
	205.00	
California Chapter members...................	180.00	
Journals...........................	1.55	
Quarterly Journals...........................	2.25	
Interest on bank balances.....................	77.05	
Interest on Investments......................	410.00	
Total receipts for the year.................		4,861.56
Total to be accounted for..................		$7,233.88

DISBURSEMENTS.

Printing Journal and expenses......................	$610.86
Administration expenses............................	1,645.11
Executive Council expenses........................	18.85
Advertising death notices..........................	81.65
Deficiency annual banquet 1917.....................	144.35
Expenses for annual banquet 1919..................	38.00
Treasurer's bond..................................	15.00

Historiographer......................................	375.00
California Chapter expenses.........................	5.00
Press clippings......................................	9.52
Miscellaneous.......................................	75.15
Purchasing books..................................	2.00
Engrossing certificates.............................	4.85
Furniture and fixtures..............................	945.00
Rent February to December 31......................	1,075.00
Exchange on checks................................	3.17

Total disbursements........................ $5,048.51

Balance cash on hand:

Emigrants Industrial Savings Bank......	$88.50	
Metropolitan Trust Co.—General Fund...	131.03	
Metropolitan Trust Co.—Foundation Fund	1,965.84	
		2,185.37
		$7,233.88

Mr. CLARKE: It is really a pleasure to hear such a workman-like report as the one just read by Mr. Barrett.

Mr. Barrett asked that a committee be appointed to audit the Treasurer's books.

Mr. CLARKE: The next order of business is the report of the Historiographer.

Voted that the report of the Historiographer be received and placed on file.

Mr. CLARKE: Now we must make a great effort to increase our membership. Now that we have a home of our own we can hold a meeting every night if we desire without any added expense, and I think if we work up this idea and if the New York Chapter takes hold in the proper manner we will double our membership in the coming year. We should have at least 15,000 members, and I am sure we can do it but it requires energy, service and time. We could not do anything last year because everywhere we went the men were away. They were in camps, in organizations, in the Red Cross and other places. But from this on we must work, because we will not be worthy of ourselves if we do not. We want to impress on the out of town members to to visit this office when in the City. I have a suggestion laid before me for a union of some other Society of this character to share the rooms and expenses of this office. I think if we look into this we will find such a one. I tried to get the Friendly Sons of St. Patrick to share this office, but without any success. Perhaps if they had joined with us we could have taken this whole floor, and if any other good Society comes forward and makes proper arrangements I think the Executive Council will be quite proper in accepting it. Now I urge the Membership Committee to get a larger number of effective workers.

Mr. O'Malley told of a scheme to secure membership. He also congratulated the Society on the reports, and suggested the only way to reach newspapers is through the medium of the check book.

On motion of Mr. Daly, duly seconded, the Treasurer-General was authorized to pay the Historiographer the usual amount appropriated for necessary expenses, or $500.00 for the coming year.

Mr. CLARKE: The next order of business is the report of the Nominating Committee.

Mr. Daly submitted the following report of the Nominating Committee:

REPORT OF NOMINATING COMMITTEE.

To Joseph I. C. Clarke Esq., President-General, and to the Executive Council of The American Irish Historical Society.

The undersigned, members of the Nominating Committee, appointed by the Executive Council to make recommendations for candidates for the various offices to be filled at the annual meeting of the Society to be held on January 4th, 1919, do hereby report the following names of members selected by them to fill the following offices, namely:

President-General,	J. I. C. CLARKE, N. Y. City.
Vice-Pres.-General,	ROBERT P. TROY, San Francisco.
Treasurer-General,	ALFRED M. BARRETT.
Secretary-General,	SANTIAGO, P. CAHILL.
Librarian and Archivist,	CYRIL CRIMMINS, N. Y. City.
Historiographer,	MICHAEL J. O'BRIEN, N. Y. City.
Official Photographer,	MISS ANNA FRANCES LEVINS, N. Y. C.

EXECUTIVE COUNCIL.

Hon. Chas. Scanlan,	Milwaukee, Wis.
Patrick F. Magrath,	Binghamton, N. Y.

Thomas Addis Emmet,   N. Y. City.
James L. O'Neill,   Elizabeth, N. J.
Patrick Cassidy, M. D.,   Norwich, Conn.
Thomas S. O'Brien,   Albany, N. Y.
Thomas Z. Lee,   Providence, R. I.
Patrick T. Barry,   Chicago, Ill.
Thomas B. Fitzpatrick,   Boston, Mass.
R. J. Donahue,   Ogdensburg, N. Y.
J. G. Coyle, M. D.,   N. Y. City.
Edward H. Daly,   N. Y. City.
John G. O'Keeffe,   N. Y. City.
Frank S. Gannon, Jr.,   N. Y. City.
Alfred J. Talley,   N. Y. City.
John J. Lenehan,   N. Y. City.
Edward J. McGuire,   N. Y. City.
Bernard J. Joyce,   Boston, Mass.
Louis D. Conley,   N. Y. City.
Thomas A. Fahy,   Philadelphia, Pa.
Michael F. Sullivan, M. D., Lawrence, Mass.

STATE VICE-PRESIDENTS.

Arizona,   T. A. Riordan.
California,   Robert P. Troy.
Colorado,   James J. Sullivan.
Connecticut,   Capt. Laurence O'Brien.
Delaware,   John J. Cassidy.
Florida,   J. J. Sullivan.
Georgia,   Michael A. O'Byrne.
Illinois,   John McGillen.
Indiana,   Very Rev. Andrew Morrissey.
Iowa,   Rt. Rev. Philip J. Garrigan, D. D.
Kansas,   Patrick H. Coney.
Kentucky,   James Thompson.
Louisiana,   James A. O'Shee.
Maine,   Charles McCarthy, Jr.
Maryland,   Michael P. Kehoe.
Massachusetts,   Wm. T. A. Fitzgerald.
Michigan,   Thos. J. O'Brien.
Minnesota,   C. D. O'Brien.
Mississippi,   Dr. R. A. Quin.

Missouri,	
Montana,	Rt. Rev. M. C. Lenihan.
Nebraska,	Rev. M. A. Shine.
New Hampshire,	
New Jersey,	Col. David M. Flynn.
New York,	Edw. J. McGuire.
North Carolina,	Michael J. Corbett.
North Dakota,	E. I. Donovan.
Ohio,	Thos. Plunkett.
Oregon,	J. P. O'Brien.
Pennsylvania,	Edward J. Dooner.
Rhode Island,	Michael F. Dooley.
South Carolina,	William J. O'Hagan.
South Dakota,	Robert Jackson Gamble.
Tennessee,	Joshua Brown.
Texas,	Richard H. Wood.
Utah,	Jno. J. Galligan, M. D.
Virginia,	Rt. Rev. D. J. O'Connell.
Washington,	William Pigott.
West Virginia,	
Wisconsin,	Patrick Cudahy.
Wyoming,	Thomas J. Cantillon.

OTHER VICE-PRESIDENTS.

Canada,	W. I. Boland,	Toronto.
Dist. of Columbia,	Patrick J. Haltigan,	
Ireland,	Michael F. Cox, M. D.	Dublin.
Australia,		
Philippine Islands,	Rt. Rev. Michael A. O'Doherty,	Manila.

FOUNDATION COMMITTEE.

John D. Ryan,	N. Y. City.
Francis J. Quinlan, M. D.,	N. Y. City.
Samuel Adams,	N. Y. City.
Stephen Farrelly,	N. Y. City.
Franklin M. Danaher,	Albany, N. Y.
Joseph I. C. Clarke,	N. Y. City.
Thomas Z. Lee,	Providence, R. I.
*Thomas B. Fitzpatrick,	Boston, Mass.
James Thompson,	Louisville, Ky.

* Dead since January, 1919.

Col. David M. Flynn,	Princeton, N. J.
Daniel M. Brady,	N. Y. City.
John J. Lenehan,	N. Y. City.
Edw. J. McGuire,	N. Y. City.
Jos. P. Callan,	Milwaukee, Wis.
Eugene M. O'Neil,	Pittsburgh, Pa.
Patrick F. Magrath,	Binghamton, N. Y.
Patrick A. O'Connell,	Boston, Mass.
Jas. D. Phelan,	San Francisco, Cal.
Morgan J. O'Brien,	N. Y. City.

Dated, New York, January 4th, 1919.

Respectfully submitted,

STEPHEN FARRELLY, *Chairman,*
P. F. MAGRATH,
THOS. Z. LEE,
ALFRED J. TALLEY.

On motion of Mr. O'Brien, duly seconded, Mr. Bernard J. Joyce was elected a member of the Executive Council.

The Secretary announced that he had cast one ballot and declared that the names read, together with Mr. Joyce's, had been elected.

Mr. CLARKE: I thank you for re-electing me to the office of President-General, but as you know for the last two years I have been trying to get out of the office on several grounds. The prime reason is that we want new blood in the office. We want new vivacity, new push. I might say that I thought to get a successor but did not succeed. Mr. Farrelly convinced me that I should hold on for another year. Now that we have a home of our own there is no reason why we should go all over town to hold our meetings. We have two million men coming from the other side and two million dispersing here and I am sure it is up to our members to take up our cause and compile the history of the Irish race in the present war.

Mr. Barrett suggested that we make known the fact that the Society is going to compile the history of the Irish and Irish Americans in the great war and that when such information was made known it would bring in a great many new members.

Dr. Coyle reported for the Dinner Committee. He stated

that they had invited some officers and men of the old 69th who would be glad to attend the Dinner, and that the following gentlemen would address the Society at the Annual Dinner: Maj.-Gen. J. Franklin Bell, Rev. Patrick J. Healy, D.D., Hon. Maurice Francis Egan, Maj. Thomas T. Reilly, Hon. Martin Conboy, and William P. Larkin.

On motion the meeting then adjourned till the afternoon.

AFTERNOON SESSION OF THE TWENTY-FIRST ANNUAL MEETING OF THE AMERICAN IRISH HISTORICAL SOCIETY

HELD AT 35 WEST 39TH STREET, NEW YORK CITY, ON JANUARY 4, 1919.

THE PRESIDENT-GENERAL: Invited Mr. M. J. O'Brien to read his paper on Franklin's letters.

MR. O'BRIEN: I have written a short paper on Benjamin Franklin's Irish Correspondence. It contains some facts that are not published in any history of the American Revolution. I found these letters at the American Philosophical Society. They are not embodied here. I have prepared a long introduction of these letters which I shall not read, the destination of that introduction being the JOURNAL of the Society. I shall, however, read extracts from the letters, and I am sure you will find them of interest, because they are not published anywhere in the world, except that the American Philosophical Society has published a calendar of these letters, from which I got the suggestion. The originals are in the possession of the American Philosophical Society.

I wrote under the name of our American Irish Historical Society to the American Philosophical Society, asking permission to take photographs of the most important letters, and they informed me they would be delighted to give permission, and I gathered from the secretary's letter that the name of our Society is pretty well known there.

This Society was formed in 1729 by Benjamin Franklin himself.

[Extracts from several letters were read by *Mr. O'Brien.*)

I did not have a chance to examine Jefferson's letters, but I am going to examine them before this document is printed in the

JOURNAL, and it may be that something will be found there indicating that Samuel Cooper of Boston sent Jefferson a copy of Molyneu's work, and I think we will find the first paragraph of the Declaration of Independence attributable to Ireland.

There are over 100 letters, and I copied only those from which I have made the short quotations, but among his correspondents was Daniel O'Connell.

MR. ROONEY: I think that we ought to express a word of thanks to Mr. O'Brien for that splendid paper. It is only one of so many contributions he has made. He is our great power-house; he is the man who is doing the true historical research, with details, with the proofs, and showing the data, and the letters. We are very fortunate in having Mr. O'Brien to do this. We ought to thank God that we have him, but we must not expect that Mr. O'Brien is going to live forever. We ought to encourage others to do this work. We have had some splendid papers and I think we have some very good papers to be contributed here to-day; but if we can encourage somebody else to take up the work as Mr. O'Brien does, I think it would keep our cause moving. I do not move a vote of thanks, because Mr. O'Brien is our own member and our own secretary, and he does not need that sort of thing; but I want to tell you what I think of it.

MRS. QUEENEY: Mr. O'Brien is the one shining star in the Society, and when I read that Lord Northcliffe and his band of fifty writers came over here and spent several million dollars in propaganda work in the last three years, it has occurred to me, why cannot the Irish Americans of this great country, numbering fifteen millions, I believe, be appealed to to pay Mr. O'Brien something like $20,000 a year, which he deserves, and employ him exclusively? In our daily papers, we are getting the most shamefully insulting advice and it is nobody's business to pay attention to it. Isn't this Society big enough to, at least, have one man? Lord Northcliffe has fifty. That is merely a suggestion, Mr. President.

MR. ROONEY: Mr. President, the good lady did not hear Mr. O'Brien this morning, or she would know such things would be attended to. Perhaps if this organization would send a committee to the newspapers showing them that anything we should send is authoritative and reliable it might change all this with our President to lead such a committee. I lay this before you just as a suggestion.

MR. MAHONEY: Mr. President, this, as far as I know, is the only organization of its kind, the American Irish Historical Society, which has as its task the unearthing and bringing to light of historical facts in connection with America and Ireland, and laying them before the whole world. At the present time, Ireland is one of those nations about which I have not seen much in the daily papers, since President Wilson went across the sea, as being one of the small nations entitled to self-determination.

This organization certainly is Irish to the core, and it ought to put itself on record and be a powerful factor in calling the attention of the American people to the fact that Ireland should be granted self-determination. Most of the other societies, Catholic University and others, have put themselves on record as demanding full self-determination for Ireland, as expressed by Congress and the President,—that Ireland should be included as one of the small nations as well as the Jugo-Slavs and Czecho-Slavs, and the Poles and the Armenians, and the rest. They want to make Ireland an integral part of England, which, I hold, should not be considered. Every country, it would seem, under the domination of the Central Powers before the war must get freedom, but any country under the control of little England must remain under the domination of England. Why do not the people in America of Irish birth come out now, as the Irish at home did in the last elections in Ireland, where they elected seventy-three members out of 103? Ireland cannot achieve her rights by force, but she can achieve her ends by right, as President Wilson has declared that all nations must determine for themselves how they shall be governed.

A short time ago a small delegation went before the Foreign Relations Committee in Washington, and the only dissenting voice against self-determination for Ireland came from a man named Fox of New Haven. He is the only man who opposed self-determination for Ireland, and when he was asked, "Whom do you represent?" he said, "Myself." What an immense man that Fox must be, representing himself as opposed to all the other committee delegates representing other societies!

I think at the dinner to-night that every member of this Society ought to come out for and vote in no uncertain terms, for self-determination for Ireland. It is only living up to our name as the American Irish Historical Society to pass such a motion.

MR. ROONEY: I move now that, to-night, a motion be brought forward, that self-determination for Ireland be endorsed by this Society.

MR. O'BRIEN: I make an amendment that this meeting of the American Irish Historical Society instruct its President-General to present the case of self-determination for Ireland and call for a standing vote on that question.

MR. MAHONEY: We will vote for it now.

MR. O'BRIEN: You will vote to present it now.

THE PRESIDENT-GENERAL: The question, of course, is really very vital to us all. The program for to-night is pretty full. It is for a very definite object, the celebration of the victory of the Allies over the forces of evil in Europe. If it is the good will of the Society that it should address itself to this question and it be done within limits of time, there would seem to be no objection; but the meeting is not going to be stampeded. It is perfectly within our province to talk of it now.

MR. MAHONEY: I know what is in the mind of the President, and it is quite proper it should be. The American Irish Historical Society will hold its annual dinner to-night, and we want to keep it along the line of the Society's work. We must keep it there, because you are strong when you hold it within these lines. We might pass a resolution here, and I think to-night it would be a very good idea to have the matter brought up in a very brief way and, within a very short compass, put the Society on record. Let the President-General introduce it in some way suitable to himself and suitable to the program of the occasion.

PRESIDENT-GENERAL: Among the speakers to-night will be Father Healy of the Washington University. His subject is "Ireland and Democracy." I have no light as to how the gentleman is going to treat it, but, at any rate, it seems to me that, at the conclusion of his speech, it might be practical and possible to present such matter as proposed in the form of a resolution or the form of a call upon the meeting to sustain the idea, only I don't want, and I will not preside over a meeting that is to be deliberately taken from my hands. I have conducted a great many meetings and I have always managed to hold my own, because I know what the dignity of the Chair requires. I know what the forces of speech demand, and if you put it in the way that **Mr.**

O'Brien has outlined, I will be very happy to fall in with that idea. I think that will be the practical and ordinary way to do it.

MR. ROONEY: Mr. Chairman, I want to suggest that the resolution be brought forward simply saying, "The following resolution was proposed and adopted," and read this resolution.

THE PRESIDENT-GENERAL: Well, we have not, as a matter of fact, adopted any such resolution. Let us first frame it. The Friendly Sons of St. Patrick instructed a committee to frame resolutions on the subject, and I was of that committee. The resolutions were formulated and we passed them around to the entire committee, and I think we signed it, every member. I signed for my membership, and that resolution stated the case of Ireland, and said, that, in accordance with the principles of self-determination, they urged upon the President of the United States to forward that idea in every way he could. That resolution was engrossed, taken to Washington by the Secretary and presented to the President. I have some means of knowing that the President has replied to some of these applications forwarded to him from all parts of the country stating his willingness and desire to accelerate in any way he could this idea. Of course, you will understand that the position,—it seems so to me,—has changed somewhat within the last three or four weeks. No such body of opinion was behind the idea then as there seems to be now, due to the recent elections in Ireland. They have 73 members of Parliament who declared themselves members of the Sinn Fein Parliament, if I may call it so, and it has always been my belief that the people of Ireland are the best judges of what is good for Ireland. I know that when I was working in the Fenian cause on the other side, we always resented what we called "dictation" from this side, even from patriotic Irishmen from this side, because, too often, they seemed to conclude, because they had been born in Ireland, or their fathers had been born in Ireland, or in England, that they knew better than we what we should be doing. We used to get surprising things in the way of recommendations from this side, that were not practical, and were foreign to our ideas.

I think that, within the lines heretofore laid down, I can very properly introduce the question to-night.

DR. COYLE: How would you suggest that the matter be introduced so we shall not go beyond your idea of the program?

THE PRESIDENT-GENERAL: What I want to avoid is general speech-making. I want to have the matter put in such shape that it can be disposed of in proper order, without undue haste, and without breaking out into a series of disorders as has happened sometimes.

DR. COYLE: The best way would be to pass the resolution here and then, at the appropriate time in the evening, report that it has been so passed and ask for an endorsement.

THE PRESIDENT-GENERAL: Why not do that? Let Dr. Coyle and Mr. Ryan repair to my office and frame the resolution.

DR. COYLE: And then the only question before the meeting to-night is its approval.

THE PRESIDENT-GENERAL: Yes.

(The committee retire.)

In the interval Mrs. Queeney urged that the Irish organizations should have a daily paper of their own.

THE PRESIDENT-GENERAL: The remarks in our proceedings, before Mr. Mahoney took up the subject of self-determination, had been directed toward Mr. O'Brien. I want to say that nobody appreciates Mr. O'Brien's work in the proportion that we of the Society appreciate it. It is not a question of raising a breed of O'Briens. They are not to be found. Before the advent of Mr. O'Brien into the Society, he had for years been devoting himself to American Irish History. Since he has come to the Society, we have managed to make it very fruitful ground for his labors; but we did not originate them; they originated with himself. Before Mr. O'Brien came, Mr. Murray, up to the time of his death the Secretary of this Society had, in some degree, the spirit of Mr. O'Brien; but the latter has proved to be the only man that really had that genius for exact research and exact report which make the historian. They are not to be found on every bush. With wise leadership and with some money, we could doubtless raise a breed of budding O'Briens, but it is a work of years and years. The great thing we need in the Society is members. We want members and we want money. We have been struggling along and have reached a membership of 1,300 members in the entire United States. It is up to every one in the Society to bring in one or two members, and, in that way, you can double it and treble it.

MRS. QUEENEY: Thirteen thousand would be a small membership.

THE PRESIDENT-GENERAL: Thirteen thousand members would be a small membership, but it would become adequate to a great deal of work. I may say that, among the historical societies of America, this Society is looked upon as something of a wonder. Why? Because with its limited membership and its limited dues and charges, it is able to accomplish so much. That has been due in large measure to the self-abnegation of the officers who have worked without pay, without hope of reward, without anything except satisfaction in seeing the work progress; but we need more active support. It does not do to attend a meeting here and attend the banquet in the evening and then go away and forget the Society for a year. There is no use saying to us, we must do more; we must have a daily paper, and we must have this and that. If we had the money, we could have them all. We made the commencement of the Endowment Fund previous to the last annual meeting, and it has been necessary to suspend the pursuit of a larger amount for the Endowment Fund owing to the various and numerous and heavy public demands upon the purses of the people. From the Liberty Loan down to the Salvation Army, they have gone on one after the other—Red Cross, Y. M. C. A., and Knights of Columbus—everyone had a "drive," but the Historical Society. We have reached a condition of peace. From now on, we should all put our shoulders to the wheel and bring members and money into the organization. The condition of the finance of the Society shows that what little we get we can care for. We show to-day a balance of $13,000 in the fund of the Society, which is a great deal for a little society like this. You have your rooms now for meeting. We need not go to the various hotels and restaurants and private offices of people. We have a room here where you can assemble and come and see your books and inform yourselves about the Society, and go out as propagandists. Do not let us henceforth bother ourselves about the number of propagandists other societies or other countries have. Let us have our own. Let us match them in that way, and then we will have big results. Nothing would gratify me beyond the fact of being able, as the President of this Society, to offer to Mr. O'Brien a handsome salary, so that he could devote his entire work to it. It is what we should do. Men of means have come here and said, "Why, Mr. President, this should be done," but they have not done it. Now, let us put them to the test, and see if they will.   Do not ask it on behalf of Mr. O'Brien; ask it on behalf of the Society.   We will see that proper use be made of it.

MRS. QUEENEY: Double our annual dues.

THE PRESIDENT-GENERAL: Then you will cut your membership in quarter.   You cannot do it.   We have not collected our dues for the past year from all our members.   It shows that the idea of increasing the dues just now would be very disastrous.

MR. MCCARTHY: Mr. Chairman, is it advisable to hold the election and the reading of these papers on the same day as the dinner?

THE PRESIDENT-GENERAL: It is not, and I would be very glad to hear from you on this.   The Society originated twenty-one years ago.   At that time, when a society of this kind held its day, people came from all over to devote the entire day to it, but in a city like New York it is impracticable.   We have never been able to make a satisfactory gathering at all three meetings. We have a small meeting in the morning and a small meeting in the afternoon, and probably a great dinner; and, even then, there are some who attend all three meetings.   I think it is a thing that ought to be considered in the coming year, the holding of the annual election and the annual meeting and the reading of papers on separate days.   I think it would make for the success of all of them.

DR. COYLE: Better to have the meeting and election and the reading of papers in the afternoon.   Then, everybody would be free and you would have a larger attendance from New York City.

MR. MCCARTHY: I should think if the annual meeting was called on a different day and also the reading of the papers and whatever business there might be of the Society, and then serve a little collation, if necessary; there would be a large gathering of the members and I think many could devote attention to it. The paper read by Mr. O'Brien is a masterpiece in itself, and yet there are not many of us here.   To come here in the morning and go home and dress, it is a little to much.

THE PRESIDENT-GENERAL: The proper way here is to make a recommendation to the Executive Council.

Mr. McCarthy moved and Dr. Coyle seconded a recommendation to the Council that the annual meeting be held in the afternoon.   It was passed.

MR. O'BRIEN: Mr. President-General, before I go, I would like to introduce to the meeting Mrs. O'Connor Olson, who has only recently heard of our Historical Society. Mrs. Olson is a direct descendant on her mother's side of the celebrated Roderick O'Connor. She signifies her intention of becoming a member.

(The President-General and the members present receive Mrs. O'Connor Olson and Captain Lawrence O'Brien gave reminiscences of the O'Connor family. One daughter of that house he was bringing to the dinner.)

The Committee on Resolution returned and presented the following:

"*Resolved*, That the American Irish Historical Society endorses the principle of self-determination for all peoples as enunciated by President Wilson and requests the President to support completely the application of this principle to Ireland."

DR. COYLE: Our idea was for the President-General of the Society to read that and to call upon the assemblage to approve it by a standing vote, without debate.

MR. ROONEY: I second the motion.

THE PRESIDENT-GENERAL: You have heard the motion as it has been read, and all who are in favor of that being read at the banquet to-night will signify in the usual manner by saying "aye."

The motion was carried unanimously.

DR. COYLE: I move you, Mr. President-General, that a copy of the resolution be cabled to the President of the United States, in France.

Mr. Rooney seconded the motion which was carried unanimously.

Dr. Coyle here read his paper.

AMERICAN IRISH IN THE GREAT WAR

BY JOHN G. COYLE, M.D.

(Read at the Annual Meeting in New York City on January 4.)

Because of the vast forces engaged, numbering something over 4,000,000 men, and the brief time which has elapsed since hostilities ceased, as well as the fact that complete casualty lists are not yet available, it is, of course, impossible to present a complete statement of the work of the American Irish in the Great War. Eventually, from the studies of the questionnaires filled out by registrants, from the reports of the various bureaus of the army and the navy, and from other governmental department records, accurate statistics will be obtainable and the history of the American Irish participation may be adequately presented. It will be the joyous duty of the American Irish Historical Society to prepare and to publish that history.

But certain features of the war, already known to us, present the services of American men of Irish blood in such striking and memorable ways as to require a brief outline at this time. Priority of service and distinction of service and sacrifice conspicuously mark the history of the American Irish in this stupendous war.

By vote of the Congress of the United States, supporting the opinion of President Woodrow Wilson, a state of war against us by Germany was declared to exist on April 6, 1917. That day was Good Friday, the day which is the anniversary of the death upon the Cross of the Founder of the Christian religion, Who prayed to His Father for forgiveness of His enemies. It is a day upon which no Christian desires to hold a thought of enmity or hostility toward any being made in the image and likeness of Almighty God. But it was on that day that the blood-lust and world-aggression of Germany compelled the United States of America to enter the war.

The very next day, April 7, 1917, the first American soldier lost his life in the service of his country. John McNamara, a private in the First Pennsylvania Regiment, was shot from ambush while guarding a bridge at Reading, Pa. Thus, the very first life given in the Great War by America was that of a boy of Irish blood. The first American officer killed in the war was likewise a young man of Irish blood, Dr. William T. Fitzsimmons, of Kansas City, Mo. He was killed by a German aviator who bombed the hospital where Dr. Fitzsimmons, lieutenant in the Medical Corps, was in service, although plainly marked on the roof were the great red crosses which proclaimed the nature of the building. The bomb killed Dr. Fitzsimmons and six nurses, besides injuring many patients. A memorial in honor of Dr. Fitzsimmons has been erected in Kansas City.

The first shot fired against the German forces was discharged by John Howard Pitman, a red-headed gunner from South Bend, Ind., son of an Alsatian father and an Irish mother. The shell-casing was sent to President Wilson as a souvenir.

The first hand-to-hand conflict on foreign soil took place in Lorraine on the night of November 2 and the morning of November 3, 1917. It is singular that at that time of the war all the soldiers of the Allied forces were on French or Belgian soil on the Western front. There were Belgians, French, Irish, Scotch, Welsh, Canadians, Portuguese, Russians, Siamese, East Indians, Moros, British and others engaged in that line. But the only non-French soldiers then serving on German territory were the soldiers from the United States.

The Germans came over in a raid with the intent of inspiring terror among the Americans and to capture prisoners for the purpose of showing the German people that the Americans were not invincible. A terrific barrage cut off one American trench section from all support or reinforcements, and when the Germans were sure that the trench was isolated they attacked, believing that the Americans, outnumbered forty to one, would surrender. But the American soldiers had not gone three thousand miles to surrender. They had gone to fight—to win or die. And they fought, and died. Three paid the last penalty that night. Their names are Gresham, Hay and Enright. The last of these three was a native of Jamestown, N. Y. and a resident of Pittsburgh, Penn., Thomas F. Enright, and of Irish blood. He is buried with the other two in Lorraine. Near where they fell the people of Lorraine have erected a monument commemorating the deaths of the first American soldiers to die in battle on foreign soil in the defense of the liberty of the world. In honor of Enright the City of Pittsburgh has changed the name of the street on which he lived to Enright street. Jamestown has likewise commemorated him.

Among the first French War Crosses awarded to American soldiers two were given to Corporal Frank Hurley and Sergeant George F. Dever, both of Irish blood.

The first Congressional Medal of Honor given in the Navy was awarded to Patrick McGonigal, son of William and Mary McGonigal, of Youngstown, Ohio. McGonigal was one of a ship's crew sent in a boat to rescue a naval aeronaut, whose balloon had fallen into the sea. The balloonist was caught in the network under the balloon and was drowning in the high waves. The heavy seas prevented the boat from reaching the drowning man. McGonigal plunged overboard, swam to the balloon, cut the imprisoned airman loose, and swam back to the boat with the rescued balloonist. For this heroic act he received the Medal of Honor and other rewards.

The first volunteer regiment to land in France was the famous Irish Ninth of Massachusetts, now known as the 101st United States Infantry.

The first engineer regiment to reach France was the Eighteenth, composed to the extent of 40 per cent. of men of Irish blood.

Two regiments known for more than fifty years as Irish regiments are the Ninth Massachusetts and the Sixty-ninth New York. Again and again during this war these regiments have been commended. They have been sent to Champagne, to Toul, to Verdun, to the Marne, the Ourcq, the Meuse and the Farm, wherever the fighting was hardest. They have served continuously in all forms of military service and hazard. Not only their line officers and their rank and file, but their chaplains, the Rev. M. J. O'Connor, of the Massachusetts Ninth, and the Rev. Francis P. Duffy, of the New York Sixty-ninth, have won military distinction as well as the gratitude and affection of the men. The Rev. Thomas J. Dunne, of New York, a chaplain of the 306th Infantry, has received the Distinguished Service Cross. Several other chaplains of Irish blood have been cited for bravery, among them the Rev. William J. Farrell, of Newton, Mass.

Not to estimate the contribution of chaplains of Irish ancestry and of Protestant faith, of whom there were many in the American service, it remains as a fact of common observation by soldiers and civilians alike that from 75 to 80 per cent. of the 1,000 Catholic chaplains with the colors were men of Irish names and ancestry.

The "fighting marines" won deathless glory in the Great War. One of the most dramatic scenes in history occurred at Chateau-Thierry when the American marines opened ranks to permit the French to retire, then closing their lines once more, went forward singing: "Hail! Hail! The Gang's All Here." It was the invincible courage, the unconquerable grit, the impetuosity and indomitable persistence of the marines and the other American soldiers that caused the Americans to hold every position under every conceivable difficulty, to fight through the Argonne forest, from one shell-hole to another, from one machine gun nest to the succeeding one, and to attack, batter through, consolidate, hold, advance again and repeat tirelessly, again and again, and at last break the German morale so that the final debacle occurred and Germany's hopes of world domination collapsed in humiliating surrender. The chaplain of the marines was the Rev. Father John J. Brady, of New York City.

To set forth even a partial list of American Irish officers would make the reading like that of a catalogue. Therefore, a few are chosen which are typical and significant of the whole.

The commander of the Twenty-seventh Division is Gen. John F. O'Ryan, of New York City, a member of this society, of whom the regulars, who do not take kindly to National Guardsmen, say admiringly: "He is good enough to be a regular." He has proved his worth as a disciplinarian, a trainer of troops for fighting and a commander of troops in fighting. Another famous commander is Gen. James W. McAndrews, now chief of staff with General Pershing. Gen. Francis J. Kernan, "the man who put the machine gun into the army," is likewise an authority on military law. Major-Gen. John E. McMahon was for some time in charge of embarkation and helped to establish that extraordinary record of sending troops across at the rate of 10,000 a day. Gen. Francis McIntyre was chief military censor for many months.

Hugh Drum, son of Captain Drum, Irish by blood, became chief of staff after General McAndrew was transferred, and received the rank of Brigadier General.

In the navy one of the most experienced and beloved chaplains is the Rev. Father Matthew C. Gleeson, who is Fleet Chaplain of the magnificent American fleet at anchor in the Hudson River. Rear Admirals Griffin and McGowan of the navy are the highest ranking officers of Irish blood in that branch of the service.

From inspection of the casualty lists, from the testimony of commanding officers, from the records of chaplains and others, one may conservatively estimate that 40 per cent. of the American forces was composed of men with Irish blood as a part of their physical make-up.

There were many notably large enlistments from certain families, among whom those of Irish names were conspicuous. Mrs. Dineen, of New York City, had six sons in the service, two of them chaplains, and Mr. and Mrs. Patrick Hogan, of New Haven, Conn., had five sons. Mrs. Brickley, of Boston, had four sons in service, while ex-Mayor William P. Connery, of Lynn, Mass., had two sons and three nephews.   James J. Hagan, of New York City, had four sons in the service.   Similar records could be produced from many parts of the country.   One case which drew from President Wilson a letter of appreciation was that of the sons of Mr. and Mrs. James H. McShane, of Omaha, Neb. Five sons enlisted in the army and the sixth was assigned to conservation work when he applied for service.   President Wilson wrote to the parents as follows:

"May I not turn from the duties of the day for a moment to express my admiration for the action of your six sons in enlisting in the service of the country?   They are making, and through them you are making, a very noble contribution to the fine story of patriotism and loyalty which has always run through the pages of American history.   Cordially and sincerely yours,

"WOODROW WILSON."

And when Mrs. Brickley, of Boston, was interviewed by a reporter concerning her four sons' part in the war she said: "As a mother I am proud to have such boys, and I feel they are going to be a credit to the country as they have been to me.   We shall be grief-stricken when they leave, but somehow I feel that they will all come back to me.   If not it will be God's will.   I am doing my duty as an American mother, and I know that my boys will perform theirs as Americans."

On April 1, 1918, there were 262 John O'Briens in the United States service, of whom fifty were married to Marys.

In service for the country in many other than military lines were many hundreds of thousands of American Irish, laboring with their fellow-countrymen for united efforts to win the war. John D. Ryan, a member of this society, rendered conspicuous and eminent service by taking charge of aircraft production and so systematizing, coördinating and directing the work as to elicit praise from our own citizens and soldiers and the commanders of the forces of the Allies.

It was a soldier of Irish blood who was first to die for America in the Great War.   Strangely, too, was it that it was one of Irish blood who was the last to die.   The Rev. William F. Davitt, of Holyoke, Mass., lieutenant and chaplain, learned on the night of November 10 that the armistice was to take effect on the morning of November 11.   He sought to reach the front to witness and participate in the scenes.   He walked as far as he could; he procured a lift by motor for some distance; he journeyed in the side car of a motor cycle for some miles, then trudged again. He reached the front in the morning and procuring a fine American flag he hoisted it to the top of a flag-pole shortly before the hostilities were to cease. He released the halyards, giving a joyous look at Old Glory, and as he did a shell struck him and killed him. He was the last man to be killed in the war. Priest of God, celebrator of the Holy Sacrifice, exemplar of patriotism, gentleman, American officer, he died beneath the Stars and Stripes, the flag of victory and freedom.

THE PRESIDENT-GENERAL: I am sure that we all thank Dr. Coyle for that very enthusiastic and warm tribute to our race in the war. All of us have been impressed by reading from day to day the list of casualties. Now, it is a curious fact—perhaps, I might mention it—that, from time to time, I took up the daily death list with idea of seeing whether "Kelly, and Burke and Shea," appeared in the one issue, and repeatedly I found them. The last list I saw them in was printed four or five days ago. The Kelly was from Illinois; the Burke was from South Africa, and the Shea from New York City. Surely, that tells something for the outspread of the race.

DR. COYLE: Mr. President, I was going to say, after we passed this resolution to-night and go forth, we are bound to hear from those opposed to Ireland's receiving self-determination and the right to choose its own government; we are bound to hear some comment as to whether or not Ireland supported the war as such, and, therefore, I think we ought to have the figures plainly before our minds.

By the testimony of Sir Eric Geddes of the British Admiralty, given in February, 1918, he said 170,000 men had been enlisted from Ireland in the army of Great Britain; that did not include Great Britain's Irish who enlisted from Scotland, or Wales, or from England. By the testimony of Major Ian Hay of the British Army (whose real name is Ian Hay Beth), of the first ninety Victorian Crosses, thirty-six were awarded to Irishmen, and, as every one knows, the Victoria Cross is the highest military honor of Great Britain. By the testimony of the Marquis of Aberdeen, Ireland had produced 173,200 soldiers. When conscription was passed and sought to be enforced, Col. Arthur Lynch, M. P., appeared in Ireland endeavoring to secure a certain number of recruits for the army, because it had been said, officially or unofficially, that unless Ireland produced a certain number of recruits—about 60,000—conscription would be applied. Now, up to the time of the closing of the war, 11,000 recruits had come from Ireland during the year 1918. It, therefore, follows that Ireland produced, by the testimony of purely British sources, 181,000 accepted soldiers and sailors in the war. The population of Ireland prior to the war was 4,400,000. What it is now I don't know, but I saw a statement that it was 4,600,000. I can't believe it, because that would necessarily show an increase in population, which would be the first increase in seventy odd years. If we take 4,400,000 people and work out what proportion 181,000 accepted soldiers represents, we may—in order to get it firmly before our minds—remember this, that the United States would have to produce 4,250,000 privates as accepted fighters in the war, every one of whom would have to be a volunteer, to equal Ireland's support of the war. This is only worth mentioning, Mr. President, because, when one goes outside, he may be told that Ireland did not support the war. That is the answer, that Ireland's contribution in which every man was a volunteer, was proportionately greater than the entire American armed forces, soldiers, sailors and marines, volunteers, regulars, and conscripts.

THE PRESIDENT-GENERAL: Have you any figures about the North and South of Ireland, Dr. Coyle?

DR. COYLE: Yes; up to December 1, 1916, the uncontradicted statement made in Ireland by the Irish leaders, also by Michael McDonogh, author of two books on Irish army service never contradicted by any British authority, and given upon the floor of the House of Commons without contradiction, was that of the first 154,000 accepted soldiers from Ireland, 100,000 were Catholic and Nationalists, not Ulsterites at all. Two thirds of that 154,000 were composed of those opposed to the Ulster Volunteers and Ulster Unionists.

MR. ROONEY: Mr. President, I am familiar, in a general way, with these figures, and I think they are correct. There is another comment to be made, which I think is worth making. At the beginning of the failure of the support of Ireland for the war—the beginning of the failure of the British government to keep its promises to Ireland (and this was a conspicuous failure of the government itself)—Lloyd George, before he assumed the Premiership, while Mr. Asquith was Premier, had been sent over to Ireland to try to get a settlement of the situation politically. In a public address, I think it was in the House of Commons, he referred to the ineptitudes of the British War Office in the treatment of the Irish regiments, and further referred to the fact that the Irish regiments had received no recognition whatever in the despatches on the front for their services. Following that, came the break-down of the Irish Convention, which, of course, was not a representative convention, but was heralded as being a possible solution of the political situation. Lastly came the report of the convention and the practical repudiation of that report,—the recommendation of the majority of the convention to the British government. So the last possible shred of belief in the good faith of the English government in its treatment of Ireland was broken down, not alone from its treatment of the Irish regiments that had gone into the war, but because of its absolute dishonoring of its own pledges, and its own promises in the political field, and as a result of these two forces, and the encouragement on the other side of the forces by Carson and a small minority in the North, even to the point of employing military domination of the country by the minority, supported by the English troops, all Ireland went into revolt, went into revolt in 1916, and it is in revolt now, and it will stay in revolt until it is separated from the British Empire. (Applause.)

CAPT. O'BRIEN: There has been a statement made here about a man living in New Haven named George L. Fox. He is a pedagogue, and strangers coming to New Haven to enter college sometimes employ him. He is a member of the Carnegie Fund Society. He is a pupil of Joe Choate's, and now that the Carnegie Fund has millions to promote an alliance between this country and England, its whole object is to belie the Irish and ridicule them. Some time ago, he went to Washington and before a Committee of the Senate, he mentioned that he did not want self-determination for Ireland, that the Irish were not with it; that they quarreled and did not know anything; and he traveled the country because that fund is at his back, with its millions.

DR. COYLE: I move we adjourn this meeting.

Motion carried. Meeting adjourned.

SPEECHES AT THE TWENTY-FIRST ANNUAL BANQUET
OF THE
AMERICAN IRISH HISTORICAL SOCIETY.

HELD AT THE WALDORF-ASTORIA HOTEL,
ON SATURDAY EVENING, JANUARY 4, 1919.

THE TOASTMASTER (President-General Clarke): *Ladies and Gentlemen, Fellow Members of the American Irish Historical Society:* I welcome you all from the bottom of my heart to the twenty-first annual banquet of our Society. Our Society becomes of age to-day, and as you may see, it is quite a sturdy young man, and from the indications present, it seems to be taking a bride or two, and I hope that in the future the growth of the Society shall be on a larger and firmer scale.

We have passed through a year of the terrible war, during which the demands upon the activities, upon the energies, upon the purses, upon the lives of our fellow citizens have been enormous. In such conjuncture the claims of a historical society could not, with any seriousness, be advanced. Therefore, the activities of the Society were judiciously limited.

But I have to say a good word, for the Society has not fallen off; it possesses 1,318 members in forty-six states of the Union. It has $13,000 in its treasury, and it has every hope in its breast that, this time a year from now, it should be increased three-fold. (Applause.)

In proportion as we have refrained from pushing the cause of our Society in the year past, we are entitled to press three-fold for members in the year to come.

We have accomplished one much desired end in the year gone by, and that is we have secured a home of our own. For twenty years, like the Jews in the desert, we wandered up and down in the city, having one repast in one hotel, another in another, and one meeting in one office up town, another down town, and a third across town; and, I should add, with the shameful condition of our books in a storage warehouse.

Now we have altered that. We have secured a home of our own, a dignified place, where the books of the splendid Irish library of John D. Crimmins have been installed with our own books; where the visitor is welcome; where you are all invited to come to read the story of our race, to instruct yourselves, and to cheer each other. We have now a meeting place for committees, and even for larger bodies, and I am sure that, with the impetus that the times are bringing to all things American, all American enterprises, that we of the American Irish Historical Society should share in the prosperity. It is really up to the members present, to the members all over the United States, to take up our cause, and push it forward.

I could dwell on this, but I cannot now go further than the salient facts, which are, that, out of so large a population of millions of Irish and Irish descended people in the United States, instead of thirteen hundred members, we could get along pretty well with thirteen thousand. If we had thirteen thousand members, you would see a very much greater output of the books and of the information of the Society. You must remember that every member you bring in, every five dollars added to our funds, ensures by so much you advance this spreading the light, of making "better known the Irish chapter of American history." (Applause.)

We have to-night with us, as we have had for years past, a gentleman whom I shall introduce to you later, whose work on behalf of original research of the American Irish type has produced a book that I will refer to later, and I simply say that it will be considered by you, if you please, as a splendid monument to Irish investigation, to Irish accuracy, to Irish truth, and the importance of this book should make it clear to every one here that each one should possess it. It will be published within a month, and I reserve to a little later any further description of the work.

Gentlemen, we meet to-night to celebrate a victory—in the largest sense a victory for humanity, a victory that has overthrown the seats of the mightiest criminals the world has ever known, a victory out of which, under God, shall issue a peace for the world, of justice and right. ("Hear! hear!") (Applause.) In a closer sense, it is the victory of America, the victory of four million soldiers and sailors, of a grand ideal, backed by ninety-six million men, women and children, who served and helped and paid as best they could. It is a victory for all Americans. (Applause.) Closer still, and with a keen thrill stirring the blood, it is a victory for our glorious flag, the radiant emblem of ordered freedom, the starry reflex of the Heavenly fires; it is a victory for the Stars and Stripes, "long may it wave, o'er the land of the free and the home of the brave." (Applause.)

(The orchestra here played "The Star Spangled Banner," the audience rising and singing the chorus.)

Closer, breathing hard anigh to us, filling us with pride and joy, it is a victory for the stuff, the stamina, the strength of the American soldier, the wonderful unheard-of complex of the American army, welded of forty-four races, but marching, drilling, fighting, conquering, carrying all before it, as one. We had staked all upon it. It stood up to the test. We asked for victory from it. Through fire and death, it answered our prayer.

And then—the deepest, warmest thrill of all—it is a victory shared nobly, shared devotedly, shared without a backward look in its superb advance by the flower of the Irish race that fought for us in France. Oh, gathered children of the Fighting Race! We thank you! We glory in you! We take you to our heart of hearts! Never, in the long history of war have your gallantry, your endurance, been put to a greater test and led to finer results! To a man we envy you while we embrace you as brothers in Granuaile! (Applause.)

I wish to propose the first toast of the evening, which we will drink with willing hearts: To Woodrow Wilson, President of the United States. (Applause.) ("Hear! hear!") ("The Star Spangled Banner" was again played, while the toast was drunk.) (A Voice: Three cheers for Woodrow Wilson!) (The cheers were given.)

One thing always disturbing on an occasion of this kind is the reading of a note of regret, but our regret at the absence of Major General Bell is one that I am sure you will all join in. The General, four days ago, was prostrated with an attack of the current epidemic, and has been confined to his bed since. He did not have us notified of the fact until this morning, because, to the last minute, he hoped that he would be able to be with us. The doctors, however, forbade it, and he sends his very hearty regret, something in which we certainly join, because General Bell is a fine soldier and a fine man, and the speech that he was prepared to make I am sure would have thrilled us with admiration of the eloquence and of the matter that he had to give us;

it was, "The Irish Soldier in the Great War and in Other Wars." His note, or rather his aide-de-camp's, says in conclusion:

He now finds, however, it will be impossible for him to be in any condition to leave his room by that time, and he requests me to send you this information as speedily as possible. He regrets exceedingly this occurrence, but feels somewhat consoled by the conviction that out of every hundred Irishmen attending a festivity of any kind, at least ninety-nine will be qualified to take the place of any speaker without previous notice. (Laughter.)

With your leave, I will direct the Secretary General to communicate your hearty sympathy to him and your hopes for his speedy recovery.[1]

Now, this absence of General Bell leads, perhaps, to a little change in the order of our speeches, and I wish to introduce to you a gentleman of the highest character, a lawyer by profession, of high standing, and a man who has made his mark in the community as the director of the draft in the five Boroughs of New York City (applause); the master and director, almost the Father Confessor, if you wish to give him a reverend title, of 189 registry boards in the city. I introduce the Hon. Martin Conboy. (Applause.)

SPEECH OF HON. MARTIN CONBOY.

AT THE BANQUET OF THE AMERICAN IRISH HISTORICAL SOCIETY, WALDORF-ASTORIA HOTEL, JANUARY 4, 1919.

Mr. Toastmaster, and Ladies and Gentlemen: Why, when the suggestion was made by General Bell, that out of a hundred Irishmen gathered together, at least ninety-nine might be found to supply the necessary oratory to take the place of the absent guest, you should have passed over the ninety and nine and seized upon the remaining one of the entire hundred and imposed the obligation upon him, is more than I can understand.

I am sure there is no one here regrets as much as I do that General Bell is not in attendance at this dinner this evening. If Captain Spaulding, who wrote the letter, explaining that the General's physical condition was such that he was unable to come to this gathering, had been thoughtful enough to have sent with the letter of regret the General's speech, so that it might have

---

[1] Sad to say, Major General J. Franklin Bell, U. S. A., Commander of the Department of the East never rose from his sick bed but passed away on January 6, a splendid soldier, of high fighting record.

been used by me, it would not have been so difficult to have engaged upon this undertaking in his stead.

I think it is very appropriate that I should say a word about General Bell, because I think that the success of the administration of the Selective Service Law in this community was in no small measure due to the splendid manner in which the Commanding General at Camp Upton, during the period of General Bell's administration, conducted the affairs of that camp. It was certainly desirable, and almost necessary, as you can readily understand, to have the best possible impression made upon the community from which these men were being taken, and General Bell was equal to the occasion, and to the requirements of the occasion. The camp was conducted upon such lines that the men were given the greatest amount of liberty compatible with proper discipline, and there was no camp in the United States where military discipline was better maintained than in that camp. He permitted, within the bounds of discipline, the men who had been inducted into the National Army, as it was called during his administration, to return to their homes as often as might properly be allowed, and he also invited the members of their families to come to the camp so that they might observe at first hand what character of institution the National Army of the United States was, and the effect upon the community itself of the impressions received by the visiting relatives and friends and conveyed by them to those who had not been so fortunate as to go there, and the impressions received by the men themselves, and expressed by them upon their return to their homes, created a spirit among the young men of this community that was of incalculable aid to us in the administration of the law. It was a farsighted policy that General Bell put into execution—a policy that I think entitles him to the thanks not only of this community but of the nation, because of its splendid effect upon the administration of the Selective Service Law in the district of its most extensive application.

General Bell had for his toast, "The Irish in the Great War." You know that is a much easier subject to speak about than "The Irish in the Draft." The draft was an all-inclusive, and an all-comprehensive undertaking, and it is difficult, if not impossible to single out for commendation the participation of any special

national group.[1] The achievements of the Irish themselves in
the Great War can be told in such stirring sentences as would
justify and inspire the highest flights of oratory. I feel that I can
do no better, in alluding to his subject, than paraphrase the
description on the walls of St. Paul's in London to the memory of
Sir Christopher Wren, and say, "*Si evidentiam requiris, circum-
spice.*" If you require any evidence of the accomplishments of
the Irish, in the Great War, look around about you in this room.

It has been my privilege to sit through this dinner with one of
the officers of the old 69th who spent five years in the organization
before its numerical designation was changed to the 165th. We
have also at this table, and will hear from him during the course of
this evening, a major in that organization, who was the captain of
the company that Lieutenant Clifford subsequently commanded,
and here in front of us in the persons of those wounded veterans of
the 69th you have visual evidence of the heroic devotion to our
national honor and the cause of Democracy of the Irish in the
Great War.

And now I shall speak of some matters that are more particularly related to the subject which the program indicates that I am
to discuss. Although the administration of the Selective Service
Law has practically come to an end and the labors of draft officers
have virtually concluded, the experience has been so recent a one
that it practically fills my mind to the exclusion of everything
else; and as I talk to you this evening, it must be in a rather
vagrant way about impressions that were gained in the administration of that law in this community.

I find it somewhat difficult to ascribe any particular phase of it,
any especial feature of it, to the Irish. This law made no dis-
tinctions between racial groups as such, and New York City is a
curious admixture of all nationalities. The President has referred
to the fact that in the city of New York there were 189 Selective
Service Boards. There were more here perhaps than there were
in any state of the Union except one. There were, upon the
classification lists of boards in this city, after the September 12,

[1] Since this address was delivered the second report of the Provost Marshal
General has been published. In the classification of aliens by nationalities,
Ireland has the largest percentage of total aliens in class 1 and the lowest per-
centage of non-declarent aliens in deferred classes of all the alien races in the
United States. (Second report Provost Marshal General [1919], p. 400.)

1918, registration had been completed, 1,483,000 names. The contribution of the city of New York to the military and naval man power of the United States is enormous. Before the first draft was made of the men within draft age the enlistment credits alone of New York City exceeded 32,000 men. To that number, there were added, by the process of induction through the local boards, 147,000 more. To that number there were added, by the process of voluntary enlistments, 45,000 additional; so that New York City, so far as men within draft age are concerned, stands credited upon the national books with a grand total in excess of 225,000 soldiers and sailors. That total does not take into account the men under draft age and the men over draft age who were in the federalized National Guard at the time that we entered the war and who enlisted subsequently in such organizations, the regular army, the navy, and the marine corps, before they were under any duty to enroll themselves among those who could be called for national service; so that it is a fair estimate to say that the city of New York furnished to the army and navy of the United States during the period of the Great War at least 300,000 men.

And these men were made up of all the nationalities that people the earth. The registrants of the New York City boards read the news of the day in daily newspapers published in this city in more than thirty languages; for, in New York City, we have a Japanese *Daily Times*, and a Chinese semi-weekly and a Chinese weekly, and newspapers that are published in Arabic, and at least six Italian dailies, and a string of Yiddish newspapers that would reach the length of your arm. I know of no more heterogeneous recorded gathering than that time honored one that is referred to in the second chapter of the Acts of the Apostles, gathered out there in front of the house in which was the upper room, in Jerusalem, from which the Apostles came down after they had received the gift of tongues and spoke to each man there present so that he understood him. Although that first congregation was composed, as Dr. Healey will remember, of Parthians, Medes and Elamites, and the inhabitants of Mesopotamia, Judea, and Cappadocia, Pontus, and Asia, Phrygia and Pamphylia, Egypt, and the parts of Libya about Cyrene, and strangers of Rome; Jews also, Cretes and Arabians, yet it was a homogeneous, solidified mass in comparison with the heterogeneous gathering that represented the contribution of New York City to the draft army.

These elements, representing the population of our great city, were mixed up in this wonderful alembic and compounded into the Army of the United States, the greatest army the world has ever known.

One day, about three or four weeks ago, I read in the newspapers that a Chinaman named Sing Kee had received the Distinguished Service Cross. He was in a New York draft regiment, and the auxiliary organization that had charge of the social affairs of that particular unit was unable to ascertain where that man had come from. His next of kin lived in San José, California. I knew that Local Board No. 94, with headquarters in Baxter street, had in its jurisdiction all of Chinatown, and I called up the chairman of that board and asked him if he had Sing Kee upon his classification list, and he said he did; and then I said, "Is he the same man who received the Distinguished Service Cross?" and he said, "Yes, he is the Chinaman." "Well," I said, "wouldn't it be desirable to furnish some sort of record of Sing Kee so that the auxiliary organization might know more about him?" "We shall do it if you want us to do it," said he, but then he explained that Sing Kee had exemplified Polonius' advice "beware of entrance to a quarrel," but when he had actually gone into the conflict carried out the rest of the advice and made the opposed beware of him.

You remember the lost battalion in the Argonne Forest, cut off from its organization, cut off from its supports, days almost with only emergency rations, weary, sleepless, hungry, and thirsty; it was a Yiddish battalion, composed of push-cart men and sewing machine operators and button hole workers, from the lower East Side of New York City. And so well had the leaven of democracy worked itself into the souls of those men who before they gave such splendid evidence of devotion to the cause in whose behalf they had enrolled, might have been regarded as the least desirable of soldier material, that when the blindfolded American prisoner brought in his message from the German officer, requesting them to surrender, they were able to manifest their attitude towards the demand in such unmistakable terms that Lieutenant Colonel Whittlesey could tell the blindfolded prisoner to return to the German officer with the message that he could "Go to Hell."

In the same connection, it is interesting to compare the "ill grace of anarchy and riot" with which the Civil War Conscription Law was received in this city, with the unvarying assistance rendered by these diversified racial groups, constituting the population, to the administration of the Selective Service Law of 1917.

The Civil War Conscription Law was passed on the 3rd of March, 1863. The Civil War had been in progress for two years at that time. The lists were not prepared until May 1st. The attempt to enforce the law began with the 1st of July, and on the 13th of July, when the attempt was made in New York City we had the draft riots. My father's regiment, the 37th New York, known as the "Irish Rifles," a two-year regiment, was mustered out after the battle of Chancellorsville. He enlisted in the regular army and was in charge of a recruiting office when the riots began. A crowd gathered about the building, where that office was maintained to secure men to protect the integrity of the American Union and the flag of the nation was displayed, and threatened to tear it down.

A more striking contrast than that, perhaps, is in connection with the entrainment of men under the Civil War Conscription Law and the Selective Service Law, which went into effect on the 18th of May, 1917.

It may have been the experience of some of you to have seen contingents of drafted men go away to the mobilization camps. If it was, you observed that before the time for their entrainment there were public demonstrations in their honor. They were fêted. Meetings were held, at which prominent citizens of the community made stirring addresses to them and the character of the sacrifice that they were about to make was extolled in the highest terms, as it should have been. When they were actually entrained, processions were formed, the civic organizations of the community acted as a guard of honor for the men, and marched to the places of entrainment. Bands played and banners waved and, as the men went away, there were cheers.

An old friend told me that in 1863 he stood on State Street in Albany and saw a contingent of drafted men marching down to the boat to come to New York City. There were no bands playing for them. There were no crowds of cheering friends. There were no banners flying. Those men were shackled. An armed guard was in charge of them. As they reached the place where this man was standing one of the number broke away and ran down Beaver Street and turned the corner. One of the guard on horseback followed him, a shot was heard, and the guard trotted back and reported to the Commandant that the man, who had attempted to escape, was lying in the street with a bullet hole through him.

In fifty-five years there has been a marvelous change in the attitude of governmental administration towards the people, and in the attitude of the people towards governmental administration, and the most sufficient and satisfactory evidence of that change is the manner in which the people received and assisted in the administration of the Selective Service Law. They established, so that the general truth is now conclusively demonstrated, that the people of the United States, under all circumstances, and in all contingencies, are fitted to be entrusted with the machinery of government and so long as that is understood, there need be no fear of inroads of Bolshevism among the masses of the American people.

I have brought with me this evening—because this being a historical society, it might be desirable for you to know certain things that are not commonly known—a statement that contrasts the manner in which the army of the United States was raised during this war and the manner in which the armies of England were raised, as typifying the differences, the different methods of raising of armies in the two great Anglo-Saxon democracies, with the consequent result, as you will observe, that the method adopted there was not so productive of beneficial results as that which was inaugurated here, and which, with greater efficiency than even the Prussianism of the Hun knew, produced the greatest army that the world has ever seen.

"On August 1, 1914, England had a regular army of 234,000 men, one-half of which was scattered throughout the vast expanse of her Colonial Empire. She had a regular army reserve of 146,-000 men available for call to the colors, but made up of older men, veterans who had completed long enlistment periods and had passed to the reserve. She had 250,000 territorials in a status like our own unfederalized National Guard—that is, obligated for home defence but without the authority which the National Defence Act gave us to draft them into the military service for all purposes—and, on the whole, the territorials were but meagrely trained. In all, England had a force on paper of less than 700,000 men on August 1st, and, out of this number could summon for expeditionary duty across the Channel less than 100,000 men knowing how to die, but little else in the awful carnage that awaited them.

"In this situation, what did England do? Lord Kitchener was appointed Minister of State for War on August 6th. On the same date Parliament authorized the calling of 500,000 volunteers to constitute the new establishment. On September 10th, an additional 500,000 were authorized. On November 16th, the Parliament had been asked for and had authorized 1,000,000 more, and an additional increment of 300,000 in May of 1915.

"There was, of course, a rush of volunteers following the declaration of war. The first 500,000 men were recruited promptly enough, in the first six weeks of the war. In the next eight weeks' period but 200,000 in all had responded. Then began the first frantic, fevered appeals for volunteers. A Parliamentary Committee was appointed and with citizen committees flooded the country with posters, literature and oratory. The superior age limit was raised, first from thirty to thirty-five, and then to forty, and height limits were twice reduced, householders were besought by personal appeals and otherwise to solicit members of their families to enlist. Every conceivable form of personal appeal was made to English manhood, through the press, the billboard and the platform, through organizations, through committees, and through individual solicitation. On January 1, 1915, results were totalled. The six weeks campaign from November 16th had netted only 120,000 additional men. After January 1st, the recruiting campaign was continued, but the flow of recruits was daily decreasing, and the cry from France for more and more men was but feebly answered. Yet exponents of the volunteer system called this result a triumph. A distinguished statesman of England was prompt to call it a 'German triumph which had meant the ruin of Belgium and the devastation of France.' Even at this early period of the war England was face to face with conscription and yet unable to command the necessary Parliamentary majority. The result of all the agitation was a halfway step—the Industrial Registration Bill passed by Parliament July 15, 1915, with ample disclaimer that it meant or even suggested military conscription." . . .

"The Parliamentary Committee, the citizens' auxiliary committees, working in conjunction with the army recruiting service began anew the cry for volunteers. Again the country was placarded with posters, the homes flooded with literature, the public harangued by recruiting orators. Parades, concerts, rallies and the personal solicitation of the recruiters put the country in an uproar. The drive ended on October 1, 1915, with the new armies more than one million short of their authorized strength." . . .

"On October 5, 1915, Lord Derby was appointed Director-General of Recruiting and with his appointment came the announcement of a final volunteer scheme called the 'Derby Plan.' I shall not burden you with the details of this scheme, except to say that all men of military age remaining on the industrial register were divided into two groups, married and single, and each of these groups divided into subordinate age groups." . . .

"An elaborate system of canvassers was again invoked. Advertising agencies again came forward and with a great fanfare. The final volunteer campaign began on October 23, 1915, confined in the first instance to 'unstarred' single men. The campaign was to have ended on November 30th, but was extended to December 15th. The men to be solicited had, of course, refused for over fourteen months to enter the service, in spite of every plea. Social ostracism was the fate to which the volunteer first sought to consign the slacker. Out of more than 2,000,000 single men only 840,000 attested. Out of nearly 3,000,000 married men only 1,300,000 attested. When the campaign ended and the results had been totalled, less than 600,000 fighting men had been secured and more than 1,000,000 single men had failed to attest. And so it resulted that on January 1, 1916, after seventeen months of war which had witnessed the disastrous fighting at Gallipolis Mesopotamia, and in the Balkans, and the deadlock on the western front, the new army of England was 1,700,000 men short of its then authorized strength."

It was after all this that the government brought forth its first draft act which was passed January 24, 1916, and made effective on March 2, 1916. These figures were not compiled by me. In fact, I have been reading for your information in this connection, from an address by the Provost Marshal General of the United States.

I bring these figures to your attention for a two-fold purpose. They may help you to form a correct judgment on those criticisms that have been made against one part of the United Kingdom with respect to the failure of the English system among the inhabitants of the British Isles. The failure was universal throughout the entire Kingdom.

I also bring them to your attention in order that you may have in some concrete form the difference between the system or series of successively failing systems that were attempted to be invoked for the purpose of raising the armies over there and the splendidly successful system that was able, before America had been in the war for one year, to put down American troops on the shores of France at the rate of ten thousand men per day.

And now it seems to me that it is fitting that I should close with a reference to the illustrious deeds of this organization which these young men, not one of whom probably was over the age of twenty-one when this war began, have accomplished. We knew that the Irish would prove themselves worthy in this war of all the traditions of the Irish in the American armies. So far as we were concerned, we took it for granted. The demonstration was something that we had expected. As evidence, it was unnecessary. The devotion of the American Irish to the flag of the Union had been already attested upon a hundred battlefields, to the undying glory of the Irish in the United States. It began with Bunker Hill and Yorktown, and it was carried through an unbroken series of valorous deeds and accomplishments to Chateau Thierry, the Marne, the Argonne Forest, and Sedan.

I feel that the draft may take some credit even in the accomplishments of the 69th, because I am told that the replacements of the 69th—the 165th—were with men who had been drafted into the National Army of the United States. Moreover the deeds of the Irish, as typified by the 69th's accomplishments, have obtained throughout all of the draft organizations. Wherever there was an Irishman in a unit of the Army of the United States, there was a man who would willingly pour out the last drop of his heart's blood to establish his devotion to the eternal principles of democracy on which this country was established, for which his forefathers had time and again made the supreme sacrifice, and for the vindication of which Woodrow Wilson, the President of the United States, is in France to-night.

THE TOASTMASTER: By contrast with the letter of regret of General Bell on account of sickness, it will be my pleasure to introduce to you a gentleman who has risen from a bed of sickness to be present. Thank God, he did not rise too soon; he will not have to go back on account of coming here to-night; but a gentleman of his standing, or his merits in diplomacy, does not need particular introduction through me. We know the gentle poet; we know the careful writer of essays; we know the teacher of scholars; we know the diplomatist who represented the United States for seven years at the Court of Denmark. We know the Honorable Maurice Francis Eagan.

SPEECH OF HON. MAURICE FRANCIS EAGAN.

"*Mr. President, Ladies and Gentlemen:* I felt when I was asked by your President to say a few words this evening that I ought to do something tremendously fine on the subject assigned to me, "The Martial Spirit of the Irish Race." I might have gone back in investigation of the career of that son-in-law of Noah, I think of the name of Mac Egan, who tried to assume the ownership of the Ark, or I might have gone back, with the assistance of my learned friend Dr. Healey, to the story of the gallowglasses and made it a story worthy of this occasion; but in my physical condition, I recall just an incident of my first and only visit, a delightful visit to Ireland. We had reached in our packet, Kingstown, and early in the morning, about six o'clock, I heard a silvery Irish voice say, "Ah, dear Mrs. Sullivan,"—it was the stewardess —"let me give you some good, warm water to wash your hands." And then a lady's voice replied, "Sure, my dear, it isn't necessary; I am going to relations." (Laughter.) And I really felt that, under the circumstances, not that the analogy is quite complete,—that, under the circumstances, I might be allowed to appear before my relations without such an arduous preparation.

For eleven years, I have learned by experience the real value of freedom. I have lived in a little country a night's drive from Berlin, under the very foot of the Colossus, where, every week and every month of the year, we never knew whether we were to be absorbed and made part of the huge Germanic despotism or not. There is nothing, ladies and gentlemen, makes you love freedom so much as to see the struggles of a little race desiring only the development of its own culture, of its own country, the use of its own freedom, in the clutch of a despot. We, whose ancestors are Irish, know what this means; but it has never been in our time brought so near to us as it was to me. I knew what they had suffered in the past because I saw here, in this little country of Denmark, in this little Danish-speaking province of Schleswig, what our ancestors had known in the time of Limerick and of Cromwell. Here, in the nineteenth, in the twentieth century, with the consent, let us say at least with the tolerance, of all Europe—and I learned one thing which is not at all a politic thing to say to-day, but, as I am entirely out of politics for the moment, I can afford to be honest (laughter)—I learned that before this war, there was no power in Europe which could be depended upon to consider for a moment the interest of freedom or democracy, when its own territorial interests were concerned. It was the United States that brought the spirit of altruism and the love of democracy, a democracy which yet, perhaps, needs to be fully interpreted into this struggle. Here was this little country of Denmark, geographically a part of Germany. In 1864, already, Bismarck, the far-seeing Bismarck, had determined to make the German Empire possible; it was merely a Prussian state at the time; and he fixed his eyes on this little country, largely because it contained the best sailors in the world and the Empire must rule the sea, and largely because it offered the opportunity for the future building of the Kiel Canal. So, he tore this little strip of territory from the Danes, who were among the most proud and freedom-loving people in the world—they may have acquired these qualities in their short stay in Ireland during the time of Brian Boru (laughter)—but just you imagine a little people—not on paper, not a part of history—but every day of one's life one saw the struggle of this little people, desiring nothing, no accession of territory, simply that they might stay, as I said a moment ago; follow their own culture, their temperament, feeling every day of the week that the next morning they might be Prussianized! In 1864, there was no power in Europe to help them. Germany, or Germany with the assistance of Austria, which has always been the tool of Germany, took this scrap of territory, and, from that day to this Denmark has hated Germany with all its heart, simply because it loved freedom, and has never rested without the cordial and fervent hope that that territory might be restored to it. It is not yet restored, but I hope that the time will come when all Danish-speaking Schleswig will be Danish.

There is a curious parity between the condition of this people and the condition of Ireland, and I think as I am the son of an Irish father, perhaps, as Providence is said to be good to the Irish, I was sent to avenge the wrongs which the Danes had done us some hundreds of years ago. (Laughter.) It was in this country that I learned what our ancestors had suffered and what the real value of freedom meant. Ladies and gentlemen, we here have been so accustomed to it that we hardly realize it, and it took this war to educate us in its value, and this war has thoroughly educated us in its value.

But when I went to Denmark at first, one of the greatest consolations was to find that there were Irish people there before me. For instance, there was a family of Oxholms. I was surprised that each member of this family of Oxholms had in his name "O'Kelly, O'Neill." The Chamberlain that presented me at court was the Chamberlain O'Neill Kelly Oxholm, and I said to him, "You appear to be Irish." "Oh, of course," he said, "we are Irish; our great-great-grandmother was an Irish woman." And one found, all throughout this country, the praises of the Irish and pride in the Irish. Probably one of the most beloved men in Copenhagen is the pastor of Hamlet's city of Elsinore— Father Flynn—an honest Irish name beloved by the Danes, beloved even by the Socialistic Danes. *À propos* of that, Father Flynn has a great bazaar of charity every year, and I happened to attend it at the behest of the various ladies and patronesses, and in this bazaar there was a tremendous cave and a fearful giant, which was considered one of the greatest attractions of the affair, and I happened to ask who the giant was. "That man," Father Flynn said, "is a good Socialist who always lays aside his prejudices and plays the part of the giant every year for me." And Father Flynn, like most Irishmen, has managed somehow or another, while martial in spirit at the right time, to be a peace-maker, and a soggarth.

I should stick to the text, ladies and gentlemen, and say something about the fighting spirit of the Irish, the martial spirit of the Irish, and I intend to do it. I hardly think that there is any people on earth who have been so little understood, so much misrepresented, as the race from which we sprung. We are all supposed to love fighting for the sake of fighting, and to fight merely for the sake of a fight.   Now, this is hardly true, because I think the whole human race loves a fight, which is a very good reason to believe that we are not at the end of wars yet (laughter); but it seems to me that the distinction—if I may be allowed to boast for a moment—between the Irish martial spirit—just a moment of pride, if you like—is that the Irish are willing always to fight for an ideal, to suffer because the martial spirit is as much evinced in suffering as in fighting, as in bold fighting.   In speaking of the fighting spirit, the martial spirit, I think that we often leave out what the Irish women have suffered in the past and how they have fought with their hearts and souls; and after all, when you consider the history of our race, one must remember that we fight because our oppressors left us no profession worthy of a gentleman except that of fighting (laughter); but the real fight of the Irish race has been always for legitimate liberty, for legitimate democracy, against the spirit of a false autocracy, which sometimes masquerades under the guise of democracy.

For instance, to-day, it seems to me there are two things— coming, as I do, from living so long abroad—there are two things that I find curiously misunderstood here; and one is the impression that there has been a change of heart in Germany.   Now, if you ask me, ladies and gentlemen, if I think of anything, what do I think of certain subjects during my experience, I shall say that I have ceased to think; to think to-day is to prophesy, and I am not a prophet; but I know this, that if to-morrow Mr. Erzburg, or the Central, or any Democracy of the Social group, should discover that the old cry of "Deutschland über alles" could be revived, they would vote out of their very bankruptcy their last cent to begin the struggle over again. (A Voice: "That's right!   That's right!")

And another thing, it seems to me that we, many of us, misunderstand really what we have been fighting for.   We have not been fighting for the democracy which is assumed to control Russia to-day and for the kind of democracy that exists in Italy, or even in our beloved colleague of France; we are fighting for, we have fought for, legitimate democracy.

As an example—perhaps it may be a rather shocking one—of the point of view of some of the democrats of Europe, I shall tell you a little story of what happened, just after the Russian débâcle in my legation. Naturally, it was my business to be acquainted with all kinds of people, from the Russian Bolshevik to the Czarina of all the Russias. Just after the downfall of the Czar, there came in to me a Bolshevik whom I had known for some time, an enthusiastic Bolshevik. He didn't speak any English and I didn't speak any Russian, so we spoke in French. "Ah! Cher ami!" he said, kissing me on both cheeks—which wasn't particularly enjoyed—(laughter) "we are friends; we are friends at last. I have never been in your great country, but I know the sentiments of your people. We have the same ideas, at last, at last we are brothers." Then I said to him, "What are you thinking of, exactly?" "I have come on a very important mission. I have discovered that throughout all the English-speaking countries, in New York, especially in London, there is what is called a Woman's Exchange. I know that in Copenhagen here your wife is a patroness of this institution; she, too, being an American woman, is emancipated as you are. I understand that as the old order has passed, the bad old laws that governed us have been swept aside; have gone; that the new day has dawned. I understand that the poor man now may have his rights. Divorce, under the old system cost too much for the poor; but now every man may have his opportunity. It has been explained to me that all I have to do is to deposit a small sum for a ticket to the Woman's Exchange, and, being tired of the woman with whom I am living, I shall see a number of photographs of the lady that I should like to live with. (Laughter.) I pay my fee and I choose her." (Laughter.)

Now, ladies and gentlemen, this must seem an exaggeration of the point of view of some of these amiable democrats who are supposed to represent the real democracy in Europe to-day. It is no exaggeration whatever. I know I have shocked the ladies horribly, but the truth is the truth.

Now, I feel sure that your boys and my boy, who is now in France, that these boys did not go into this war for the sake of mere fighting. They could have had a taste of that at an ordinary football game; but they went in heart and soul with the full spirit of sacrifice for an ideal, that ideal that forms the real martial spirit of the Irish race. They went in for freedom, for the honor of their country, and for the legitimate freedom of Ireland and all the little nations." (Applause.)

THE TOASTMASTER: We have been coming nearer and nearer to the goal.

We have with us to-night, as you have observed, a group of the wounded men of the 165th Regiment, men who fought in France, who have revived the glories of the battlefields of the old Brigades of two centuries ago that fought in the service of France. These men before us have added a new glory to the Irish name, to its fighting spirit. I give you the health of the 165th Regiment, and I call on you to stand and give them cheers. (Applause.) (A Voice: "Three cheers for the wounded of the old 69th, at the head of the table there!") (Cheers.)

And I call upon one of the men who led that regiment through the battles of the Argonne. I call upon Major Thomas T. Reilly, to tell us a little of his story. (Applause.)

ADDRESS OF MAJ. THOMAS T. REILLY.

Mr. President, Ladies and Gentlemen: I am sorry to state that, in my opinion, while Mr. Conboy started out to prove that he was the 1 per cent that General Bell speaks of and wound up by proving that he was one of the foremost of the ninety-nine, I am sure that I shall have to claim to be the 1 per cent.

Last Sunday, in the *Times Review*, I noticed a reviewer, who is evidently tired of hearing so much about certain organizations, stated, in reviewing a history of the marines, that, according to the writers of to-day in the newspapers, the armistice was entirely brought about by the sole and unaided efforts of the marines and the 165th Regiment, "which always must be referred to as 'the gallant 69th.'" (Applause.)

I am afraid he overstated the case—none of us claim that. It would be too silly. I don't think that any members of the old "outfit" ever came back with any such bragging spirit. The thing was too large. Of course, there was the British effort on the west; there was the effort of the French, which, when all is said and done, far outweighed any others, for they met the Germans when they were at their best; they fought them through four years; and though they were driven back by vastly superior numbers to the Marne in the first year of the war, and although outnumbered eight to five they then fought that great battle which turned the whole tide of this war. They caused the Germans to reel and retreat, after themselves being driven back for ten days. The French soldier will tell you that they owed that possibly to the old strategy of the open square that Napoleon invented. The French peasants (by the way, before we went over there, we had been reading before the war that France had lost its sense of religion, but the majority of us discovered that this was not so) the French peasants still maintain that the only thing that saved them that day was an act of God; and a peculiar thing about that battle was that before it was fought, General Foch called for the prayers of the French people, and, in his order of the day after the battle he makes a very pretty reference to the fact that the prayers must have been heard. That might seem strange to any one who thinks of these soldiers as simply killing each other; but you get a sense of the religious over there.

Now, to return to the 165th Regiment, we were only a small part of one division, the 42nd. It was nicknamed "The Rainbow." That division, with three others, saw more fighting than the remaining ones. In France the Rainbow was with the first four over there. These were First and Second of the regulars, the 26th National Guard of New England, and the 42nd. There was nothing, from the American standpoint, that the 42nd Division did not get into. And in every battle phase, the 165th was there. The men will never contend that they did all the fighting there, but one thing I will say for the old "outfit," they did all that was asked of them. They never did take a back step, and every time that they were put in, in the center of some of the hardest fighting there, they "delivered the goods." (Applause.)

I do not say this in a spirit of boasting, because we are not boastful about it; but it is a poor fighting man that will depreciate his own fighting ability, and will side-step and kowtow to the enemy; and I will admit that that old "outfit," after they got their men into training, had a bit of a swagger to them. We noticed that later, when we had lost the old men.

We assembled in Camp Mills, as most of you know, with the other elements of the 42nd Division. Then, suddenly orders came, and we sailed away to Canada. The First Battalion took boat at Montreal, landed in London and in Liverpool, and then finally reached France. The other battalions, several days later, sailed directly to France. The first place that the regiment hit was directly behind the Toul sector, which was finally to become the American sector.

Our greatest struggle, at that time, was with the French climate, with the housing facilities of the men, which were in barns, pretty open to the weather, and with the men's attempts to say the French word for "eggs." (Laughter.) As you would go around the small towns, you would find them in every house saying (imitating) "Oeufs! oeufs!"; the French people finally understood what they meant, and gave them whatever they had of that kind of fodder. (Laughter.)

We trained in that sector, and finally reached the trenches. Before I went over, I had a very vivid picture of the trenches. I heard the sad stories of troops from other nations as these stories drifted over here, and I thought they must be a terrible place. They were not so bad. There was many a time later when we wished we were back in those same old trenches. They have many advantages over the real warfare, which is the open warfare. There are two kinds of war: warfare of position— trench warfare—and warfare of movement, which is the only kind that wins wars, or wins battles. So, in our last stages, we sighed for the little wooded hills where we had our trenches, where the men had places to sleep, and could keep warm once in a while, and you could pretty well depend upon the food supply.

We went through all the phases of trench fighting. We went to a "rest sector" up in a corner of France, near the Vosges Mountains. The French and the Germans called them "rest sectors"; that is, when wearied after three and a half or four years' fighting, a division would be shot up, many of its men gone, they would then send the remainder to one of these so-called "quiet sectors," to rest, and they had a kind of gentlemen's agreement that they wouldn't bother each other much there. The Americans came in fresh and vigorous. There was hardly an American Division that came in that didn't change all that. The first thing we knew the American artillery wanted to try out their new guns, and the captains or some lieutenant over them kept lobbing over some "hot stuff," and our infantry men wanted to send over little patrols into No-Man's-Land. Thus it got so that in our restlessness we were "running around" pretty much. There were not many German patrols out, for it was a "rest sector." But it was varied somewhat, as our battalion found in the first rest sector they went into.

We had great fear of the gas. It was the thing that we feared most; it was the most mysterious to us. Towards the end we didn't fear it so much; we had become accustomed to it.

Our first experience of the trenches was on the sides of the mountains and anywhere from two to eight hundred yards away would be the enemy's trenches. You could hear the gas alarm go; possibly one or two shells would come over in the night. That alarm would be taken up for ten miles along the line. We were told to play safe. We did. The men would be putting on their masks even though the danger did not seem to be there. But the danger was there. The Germans in the "rest sectors" didn't fight so much with patrols; they had their favorite little weapon, the gas.

The Third Battalion went in and they lost about 450 of their men with a mustard gas attack in which the Germans poured about 2,500 shells in a small area. The Major of that Battalion and two Captains, with many of the officers and men were gassed and forced to go to the hospital. So, the gas deserved all the respect that we gave it. But yet, at the end, you would be surprised how the men acted toward things of that kind. In the last great forward movement of ours, shells would come over and spatter up the landscape. We would hear them coming through the air, or a dull explosion, and where, six months before, would be a cause of great alarm, we would all wait until we got a good sniff of it before the masks went on.

In the trenches, in fine, we had some patrol fighting, captured prisoners, went out on raids, lost men, and in the R—— sector, occurred the incident of which Joyce Kilmer wrote his little poem. There were twenty-one men and one lieutenant buried alive by a minnenwerfer attack. The minnenwerfers came over, smashed down the tops—they were flimsy dug-outs at best—and the men were never able to get out, and others lost their lives trying to dig them out. We had our casualties, yet, on the whole, it could be said to be just what the French and Germans called it—a rest sector—compared to what came later.

We were with the French all this time, and words of mine cannot express the opinion I hold of the French soldier. Our unqualified opinion of him—and I heard other men express it before I ever even saw them in action—is that he is the most wonderful soldier in the world. (Applause.) We had wonderful stuff, wonderful material, but, when all is said and done, the

Frenchman had acquired something in four years which it would take us another year to get. He was and is a finished product. Of course no nation's men surpass the "doughboys," as they were called, in the way of ordinary fighting men, in just dash and courage. They were even too rash. The Frenchman knew how to protect himself, and, when occasion called for it, he was as rash.

As to their staff work I think their high generals are beyond compare. I know every time we were under their dominion and received orders from them, they were works of art. Never was anything left unprovided for. They seemed to foresee and have an intuition which told them everything that will happen in the future, as Marshall Foch pretty well proved it within the last three months.

We left that trench sector finally and went to other sectors. We knew that action was ahead. The British had recoiled twice in the spring drive of the Germans. The French had been caught asleep—one of the few times in the war—at the Chemin des Dames, with a thinly held line. The Germans had rolled over and down towards the Marne and were on their way towards Paris—although even if they had punctured deeper into that salient, that would not have determined the war, by any means; but it was a crucial time.

At this time I wish to correct an impression which seems to be in most minds about the Second Division. The papers kept referring to it as composed of "Marines," "Marines." But there it contained only two regiments of marines, making one brigade; the other brigade of that division was regulars; the 9th and the 23rd regiments were artillery; all the rest of the brigade were regulars. Out of 27,500 soldiers, there were only 7,400 or 7,500 marines. The whole division did wonderful work. But, yet even at that time at Chateau Thierry, while it was the 9th and 23rd which captured the town—and did the fighting—the marines, nevertheless, got the credit in many articles for the work of the regulars. They were on their way back to a "rest sector"; they were thrown in across the road; they did their work. The other regiments which were following were thrown in and also did wonderful work. The result was the Germans halted; they gathered up their forces for attack but the salient was too narrow. It was necessary to widen it. So, the next proposed attack was to the east of the salient. The Germans prepared the heaviest artillery barrage which had been seen in the war, according to French authorities. Our division was the only division to the east of Rheims, with the French in Gourard's Army. The German offensive came on July 15th. It was their last. The German of that hour was far different from the German that was fighting at the end of the war. He was at that time a victorious German, and he was trying to finish up the war. He was going to smash right through and roll right on to Paris, which would give him more elbow space, more room to manoeuvre in, and he could not see anything else but ultimate victory. It was at this battle that General Gourard used his famous strategy of vacating the front line trenches, leaving just a sentinel out there, putting machine guns in before the front line trenches and intermediate trenches, and when the Germans came on, the front line gave the signal, the machine guns split the attack, and the enemy was stopped one kilometre back of the intermediate position. Right astride of the Chalons Road was our division, with three other regiments right on the road, and with some French chasseurs. It was the first real open fighting the men had. It was different from the trench fighting, but the regiment was in wonderful shape. It had had every experience that it could possibly have, except the open fighting. It hadn't suffered very heavily; it had its officers and its men and it was ready for battle. As the Germans came along they were stopped without gaining an inch past the position at which Gourard determined that they should be stopped. But our men could not be held in their position; they were too eager. They went over the front. The Germans came piling down through ravines, through communicating trenches, pushing their old machine guns—which was the most effective weapon they had in this war for putting men in the hospital—ahead of them. Every one of our men went over with the bayonet. They met the Germans at the wires and stopped them, and drove them back after five days' fighting. The German attack was really stopped in the first four hours, but the fighting continued for four more days.

We were then told that we were due for a rest period. We were told to go back. We did, but after hiking a bit, the camions appeared. We later learned to know that the camions always meant trouble when they came. Instead of a nice, soft drive, it meant a rush into another fight. We were no more than

mounted on the camions than we were being pushed up into the
Chateau Thierry section along the Marne. At that spot we
encountered the best troops the Germans had. There were the
Fifth and Sixth, Crown Prince Regiments, the Fourth Prussian
Guard, the First and Second Bavarian Division. They had no
better troops. They still felt victory. They had been stopped
temporarily, but they were full of fight, and fought very hard;
but the regiment was in great shape and eager for battle. It was
in this section during this desperate push that occurred the so-
called battle of the Ourcq River. It was very costly to us. The
regiment was never the same again, but we had crossed the
Ourcq.

About August 3rd we were pulled out of the sector. In the
course of the battle, the Germans had been pushed back to the
Vesle River. They had been driven back a distance of 16 kilometres. We had taken prisoners from eight different divisions
on our front, but when the count was made afterwards, we found
that in the twenty days, of which we had been fighting fourteen,
we had lost 77 officers and 2,300 men of the original 3,500 that
went into the Champagne fight.

Now in figures, of course, that is large enough. Those figures
were given to me by the colonel of the regiment himself; there
are no official figures. In figures they are large enough, but
when you come to think that included in that was one of the
three majors, nine of the line captains, and scores of the best
lieutenants, and one of the most regrettable of all, the loss of our
experienced non-commissioned officers, the seriousness of it
becomes impressive. Good sergeants are the back-bone of any
regiment, and I am sorry to state that in that fight we must have
lost about 70 per cent of our best non-commissioned officers. At
any rate, the regiment was never the same. We had been
accustomed to hearing the different brogues floating out from
barns, as we passed the mens' quarters, and the East Side dialect,
the West Side dialect, and even accents from Jersey City and
Brooklyn. (Laughter.)

We went back for a couple of days' rest, and they started us
training again. Then came the replacements, when we added
a few new languages which Mr. Conboy didn't allude to. They
came from Kentucky, North Carolina, South Carolina, Texas,
Oklahoma, and we had sixteen Indian tongues, because we got

sixteen full-blooded Indians from Oklahoma, from as many different tribes—sixteen different tribes. All of these men proved good men. They had the grit that the average soldier had—the average American—that came in. The Texas and Oklahoma men were especially good; but, the old-time officers—possibly it was due to clannishness—never felt that the regiment had really been replaced. We had the same numbers, possibly, but they never seemed to have the same spirit; they didn't measure up to the old men; they didn't fight like them, though they fought, fought well.

Well, we went back after this fight. There weren't many of us entitled to that seven-day leave you read of, and which my sister so dutifully cut out of the paper and sent to me asking, "Is this you?" and I would have to answer back, "No." As a matter of fact, the division never did get the leave; some divisions did; but despite the fact that our regiment was over there one year, we were too busy.

The next thing we found, after training a short while, we were enrolled into the St. Mihiel salient attack. The First and the 42nd Divisions were on the longest dimension of that salient, and on the defence line of 19 kilometres in length, the largest thing from the American viewpoint tried yet. We had about 500,000 troops. When the attack was made the gains in territory were enormous, as well as in prisoners. The American papers made much of it, but we always regarded that as one of the finest cake-walks we had there. We did not lose many men; we got big results, and the position was assured. We ran into some Austrians, some Wurtemburgers, some Saxons, and, somehow they did not fight like the Prussians, or the Bavarians.

After that affair, we held the front line for twenty days. Then October 2nd came along. We went out again. Someone said, "Well, we are going to get that leave." We knew different, when we saw the camions waiting. (Laughter.) We were on our way after the Argonne fight, which had started on September 26th. Most of the division started in the fight were our new troops—National Guard and National Army troops. They had not been in many of the bigger things. The veteran divisions, which included the First, Second and Third Regulars, the 26th, 42nd, and 32nd Divisions of the National Guard, were not included in the first drive, but they all came in later, seven days

after the first push, and joined in the famous Argonne-Meuse
drive, which covered a front of about 25 kilometres. It had
three different phases, the first starting September 26th, and
another drive October 14th, and another drive on November 1st,
and we were not in at first. We were in the other sector still
under fire, but, after the camions came, we were brought up.
We were pushed in the Argonne drive, right through the First
Division, which had been in, and we were driven against the Côté
Chatillon over several hills in the village or town of Lyons-St.
George; and here, as usual, we got a very bad cutting up. The
regiment, somehow or other—I don't know whether it is the
natural impetuosity of the Irish or not—seemed to have a habit
of getting out a bit in front of the others. Well, that gets you to a
point quickly, when you have an objective, but there are some
objections to the system, the worst that I know being the objection that you get machine gun fire from both sides, as well as the
front machine gun fire and direct fire of artillery. We were
hung up at Lyons-St. George, where, after advancing about four
to five kilometres without any artillery preparation, we were
pretty badly shot up. The battalion I was in command of started
with 876 men and lost 475. The First Battalion was cut up
possibly a bit worse than that. Then we held that position,
advanced beyond the German wires, and the division checked
the enemy at Chatillon. This check it was that made the
November 1st drive possible. They were behind wires in a very
strong position.

We occupied that position for twenty days, held the line, and
then, on November 1st, the Second Division jumped over. I
think you will realize the importance ascribed to this part of the
sector, the Argonne-Meuse fight, when you hear that the 1st,
42nd, and 2nd Divisions of the army supposed to be three of the
most experienced divisions, were all engaged in this fighting.
The spirit of the men of the divisions was the same spirit as in
all previous affairs. The Germans were coming up. After hanging back a day or two, we moved up again; and, in the early part
of November, we jumped through the division in front and went
at the Germans, who by this time were pretty well pulled back.
They fought doggedly on every hill. As our column advanced
we would get their artillery fire from the front, and get their
machine gun fire later on; but they were pulling back unmis-

takably. From that time on it was a smash and a push, over hill, through woods; but we lost men on the way.

The Germans' light machine gun is a wonderful weapon, and they certainly knew how to use it. About November 7th, the Third Battalion, of which I was the commander, left a hill on the right, near the town of Sedan, the town famous in French history. We pushed our patrols into the outskirts of Sedan, but, despite the statements of the American newspapers that we entered Sedan, it was permitted to the French to go first into Sedan. We really had the town; took it; had the outskirts; but, through an act of courtesy of the division, the French were the first in the town proper. It was nearly fifty years since they had left it. November 11th, we had heard rumors that the armistice was coming. We were ready to pull back. That morning the French came up, and we were relieved; and, as we were hiking back, about one minute to eleven, every big gun in the American sector sent over one last parting shot. They all had watches in hand ready to time the sending over.

We then hiked back to a town to rest up. We were told that our ranks would be filled up. Of course the men had their usual rumors: "now we were going to be relieved"; "we were going to see this leave they had spoken of"; but, the next bit of news we heard was that the Regiment was going to be re-equipped, refitted, and filled up, and then sent into Germany with the Army of Occupation.

We had about 175 men left in our battalion. We had been fighting from about October 11th to one month later. The battalion started out with 875, and when we halted in front of Sedan, we had 175, 50 men out on listening guard, 53 men back with the kitchen. We had added some men during the interval, men who had come back from the hospital. At this stage, my battalion, I know, the very day I left, November 15th, received 400 replacements from the pioneer regiments. They are supposed to mend roads, do engineering and laboring work—work of that sort. The papers said the regiment is in Germany on the banks of the Rhine, but it is not the regiment that did the fighting. At best I cannot see that there are more than 700 men left of the old 3,500.

I left the regiment then, and there were very few familiar faces in it; although I have read recently that Lieutenant-Colonel

Donovan and other officers have returned from the hospital since I left. One of the most familiar figures was Father Duffy. (Applause.) He seems to have had more lives than a Kilkenny cat. I think the papers have had him killed ten times and wounded a dozen. He has exposed himself and did wonderful work. Up in the Champagne fight, he was out in the first front trenches helping the wounded. He is a marvellous man in every way. Every man in the regiment swears by him. He knows pretty near every one by his first name, and if he didn't know it, he would call him by a first name and let it go at that (laughter); and he has been a great factor in the bringing up of the morale. I am glad to state that in the whole course of the war he has never been wounded. Only once did he have to leave the regiment, and that was right after the fight at the Ourcq River. He was broken down by the sights and the sorrows he endured at burying so many of our dead.

The fighting had been tough, especially in this Argonne-Meuse drive, where we charged over the hills and through thick woods, sleeping in little holes in the ground, living in any kind of broken huts, and where the cold November rains came down and soaked us through to the skin. The kitchen never did catch up with the regiment. We were lucky if we got one meal every second day. That was hard work. Over the hill we would come and there we would have to keep doggedly on through machine gun bullets, and, worst of all, the direct fire artillery. In their rear guard actions, the Germans always figured "Here we will sacrifice a couple of big guns." They planted them where we would have to come over the hill, and, as we would approach very close to them, the high explosives would come whistling over the line. We would get very close. They fire until the enemy gets within five hundred yards. Through obstructions of every kind we had to burst under direct fire of artillery. Then, as we came closer, they would destroy the breech mechanism of the gun and run away from it.

That is, in my estimation, the worst thing except one that we had to face. The hardest thing I know of is the job of a chaplain of a regiment, a chaplain, such as Father Duffy is. He is not the ordinary chaplain, a man who has been added at the last minute, who might or might not leave his impress on his regiment. He is different. He has been with the "outfit" for years. He was down at the Texan border with us. He has a parish up in the Bronx, and I think every eligible man of his parish, almost, is or was a member of the 69th. He has seen them grow up; he has baptized them,—a good many of them,—and then he has the pleasant little job of going over the battlefield—which is a most unpleasant scene after a fight—with a burying squad, and burying the dead and saying prayers over them. Time upon time he has come upon those very men lying dead that he has tenderly loved as he saw them grow up. He is a most remarkable man, but that awful repetition was too much for him. After the battle of the Ourcq, as I have said, he collapsed, broke down; couldn't go any further; so the colonel sent him to the hospital, where he remained and rested up, and then rejoined the regiment. There have been many inquiries from different sources as to how he was hit or wounded. He was never hit; never wounded, I am glad to say. He had a break-down, as I have told you, but recovered from that.

I am afraid I have taken too much time. There is much else to tell but not now. That has been in outline the history of the regiment. It has done its work in the trenches. There were four big American efforts, the battle of the Champagne, the battle of the Marne salient, the battle of the Saint Mihiel salient, and the Argonne-Meuse fight. It has been in every one of the first three, and at two places in the last one. The old regiment to-day? If you wish to see it, I am sure you would have to comb the hospitals. What we know as "the regiment" is on the banks of the Rhine, and I think I voice the sentiment of every man at that table when I say that they would like to be there with them to-night. (Loud applause.)

THE TOASTMASTER: I am sure that I voice the sentiments of this gathering in thanking Major Reilly for his clear, simple story of great deeds.

I turn now to another subject and to another man full of the Irish soul, full of the Irish spirit, a scholar and a priest. He comes to us from the Catholic University of America—the Rev. Father Healy, who will address us on the subject of "Ireland and Democracy."

ADDRESS OF REV. FATHER HEALEY.

Mr. President, Ladies and Gentlemen: I am afraid that any person who is suffering from a bad attack of hoarseness and attempts to make a public speech places his audience somewhat in the position of a man who, for a long time, had had a sick wife, and, to a sympathizing friend who asked how she was, he replied, "Poorly"; and after a pause he added, "I wish she was well, or——something." (Laughter.)

As I can hardly hope that a miracle will be performed, even at the hospitable table of the American Irish Historical Society, the alternative places me in the position of not taking full advantage of the opportunity which is usually offered to speakers on such an occasion as this, and of not doing full justice to the subject on which I am going to speak. Nevertheless, the privilege of speaking to the American Irish Historical Society on the subject of "Ireland and Democracy" is one which I could not easily forego, and especially of speaking to the American Irish Historical Society at its Victory Dinner.

The victory which we celebrate is a victory for democracy, and every victory for democracy brings Ireland and America closer together. (Applause.) Every American can take reasonable pride in the fact that the aims and purposes which sustained the forces of the Allies in the last desperate battles of the war were the aims and purposes which were formulated by the President of the United States. Every American can also take reasonable pride in the fact that the final victory was achieved by the skill and valor of the American soldier and the American sailor. (Applause.)

It is a source of special gratification to the members of this Society to know that the aims and purposes of the United States in the war have been the aims and purposes of the Irish people during seven hundred years of their troubled history. (Applause.)

What the final outcome of the war will be, it is useless for me to attempt to forecast. At most, it can be said that no Peace Conference can entirely undo the verdict of war. Democracy is triumphant in principle, if not in fact. It is triumphant in the Orient; triumphant among peoples who have known the blessings of free institutions. It is triumphant in the Balkans; it is triumphant in Hungary; it is triumphant in Poland; and, to a certain extent, democracy is triumphant in Germany. The German people have rid themselves of the Prussian dynasty under whom they have so long lived; and, to a certain extent, also, democracy is triumphant in England, because the English people have rid themselves of the German dynasty under whom they have so long lived. It is true they have not sent their ruler to Holland, but they have made the royal family English by Act of Parliament.

Now, as this victory for democracy is a victory for democracy because it is an American victory, so, too, the result of the Peace Conference will be a victory for democracy if it is an American victory. It would ill become me to say whether it is necessary that each and all of the fourteen points should be adopted in order that the victory should be an American peace. Many distinguished statesmen at home profess not to understand all of those points; and probably warned (?) by their ignorance, the President of the United States has felt it incumbent upon him to see that distinguished statesmen abroad will not lack due enlightenment on the subject. (Applause.)

In spite of the peevishness of the suffragettes who burned the President's speeches, and in spite of the peevishness of certain senators who assail his policy, the American people realize that their aims and purposes in the war have been fully and adequately stated by Mr. Wilson. (Applause.) They realize that their ideals are safe in his hands. (Applause.) Nobody questions his eminent fitness for the task which lies before him. He is a man of more than ordinary academic attainments, and he is also a man of unusual political sagacity. He goes abroad as a scholar and a statesman. As a scholar, he will have an opportunity at Buckingham Palace and elsewhere to observe at close range some of the few surviving specimens of that rapidly disappearing species, the king (laughter); and in his capacity as statesman, he will have an opportunity, at Versailles, "to make the world safe for democracy." (Applause.)

Now, no peace can be considered a just peace, and the world can never be considered the home of democracy, if the historic claims of Ireland to democracy and nationality are not heeded. (Applause.) The Irish people have proved their right to take their place as a free democracy alongside of the other free democracies in the world. (Applause.) They have proved their right by the way in which they have presented their claims.   For years, they followed, in the presentation of their claims, the methods which commend themselves now to the enlightened minds of the twentieth century.   They have appealed to the sense of justice and fair-dealing of their fellowmen; and time after time the English democracy has gone on record as conceding their claims, and, time after time, the will of the English democracy was nullified by the power of English junkerdom as represented in the House of Lords.   And when English junkerdom as represented by the power of the House of Lords was rendered powerless for further evil, Ireland was robbed of justice by militarism, by the crude militarism of Carson and by the brutal militarism of the Kaiser, a combination which terrified the English government and made it fail to do for Ireland what it afterwards professed to do for Belgium—to fight for the immemorial rights of a small and subject nationality.

The Irish people, in a very short time, will be represented in an assembly which will gather in Ireland, and that assembly will find justification in the fact that during the late war the Irish have proved their right and title to a share in the blessings which are to arise in the new order as a result of this war.   When it was announced that this was a war for justice and for small nations, the Irish people volunteered out of all proportion to their military population; they fought wherever fighting was to be done.   They fought in the Orient and they contributed in no small fashion to the result which was there attained, and if the people of Syria, and the people of Mesopotamia, the people of Armenia, and even the Turk, are to enjoy the benefits of free institutions, why is it that the Irish who helped to lay the foundations of those institutions are deprived in their own country of the right of self-determination?   (Applause.)

The Irish fought in the Balkans.   It was an Irish regiment that threw itself across the path of the victorious armies of Austria and Bulgaria and saved the fleeing armies of the Entente, and, because of that deed, the Slovak peoples in the Bulgarians are today laying the foundations of their free institutions, and those foundations of free institutions rest in Irish blood.   If those people are to enjoy the benefits of self-determination, why is it that the Irish at home are not to enjoy the same blessings that they purchased for others in foreign parts?   (Applause.)   ("Hear! hear!")

The Irish fought on the western front, in every great battle during the four years of the war; fought on the northern sector. On the western front, the Irish poured out their lives and their blood. They fought on the sea and they fought in the air, and why is it that they are not to enjoy the benefits of that liberty which they vindicated so nobly and so bravely?

At this coming conference in Ireland, a constituent assembly will be formed by men drawn together according to a due form, representing all parts of Ireland, and representing all classes in Ireland. This assembly will have a mandate from the Irish people to draw up a constitution for Ireland. They will find legal justification in everything that they may do in the avowed and expressed purposes of all the Allied Powers during the early years of this war, those Powers which declared that their purpose in entering the war and the purpose which they hoped to attain was the freedom of all nations. Everything that that assembly will decide upon will be ratified by the conscience of liberty-loving people everywhere.

The Irish, in entering into this conference, are not moved by animosity or hatred of any other people. They do not seek for indemnities, or reprisals. We hear from them no talk of violence or bloodshed. The only statements of that kind that have come forth have been those which have been made by Mr. Lloyd George's Coalition Chief Secretary for Ireland, Mr. Shortt, who has declared that Ireland, during the coming year, will see peace or bloodshed,—peace if they submit, bloodshed if they claim the rights which the enlightened conscience of the twentieth century, as illumined by this war, confers on them.

That is no new threat to the Irish. That is the threat which has been ringing in their ears for centuries. That is the threat which was made to Belgium, and the answer to that threat is found in the record of the past war and in the fate of those who made it.

The Irish people have no desire but the desire for democracy, the desire for self-determination. They protest against military occupation of their country, against having foreign soldiers quartered on them; against being commercially exploited by an alien race. It was that plea coming from Belgium which moved the entire world against the Central Powers. That plea of Belgium rang through the world for four years. A plea of Ireland of the same kind, and representing just the same outrages, has rung through the world for seven hundred years. The humane utterances of Cardinal Mercier pleading for his people have no more weight, have not the same weight, as the utterances of Cardinal Logue pleading for his. (Applause.)

Now, my subject was "Ireland and Democracy." "Ireland and Democracy" means the union of the hearts of Ireland and America, a union which has stood the test of years. Let us hope that, at the next gathering of this Society, what we now look forward to as a hope we may then celebrate as an accomplished fact (applause); and that the hopes of Ireland throughout her history, to realize among her people the ideals which she admires among the people of this country, will be attained, and that Ireland will have taken her place among the free democracies of the world. (Applause.)

THE PRESIDENT-GENERAL: Following the wonderfully eloquent address of Dr. Healy, I wish to read to you a resolution that was passed at a meeting of the American Irish Historical Society this afternoon, passed with the resolve that it should be submitted without debate to this gathering and that those present should signify their approval or the reverse, those who approve to arise, and those who do not approve it remaining seated.

This is entirely in the spirit of the Doctor's address. It is in line with the movement made by Irish-American Societies all through the country. It is the first opportunity that we have had to make it. It was made, for instance, a little while ago, by the Friendly Sons of St. Patrick, and the resolution, engrossed, was taken to the President, with the signatures attached of all the members of the committee that formed it. Our resolution reads:

"*Resolved*, That the American Irish Historical Society endorses the principle of self-determination for all peoples as enunciated by President Wilson, and requests the President to support fully the application of this principle to Ireland."

All in favor of that resolution, please rise.
(Nearly all of those present rise.)
All on the contrary.
(Some of those present rise.)

THE PRESIDENT-GENERAL: I think I may say that the "Ayes" have it. (Applause.)

We have heard from the history side of the recent war, and the Irish share in it, and I wish to call to the attention of our meeting that particular book about to be issued, to which I alluded earlier in my remarks. It relates to the share of the Irish people in the War of the Revolution in America. It has been compiled by the Historiographer of our Society, Mr. Michael J. O'Brien (applause), to whose distinction as a scholar and as an investigator I have paid frequent compliments, and which I can only endorse and add to.

The book will be published by the Devin-Adair Co., probably within three or four weeks, and I wish every person present to carry away with him the idea that he must buy a copy of that book and commend it to his friends; and I ask Mr. Michael J. O'Brien to favor us with a few words upon the subject. (Applause.)

ADDRESS OF MR. O'BRIEN.

Ladies and Gentlemen: One of the human weaknesses is a little bump of vanity that some of us are ready to develop occasionally, and I fear I must confess that I am possessed of that to some extent. Since you have acceded so kindly to the request of our Toastmaster that I inform you somewhat of this work to which he made reference, then I would like to assure you, however, at the outset that neither is he nor am I boosting any commercial enterprise. Far from it; because the work to which he refers was undertaken solely as a matter of race pride and for the purpose of filling what I know you regard as a long-felt want, to tell the true story of the contributions of the Irish to the winning of American independence. (Applause.)

I am sorry I am not prepared, on account of being called upon so suddenly, to inform you of the contents of this work in the manner in which I would like to do. You all know, I am sure, as I do, that the American historian has very scantily treated the Irish element in American history. Any man unprejudiced, no matter of what race, who examines the public records of the country will at once admit that there is considerable ground for our complaint on that score, because whatever evasive references are made to the Irish pioneers in America have been written mainly by persons whose minds were warped by religious or perhaps racial prejudices, and some of them, to my certain knowledge, suppressed the truth when they found it.

However that may be, we Americans of Irish blood have no one to blame but ourselves, because we have not investigated the history of our race in this country like, for example, the descendants of the Dutch and the English colonists. They have had historians who made it a sort of a business and a trade to give the world histories of their own making, which is the reason why the so-called "Anglo-Saxon" has for so long occupied the center of the historical stage, with the lime-light turned on himself in such copious effulgence, to the exclusion of all other peoples. The Anglo-Saxon, it is said, has given us whatever power or prowess or culture our country possesses, and the Irish, who contributed so much to that end, are hardly mentioned at all.

Now, some American historians disclaim altogether that the Irish took any part in the winning of the American Revolution. They have thrown us out of court; we had no case. Others of them let the case go to the jury, and the jury rendered a Scotch verdict, "not proven"; and let me whisper to you there is some justification for that verdict, because oratory never proves the case, and rhetoric never convinces a jury. Oratory and rhetoric are all we have been giving; we have not produced the facts.

What part did Ireland take in the American Revolution, and what is the evidence to support it? There are two features of Ireland's connection with the American Revolution, one being the aid and sympathy which the people of Ireland in Ireland gave to the struggling colonists, the other being the actual contribution in the field, in this country.

The work to which the Toastmaster refers produces evidence of the most indubitable character proving our case. You may recall, at this table last year, I exhibited photographs of documents which I secured in the Public Records Office in London, in the Tower of London, and from the Historical Manuscripts Commission. I showed you a letter from the commanding general of the British Army, Gen. Sir Henry Clinton, to Lord Germaine (?), the Secretary of War, in which he said that their most serious antagonists in the Continental Army were Irish emigrants; I showed you a letter from Andrew Cyrill (?), an official agent of the British Cabinet, addressed to the Earl of ———, the English

Secretary of State, in which he said "vast numbers of Irish emigrants are in the rebel army." I also exhibited two letters from the noted Tory, Joseph Galloway, in which he referred to the great numbers of Irish immigrants in the rebel army, as well as the diary of that English officer, Major Joshua Pell (?), who wrote, the very first entry in his diary, under date of June 1, 1776, that the rebel army was composed chiefly of Irish redemptionists, and he paid them the very distinguished compliment of saying that they were the greatest rascals unhung. (Laughter.)

Now, what better evidence can a historical writer have to illustrate this case than to point to the address sent on the 25th of July, 1775, by the Continental Congress to the "People of Ireland," fortified, three years later, by the celebrated Address to the Good People of Ireland in behalf of America which Benjamin Franklin sent them on the 4th of October, 1778? What better evidence can there be that the Irish in Ireland supported America than the exclamation of Lord Chatham in the House of Commons (?) in 1775, when he said, "All Ireland favors the Americans" (?), followed, on the 1st of July, 1776, by a statement of that distinguished Englishman, the great Horace Walpole, when he wrote to the Congress in Upper Ossory (?), "All Ireland is America mad!" (Applause.)

Ireland's contribution at home to winning the American war is illustrated also by their refusal to enlist in the regiments recruited for the American service. "High treason" was, all these years, rampant in Ireland, and the people of Ireland gloried in it, because, as they said in their newspapers, "we are helping our American friends to win their independence." They even went so far as to burn down in Cork, Belfast, and Dublin the factories where the clothing and supplies for the British Army were being manufactured. They burned up the consignments of supplies going to the troopships. In Irish harbors the American privateers were secure, and their depleted crews were recruited. All over Ireland meetings were held, in the North as well as in the South, at which money was collected and sent to the aid of the Continental Army, and I find in the newspapers and public records of the time, numerous statements, as well as in the speeches of English members of Parliament, that the English lenders complained bitterly of the large quantities of powder, ammunition, and other warlike stores, which were being sent out of Irish ports to the West Indies, whence they were being shipped to Charleston and Savannah for the use of the American Army.

There is no book ever published upon the subject of the American Revolution that has mentioned any of those facts which I have just stated. I said to you I obtained some of this information from the newspapers of the time, and, when I say that, let me remind you that newspapers of those days could be relied upon for the truth, because the day of the conscienceless newspaper writer had not yet arrived. (Applause.)

What contribution did the Irish make in America to winning the war? I told you at the dinner last year that I had examined the muster rolls of the Continental Army and the Navy of the Revolution. I illustrated by figures that out of every one hundred men in Washington's Army, thirty-eight were either of Irish birth or were born in America of Irish parents. There is no man or woman can dispute this statement; because, in order to do so, those disputing it would have themselves to challenge the accuracy of the muster rolls.

One of the late histories of the American Revolution, and one of the most quoted histories of the Revolution, was written by Sir George Trevelyan (?), whom some of you will perhaps remember as a distinguished Englishman who was in the cabinet of the great Gladstone. He wrote a voluminous work on the American Revolution and it indicates that he had spent many years in its compilation. There is a statement in that work which is to this effect, that less than three hundred Irishmen were in the rebel army. He quoted as his authority for that statement a Harvard professor named Louis Clinton Hatch, who wrote a book that is also much quoted, *The Administration of the American Revolutionary Army.* Professor Hatch is alive. I asked him by letter what was his reason for making this extraordinary statement. He came back and he said, "Well, that is how I found it, except that Trevellyan misquoted me, and what I meant to say was that there were less than three hundred Irishmen in the Pennsylvania Line, not in the Continental Army,"—meaning the Pennsylvania Line of which the great General Lee, "Light Horse" Harry Lee, of Virginia, says, in his personal memoirs, "They are known by the name of *The Pennsylvania Line*, but they might, with great propriety be called *The Line of Ireland*." (Applause.) And so I followed up the question with Professor Hatch. I picked out of the muster rolls ten prominent Irish names. I gave him a list of all the soldiers in the Continental Army and the Navy of those selected ten names, so as to offset his three hundred. There were 795 Kellys (applause); there were 590 Murphys (applause); there are 450 O'Briens (applause); there are 385 Sullivans (applause); and there you have the O'Rourkes, the O'Reillys, the O'Donnells and the O'Connells. I gave him a complete list of the men bearing those ten surnames, and there were 4,500 soldiers and sailors. I then selected as supplement another list of 100 particularly Irish surnames. I selected the Flannagans and the Brannigans, the Coyles and the Doyles, and the O'Connells, and the O'Donnels—they were all in that list—as well as "Kelley and Burke and Shea" (laughter and applause). I sent Professor Hatch this list and asked him if he would be kind enough to eliminate from it all the non-Irish names (applause). He replied by saying that the list is very interesting indeed, but he did not think it important enough, when writing his book, to investigate the Irish in the rebel army; and yet he was willing to use a statement of another historian, because he informed me that he was not the author; he told me that he received this statement from Charles J. Stilley, a Pennsylvania historian. I got after Stilley, and I asked him how he came to make this statement. He said, "I got it from William H. Eagle, who was the librarian and archivist of the state of Pennsylvania. Eagle was dead, so I couldn't tackle him. (Laughter.) So, you have all four of them, Trevelyan (?), Hatch, Stilley, and Eagle, all claiming that there were less than three hundred Irishmen in the Revolutionary Army, or in the Pennsylvania Line, and I sent Mr. Hatch a list of over thirteen thousand names of those selected Irish surnames, and I have collected, all told, 74,000 Irish names, all of men born in Ireland, who served in the Continental Army. (Applause.) It has taken me twenty years to do it, but I had lots of fun.

The hour is getting late; I won't delay you any longer. Let me say, however, that the work to which the Toastmaster so very kindly called your attention will be published and on the market by the 1st of February,—at least so I am promised by the publisher. It contains absolutely nothing but facts, and every statement of fact is backed up by a reference to the authority. Let me also assure you that none of those asperities that usually are allowed to creep into a book where the Irish and the English are spoken of are contained in this book; there is no "twisting of the Lion's tail." I tell the facts and let them speak for themselves.

And, in closing, let me just make this remark: That we owed, before the recent war, a great debt of gratitude to one of the other European countries, our beloved France, for the aid that she rendered to us in 1778; but I assert now, and I am producing the evidence which proves it beyond any question or (of?) doubt, that the Unities States of America owed a far greater debt of gratitude to Ireland for the aid which she rendered here in winning her independence. (Applause.) America is a country of honest men; they want to pay their debts. The psychological moment has arrived when America should pay that debt ("Good boy!") (Applause.) And let us hope, ladies and gentlemen, that the great President of the United States will carry out that policy referred to by Dr. Healey, and will apply to that little nation to whom she owes so much the great principle of self-determination. (Loud applause.)

THE PRESIDENT-GENERAL: We have heard from all sides of the military spirit—and also on the disputatious side of things. It now remains to hear something from the benevolent side, from the philanthropic side, from those who staunch the wounds of war, and help restore to calm and beauty the battered face of the battlefield once more.

I call, with great pleasure, upon Mr. William P. Larkin. (Applause.)

SPEECH OF MR. WILLIAM P. LARKIN.

Mr. Toastmaster, Ladies and Gentlemen: I do not know whether the Society is affected by the one o'clock closing law or not (laughter), but if it is, we are going to come perilously near to being under the ban this morning, because we are coming near the "wee, small hours."

I do not intend to inflict myself at any length upon you at this very late hour, but I am very appreciative of the opportunity which has been afforded me to appear before you, even for a brief moment, to say a word concerning the work of the Knights of Columbus.

At first blush it might appear as if the topic were not particularly germane to the purposes of this organization and that there might not be a very close affiliation between the disciples of the Genoese Mariner and the Sons of the Gael—who have their own St. Brendan, although, even then, the war work of the Knights of Columbus considered solely as a patriotic American organization would be a fitting theme for discussion at this or any other American board. But when it is remembered that among the original incorporators of the Knights of Columbus were a McGivney, Lawlor, O'Connor, Driscoll, Mullen, Kerrigan, Colwell, Geary, Carroll, Healy, and Curran, and that on its present day roster of supreme officers are a Flaherty, Carmody, McGinley, Callahan, Reddin, Dwyer, Martin, Monaghan, McGraw, Hart, McGivney, Fox, Mulligan, and Larkin, not to mention the "fightingest" Irishman of them all—Pelletier, Mr. Clarke's cousin from Boston, who gets his name from his father and his nature from his mother—it will be quite evident that the Knights of Columbus have a much closer affinity to this Society than mere step-children. (Laughter.)

When the army was at the Mexican border, owing to innumerable requests that came to us from various sources, the Knights of Columbus erected fifteen buildings at various points along the frontier to provide for the little creature comforts, so far as our slender resources would permit. Recollect, at that time, all of the expenses were defrayed from our own treasury, but, we did particularly supply central headquarters where Catholic boys, and Protestant boys, and Jewish boys—American boys, regardless of their religious affiliations—(applause) might come together for social and recreational purposes, and where, too, the boys suddenly withdrawn from the refining influences of home environment might feel that they were not entirely unbefriended.

When, therefore, the military autocracy that ran amuck in Europe, and became the common enemy of civilization, directed its piratical energies against our peace-loving people, and we were left with no other alternative than to take up arms and vindicate our national honor, or submit to degradation and slavery; and when the President and Congress of these United States had made the only choice that free men could make, and we were drawn into the maelstrom raging across the Atlantic,—it seemed obvious and logical that the Knights of Columbus could undertake no bigger, better, or more worthy, or more patriotic project than to continue the work which we had inaugurated on the Mexican border, but on a much more extended scale.

Our plan was indeed a pretentious one, and yet it might be summarized in the single thought that we wished to make life a little better and brighter and happier for the boys here and across the seas; and to send along with them a chaplain to comfort, and guide and console, when war's grim night was upon them.

And so we set about this labor of love, and if you will indulge me for just a moment, I shall endeavor to visualize some of our activities by a few excerpts, facts, and figures, rather than by any attempt at rhetoric, realizing that they will tell much more eloquently than any trick of speech of the Knights of Columbus contribution in the great world struggle.

The number of buildings the Knights have erected in this country is 320. The cost of this work, $2,775,000. The number of secretaries in this country, 692; the number of chaplains, 100. Cost of some of the equipment: Pianos, $90,000; victrolas, $30,000; moving picture machines, $225,000; athletic equipment, $72,000. Cost of work overseas: Buildings in France, England and Belgium, 100; number of secretaries and chaplains, in all, 992 (applause). In addition to $2,000,000 worth of materials purchased over there by our commissioners, these are some of the items that we furnished that have been shipped direct from New York: Athletic goods, a total valuation of $221,000; automobiles, in parts, $125,000; beef cubes, 6,000,000, $82,000; candy, gum-drops, hard candy, gum, $283,000; cigarettes, 550,000,000 at a cost of $2,195,000 (applause); cigars, $31,000; coffee and tea, $38,000; condensed milk, $59,000; drinking chocolate, $33,000; pipes, two million, $34,000; smoking tobacco, $181,000; soap, $151,000; talking machines,—a few special machines for the transports,—$3,000; towels, $20,000; making a total of $3,713,000 purchased in New York, already in France.

Now, ladies and gentlemen, in this great patriotic and humanitarian work, the Knights of Columbus were not striving for any particular honor or glory, except such as shall come to them from the consciousness of having "done their bit" and played the part that Americans always have played, and always must play, please God, in times of stress. (Applause.) We have regarded ourselves merely as the instrumentality in the hands of the American people to discharge a sacred trust and to enable the great heart of America to reach out across the seas, to form points of contact between the boy who was risking his all in the shadows of No-Man's-Land and the loved ones who were left behind choking down their grief and battling with the greatest uncertainty.

How faithfully we have discharged that trust is for the soldier boy to say on his return. We might anticipate by reading into the record innumerable tomes, volumes of eulogies from government officials, from military commanders, from directors of hospitals, who watched the work of our secretaries as they labored among the wounded and the dying, frequently for several hours at a stretch until they dropped in their tracks from sheer exhaustion. We might tell of secretaries far advanced in years,—for, from the beginning, our minimum age requirement was well above the draft limit,—who gave up home, and honorable position, and luxurious surroundings, in order to take up this labor of love; we might tell of men who died here and on the high seas, and "somewhere in France"; or of others who dropped in their tracks in order to help the soldier boy that they were sent over sea to aid; but for a verdict on our work, we prefer to await the homecoming of the boys, realizing that in this, as in everything else, for the next fifty years to come, if justice shall continue on her throne, the only voice in America, should be, shall be, and must be the voice of the boy who went out from home and loved ones and everything that life holds dear into the Valley of the Shadow of Death, in order that freedom might not perish from the earth. (Applause.)

Of course, there have been shortcomings and mistakes in our work; delays in obtaining necessary permits of one kind and another; or delays on the part of contractors already staggering under the burden of purely governmental work. We realize that there have been these mistakes,—but we submit, in all humility, that, 450,000 strong, our organization gave the best that was within us; and if, through having travelled the Via Dolorosa, and trod the wine press, we shall have won a little niche in the heart of the American boy, and if we can feel that through our ministrations we brought a ray of comfort and consolation into the hearts of fathers and mothers and loved ones in the thought that their boy was not forgotten, that will be recompense enough for us, and will sufficiently compensate us for any and every sacrifice entailed. (Applause.)

Out of the tragedies of this dreadful war cataclysm, the flowers of love and generosity have blossomed into fullest bloom, and sectional and religious differences and old time animosities have been set aside, please God, forever. The green grass that breaks lovingly over the graves of our boys on the battlefield of France has quickened the American spirit and has developed in us a national consciousness so that with the Catholic and the Protestant, Jew and Gentile, North, South, East and West, our only rivalry has been as to who shall strive the hardest and dare the furthest in defence of the flag,—the old flag that means so much to us, oh! so much, now more than ever before!

"For there's many a flag and many a land
    And flags of every hue
  But never a flag, however grand,
    Like our own Red, White, and Blue."   (Applause.)

So that, ladies and gentlemen, varied and beneficent as has been the activity of the Knights of Columbus in the years that antedated the war, it would appear as if its true mission had been concealed in the economy of an all-seeing Providence until the dastardly invader of the world's liberties made further toleration on the part of our country insufferable, and the sword of America was thrown into the balance in the sacred cause of humanity. Ever since the drum beat of the nation sounded the call to arms, the order of the Knights of Columbus has stood revealed as one of the most potent agencies to develop the morale and strengthen the arm and steel the nerve of the boys who have liberated the sons of men from the scourge of vandalism and autocracy, and who, at this very moment, are standing fast and true, a new watch on the Rhine, resolved that the flag which floats over them shall float over a liberated parliament of peoples among a federation of nations. (Applause.)

And now, ladies and gentlemen, at the risk even of an anti-climax, I feel constrained to echo the prayer which has been so eloquently voiced by Dr. Healy in discussing Ireland and the Peace Conference. It is in no spirit of belligerency, but rather with the keenest appreciation of the splendid contribution of Britain and her colonies in the great world struggle, and with the hope that the heroic sacrifice of her sons may redound to her undying glory, that we record here our unalterable conviction that this consummation devoutly to be desired can never come to pass until the just grievances of Ireland have been redressed and until she, too, like Belgium and Poland and Servia and Bohemia and Alsace-Lorraine, shall have a proper measure of justice meted out to her. (Applause.)

Forget, if you will, the 173,000 Irish who enlisted in the British Army prior to 1916, which would be the equivalent of four million volunteers here in our country (applause); the Irish who enlisted in every British regiment that marched to the front from Glasgow and Liverpool, and Birmingham, and Manchester, and London, estimated by John Redmond at 150,000; the stirring rôle enacted by the Irish in the armies of far-off Australia, New Zealand, South Africa, and in the magnificent body that went out, 400,000 strong, from our sister country to the north—and still would it be true that the just grievances of Ireland can never be ignored as long as men shall read with quickening pulse the casualty list of the boys of Irish blood here, who, under the starry banner that they loved so well, but with the hope that somehow their sacrifices might inure also to the rehabilitation of Ireland, offered themselves a willing sacrifice, comforted in their last moment by the thought that they had fought and died to make the entire world, not merely a section of it, "safe for democracy," and to vindicate the doctrine enunciated by President Wilson that "no people must be forced under a sovereignty under which it does not wish to live, and that self-determination is the inalienable right of all men." (Applause.)

A hundred years ago, Henry Grattan, in demanding justice for Ireland, cried out in the British House of Commons, "I appeal to the hospitals that are thronged with the Irish who have been disabled in your cause, and to the fields of Spain and Portugal yet drenched with their blood!" Fifty years ago, Thomas Francis Meagher,—the illustrious Meagher,—called upon "the woods and the swamps of the deadly Chickahominy, the slopes of Malvern Hill, the waters of the Antietam, the defiant heights of Fredericksburg, the thickets of The Wilderness—a thousand fields billowed with Irish graves, to declare that love for Ireland blends in ecstasy with loyalty to America, and that America had been served by none more truly than by those who carried in their impetuous hearts the hopes and memories of Ireland!" (Applause.) And so, to-day, we say to lovers of freedom the world over, that when France was breaking under the weight of the intolerable odds confronting her, and when Field Marshall Haig had issued his tragic message, "We have our backs to the wall; we will do what we can; we cannot do more,"—at that zero hour, when the fortunes of the Allies were at their lowest ebb, Gen. Jack Pershing, as if in the fulfillment of his pledge made before the tomb of America's greatest friend, "We have come, Lafayette," hurled the American Army straight at the apex of the German advance, and, from the very moment in which they started their offensive until the task was consummated and nothing but an armistice or surrender could save the Germans from complete annihilation, the Americans never backed an inch and every man who fell lay with his face toward the east! (Applause.)

In that illustrious army were countless thousands of men of Irish blood, like these boys here to-night (applause), and Major Reilly (applause), Father Duffy (applause), and the lamented Major McKenna (applause), to whom America was dearer than life itself, but to whom also the hope of a happy Ireland was ever present. And so, ladies and gentlemen, surely we may be permitted, because of the heroic sacrifices of these Americans of Irish descent, to venture the hope that Ireland shall not be left an outcast among the peoples of the earth, but that her just claims shall be adjudicated along the lines laid down by Woodrow Wilson, so that men of good will everywhere shall realize that the true spirit of peace has indeed come upon the earth, that the time of the singing of the birds is at hand, and that henceforth the rifle and the bayonet and the rest of the grewsome paraphernalia of war shall be superseded by the reaper and the scythe, the ploughshare and the other tokens of man's peaceful bent, and that the mighty leviathans that now convulse the waters of the sea bent upon missions of destruction shall be converted into richly laden argosies that, plying between every people and every port, like the shuttles of a gigantic loom, shall weave together the peoples of the earth into bonds of unity and amity that shall endure until time shall be no more. (Applause.)

THE TOASTMASTER (President-General Clarke): I declare the twenty-first annual banquet at an end.

THE SECRETARY OF THE BANQUET COMMITTEE (Mr. Santiago P. Cahill): It is proposed that we send a cable to President Wilson embodying the ideas expressed by the speechmakers this evening, to the effect that we desire that Ireland have the right of self-determination. All those in favor will say "aye." (Cries of "aye.")

The motion is carried.

Historical Papers.

HOW THE DESCENDANTS OF IRISH SETTLERS IN AMERICA WERE WRITTEN INTO HISTORY AS "ANGLO-SAXONS" AND "SCOTCH-IRISH."

BY MICHAEL J. O'BRIEN.

The study of race differentiation in the make-up of the American people is captivating in its possibilities. Although the available statistics on the subject are incomplete and confusing, and although there has been a mass of contradictory testimony and conclusions on the subject, there is one fact that cannot now be disputed, namely, that the Celtic element was a large and important factor in the population of the American Colonies.

Many there are who try to controvert this statement and say there is no historical foundation for it. They point to the place-names in the United States, and to the names of those who have been prominent in American history, as evidence that the English were not only the predominant element politically in the Colonies, but that they formed the major part of the early settlers. Those who argue in that way as a rule do not understand the genesis of so-called Anglo-American names, so that the possessor of any name of apparent English sound is deemed as a matter of course to be of English stock, or, as some are so fond of calling it, "Anglo-Saxon!"

In a former series of papers, I referred to the large Irish immigrations to the American Colonies during the first half of the eighteenth century. The extent of this Celtic element in America cannot now be ascertained, although it is, in some measure, evidenced by the number of Irish surnames that are found in the records of the Colonies.

But, even numerous though the old Irish names are in these records, they do not by any means indicate the full extent of this Celtic element which crossed the ocean and established itself principally in the Colonies from Pennsylvania south. Not alone were Irish names changed and assimilated to names of English origin after their owners came to America, but we know too that a great number of such names had already undergone considerable change in their original home. Hence it is clear that far

more people of Celtic blood came to America in the early days
than there are Celtic names in the records, many of these latter
having become anglicized beyond all hope of recognition.

I have already pointed out that if the true history of the Irish
element in America and what it contributed to the formation of
the American people is ever to be written, there must first be a
complete inquiry made into the multifarious changes which
Celtic names have undergone during the past two centuries, not
alone in Ireland but in this country as well. The names of many
of the Irish settlers, and especially of their descendants, have
become so disguised that it would be useless to look for them now
under their modern forms.

One of many striking instances of this is the name, Whitcomb.
A few years ago a lady in Boston wrote me, stating that, according to a tradition in her family, she is "descended from an Irish
Catholic immigrant to New England named Whitcomb"; that,
being "unable to understand how a person of that name could be
Irish," and her family having been "strict Congregationalists for
several generations," she had asked two professional genealogists
to trace her family. They found that the first of the Whitcombs
in New England had settled in Boston about 1720, having come
over as part of an Irish colony which arrived in that year, but
they were unable to trace the name or the family further back.
On my informing her that the Irish Whitcombs were originally
Kirwans or MacKirwans, she secured the services of an Irish
genealogist, who found that one of her ancestors was a Kirwan
from Galway who settled in County Meath, Ireland, sometime in
the sixteenth century, and one of whose descendants had come
out to the Colonies. Under the operation of the Penal Laws,
Irish families living within the territory known as "The Pale"
were compelled to change their names and adopt English names.
Some made the change by simply dropping a prefix or an affix and
others by transposing letters or syllables of the name, or trans-
lating it into what it meant in English. The name, Kirwan, is
an example of the last-mentioned method. Kirwan was derived
from two Gaelic words, *cior bhan* (pronounced "keer waun"),
which mean literally "white comb," that is, "a man with a white
tuft of hair on his head." But, the name "Whitecomb" was not
euphonious, so in course of time they dropped the "e" and the
name became "Whitcomb!" The name, Masterson, which

many think is of English or Scotch origin, is a similar example. This name is but a literal translation of the old Irish name, Mac-Tiernan, which means "the son of the master."

Irish patronymics are generally easy to recognize, but, on account of the changes they have suffered, and their conversion into English forms, they are often mistaken for English names. American historians paid no attention to this, even if they knew anything about it. Consequently, they describe such a family as the Clintons, for example, as of English origin. They found one of the early Clintons fighting in England by the side of Charles II, and they necessarily concluded he must have been an Englishman. Inquiry in any well-informed quarter, however, would have shown that the name of the Irish family of Clinton is not of English origin, but that it is derived from the ancient Gaelic name, *Mac Giolla Fintain*, and which, in the mutations of time became, in succession, *Mac Gill Intain*, *Mac Clintain*, *McClinton*, and finally, *Clinton*. The ancestors of George Clinton, first governor of the state of New York and vice-president of the United States, and of General James Clinton of the Revolution, were from County Longford, Ireland.

And so it is with other families who have distinguished themselves in America. Ireland is denied much of the credit that is hers, and the influence of her sons in the making of American history is proportionately lessened!

During the eighteenth century, when the largest Irish settlements were established in the American Colonies, education was banned in Ireland. The priest and the schoolmaster had a price set upon their heads. Many of the people gradually lapsed into ignorance and despair, and it is no wonder that they knew little or no Irish history and were ignorant especially of the meaning and significance of their grand old Clan names, and of the system by which many of these names were derived from the most pious and heroic origins.

Tomas O'Flannghaile, in a series of essays entitled "For the Tongue of the Gael," published in Dublin a few years ago, gives an admirable description of the Irish method of name-making. He shows that no people has had a more beautiful system of name-formations than the Irish. Every old Celtic name "means something," and many have their origin in the most beautiful conceptions; such, for example, as the names which begin with "Gil,"

"Kil," or "MacGill." Gillmore is the anglicized form of the ancient Irish name, *Mac Giolla-Muire*, meaning "the son of the servant of (the Virgin) Mary." Guilfoyle is the modern form of *Mac Giolla-Phoil*, "the son of the servant of (Saint) Paul." Gilchrist comes from *Mac Giolla-Chroist*, "the son of the disciple of Christ," and Gilpatrick from *Mac Giolla-Padriac*, "the son of the servant of (Saint) Patrick."

There are numerous Gilmores, Gilchrists, Guilfoyles and Gilpatricks described as Scotch or "Scotch-Irish," and there are Americans of such names whom one would have a hard time in convincing—if they can be convinced at all—that they are of ancient Irish lineage.

How simple it was for the ancient O'Heas to change their name to "Hayes"; the O'Culliens or O'Culanes to "Collins"; the O'Neachtan or O'Naghten family to "Norton"; the O'Creehans to "Creighton," and the O'Clerys to "Clarke," for in the Irish language O'Clery means literally "the grandson of a clerk" or of some person who occupied the position of secretary or amanuensis. Likewise, the Irish name, O'Knavin, meaning literally "a small bone," became "Bowen"; O'Muloghery, signifying in Gaelic "early rising," became "Early"; MacRory became "Rogers," because "Roger" was assumed to be the English Christian name of the Irish "Rory." The Irish family of Ford derived their name from the original MacConnava, on the erroneous assumption that "ava," the final syllable of the name, meant a "ford," and in the same way the Irish family of "King" formed their name from the original, MacConry, on the assumption that the "ry" is derived from "righ," a king. One of the clearest and most scholarly contributions to this subject that has appeared in many years was that written by Mr. Charles O'Farrell, and published in the *Irish World* during the past few years.

What an ignorant person he was, who was reported in the New York papers a little while ago as applying to the courts to change his name from MacGillacuddy to "Gill," on the ground that "people ridiculed his name!" The first of the Kerry Mac Gillacuddys got his name from *Giolla Cuda*, meaning "the disciple or devotee of Saint Cuda," his descendants becoming *Mac Giolla Cuda*. His parent was a pious Christian. and a devoted admirer of Saint Cuda, and deciding to dedicate his first-born to the saintly priest, he conferred on him the name which meant in English "the disciple or devotee of Saint Cuda." Hence, "Mac Gillacuddy."

Some of this class of surnames begin with *Kil*, which is but a hardening of *Gil*. Such, for instance, is Kilbride, from *Mac Giolla-Brighde*, "the son of the servant of (Saint) Brigid." Kilpatrick, Kilmartin and Kilkelly have a like origin.

In anglicizing the old names, it is seen that the *Mac* was often rejected, although in some few names it was the *Gil* or *Kil* that was rejected. An example of this is Mac Bride, also from *Mac Giolla-Brighde*. Mac Bride and Kilbride, therefore, are of the same identical origin. When the *giolla* was not joined to a saint's name, it had the meaning of boy or youth. Gilroy, for example, is derived from *Giolla-ruadh* (pronounced "gilla-rua"), meaning "the red-haired boy."

It is from the same system that names beginning with *Mal*, *Mel*, *Mol* and *Mul* are derived, these being the abbreviated forms of the Irish word *Maol*. This word has three different meanings —(1) a lord or chief; (2) bald, shaven or tonsured, and (3) a servant.

Most people think that Malcolm is distinctively Scotch, and while it is an old and popular name in Scotland, it is a purely Irish name. It is derived from *Maol-Coluim;* i. e., "the disciple or servant of (Saint) Columkill." Daniel Malcom, a Revolutionary patriot of Boston and a native of Ireland, friend and associate of John Hancock and John and Samuel Adams, is described by a New England historian as "a Scotch-Irishman," on the assumption that he was of Scotch descent. Malone is from *Maol-Eoin*, meaning "the servant of Saint John"; Meldon or Muldoon from *Mal-Duin*, "the lord of the fort," and Molloy from *Maol-Muaidh* (pronounced "mull-mwee"), meaning "the lord of honor." Mulready is from *Maol-Riada*, "the lord of Antrim," and Mulrennan from *Maol-Bhreannain*, "the disciple of Saint Brendan."

Once I heard the name of Mullhooley ridiculed in a very annoying sort of way by a person of Teutonic blood. To try and explain to him how the name was derived was waste of breath; but, being curious to know what the scoffer's name might mean, I asked a German scholar and was informed that it came from a word which was of a decidedly low and mean caste. On the other hand, Mullhooley, as well as its synonym Gilhooley, comes from an Irish name meaning the "servant of humility," which I think is a very beautiful conception. It partakes somehow of a saintly flavor. The letter which I wrote the critic referred to, comparing the two names, must have given him "a bad quarter of an hour."

Cu is a word that was much used in name-making by the old Irish. The word means, literally, a hound, but, in figurative language, a hero. When such names were prefixed by *O* or *Mac*, they took the genitive form of the word, which is *Con*. The word is preserved in such names as Conway, Conroy, Conmee and so on. The Conways of Virginia, an old and wealthy family, descendant of a colonist who "came from England" in the seventeenth century, are referred to in Virginia histories as "English" and "Anglo-Saxon." One of the family, Moncure D. Conway, the noted litterateur, himself says so. "Came from England" made it appear to the genealogists that the original settler must, necessarily, have been an Englishman. I wonder how Pat. Conway, the popular president of the Irish-American Athletic Club, the greatest single aggregation of athletes in the world, would feel if we called him an "Anglo-Saxon?"

Some of these names have retained the *Mac* and discarded the *Con*, but supplanted the latter by the syllable *na*. An example of this is MacNamee, from *Mac Con Midhe* (pronounced "mac-con-mee"). Also, MacNamara, which is from *Cu-Mara*, a sea-hound or shark.

In a great many cases, the prefix *Mac*, instead of being dropped, was translated and its equivalent, "son," was added to the name. Such pure Gaelic names as Mac Fergus thus became Ferguson; Mac Donald, Donaldson; Mac Neill, Neilson and Nelson, and so on. Mac David became Davidson by the same process. This is the same name as McDavitt and McDevitt. Some names derived in this way cannot now be distinguished from English and Scotch names.

Instances can be cited of men who have distinguished themselves in America whose names were but translations from the Irish into names of English sound, but bearing the same identical meaning. It is claimed by Irish scholars that one of Andrew Jackson's Irish ancestors was Shane O'Neill. Sir William Johnson, the celebrated colonial governor of New York, who was a native of Westmeath, Ireland, came from the Mac Shanes, and

James Smith, one of the signers of the Declaration of Independence, who was born in Dublin, from a Mac Gowan. These names were, of course, changed in Ireland. Mac Shane means "the son of John" and Mac Gowan means "the son of the smith" (or blacksmith), hence the transition of these names into "Johnson" and "Smith" respectively, when, under the operation of the English law before referred to, Irish families of the "Pale" were compelled to adopt new names.

The most common method of changing Irish names in America was by suppressing the Milesian prefixes *Mac* and *O*, and sometimes by transposing the syllables of the name, by which means the original Irish name entirely lost its distinctive character. I have even noticed such a grossly ridiculous transposition as "Navillus," and pitied the ignorance of him who bore it. If this American descendant of the O'Sullivans desired to disguise his Irish name, as is apparent, certainly he did not succeed, for the silly attempt is only too palpable.

The name McGuire or Maguire furnishes a good example of what Irish names have had to contend with, not alone from the keepers of early American records but from people of that name who evidently lacked racial pride. For instance, some New England descendants of Patrick McGuire from Fermanagh, who settled in Boothbay, Maine, in the year 1730, are now "Megquiers" and they themselves think they are "Scotch-Irish!" In Pennsylvania records the name is often spelled "McWier" and "Makquire"; in Virginia I find "Mogguire" and in North Carolina "Mekuier," all descendants from the Irish McGuires. A striking case is that of Patrick McGuire of Virginia, who so signed his will, yet in colonial land books recording a grant of land to Patrick McGuire his name is down as "Makwire" and on a survey warrant the same man was written down "Megwire." The changes wrought in this name in America serve as a good example of many other of the "Mac" families and this, I am sure, largely accounts for much of the ignorance displayed by genealogists and historians as to the racial origin of the first bearers of certain misspelled Irish names in American records and why these people are so often miscalled "Scotch-Irish."

But, there are also many instances of historical writers who had no earthly excuse for assuming that certain persons appearing in American records were other than Irish, but whom they deliberately wrote down as "Scotch-Irish." A book which I notice is often quoted by shallow commentators on this subject is *The Scotch-Irish*, by Charles A. Hanna, published in New York in 1902. In this book the author gives what he describes "the names of the following Scotch-Irishmen, taken from a list of the non-commissioned officers and soldiers of the Illinois Regiment and the Western Army, under the command of General George Rogers Clark in 1778." Among the "Scotch-Irishmen" he includes men bearing such names as:

Patrick Conroy	Dennis Coheron	Lazarus Ryan
William Barry	John Doyle	Patrick Riley
Thomas Connolly	Patrick Maher	Hugh Logan
George Burke	John McGann	John McGuire
John Murphy	Richard McCarty	Francis McDermott
William Munroney	Barney Higgins	Patrick McClure
Sylvester Munroney	Peter Loughlin	James McMullen
Edward Cockran	John Lyons	
George Cockran	Andrew Ryan	

This needs no comment, except to say that it is a palpably dishonest and deliberate attempt to deprive Ireland and the Irish of the credit of having furnished these soldiers to the Revolutionary cause. It brings to mind Mr. Henry Cabot Lodge's letter to me some years ago, wherein he said that "General John Sullivan was a Scotch-Irishman!" Now, if General Sullivan had not been such a distinguished American soldier—if, let us suppose, he had been only a member of the lower ranks of society— we can safely assume, if Mr. Lodge mentioned him at all, he would call him a plain, ordinary "Irishman!" A strange thing about this "Scotch-Irish" theory is this—its advocates claim that the "Scotch-Irish" in the Revolution acquired their sterling American patriotism and their fine fighting qualities from the Scotch end of the hyphen, forgetting or ignoring the fact that nearly all the Scotch in America during the Revolution were active Tory partisans and faithful adherents of the Crown, and that Thomas Jefferson's original draft of the Declaration of Independence contained a reference to "the Scotch mercenaries" who were sent over to fight the Americans, but that it was stricken out in deference to the Scotch patriot, John Witherspoon!

Changes in names by the dropping of the Irish prefix, *O'* or *Mac*, are also illustrated by such names as "Kneill" from O'Neill or MacNeill; "Knult" from McNulty; "Moness" from Mc-

Manus; "Mahan" from McMahon, and an extreme case is the name "Claflin," from MacLaughlin. In exactly the same way the American names, Laflin and Loffren (from Loughran) began.

These are not suppositious instances, but actual cases which I have found by comparison of certain names mentioned in historical and genealogical works with land, probate and church records. In some cases, it is very amusing, if indeed not tragical, to follow such names through the records and the reasons given by the genealogists for changing them. Some of the O'Neills, a very prolific family of South Carolina, dropped the "O' " because of their "ignorant assumption that the O' in their name was some aristocratic distinction, instead of meaning 'the grandson of,' they struck it off and wrote their name Neall or Neill." This we are told by Judge John Belton O'Neall in his *History of Newberry, S. C.*, a town where an O'Neill or O'Neall family from Ireland were among the pioneer settlers in 1752.

There is also a family named "Gerrald" in Massachusetts who are descended from one Edward FitzGerald who came from Ireland to Palmer, Mass., in the year 1719 with a colony of his countrymen and located at a place they called Dublin, and which is still known locally by that name. And in North Carolina, I find a family named FitzPatrick who, in course of time, came to be recorded as "Fitch Patrick," from which we can readily see how the name "Fitch," borne by some of their descendants, was formed. The name "Pherl" is another interesting example. Michael O'Farrell or O'Ferrell was a Revolutionary soldier who served in the Second Regiment of the New York Continental Line. He is recorded several times on the muster rolls as "Michael Opherl," and I have very little doubt that the "Pherls," or some of them, whose names are found on land and church records of New York state are descendants of Michael "Opherl," the Revolutionary soldier.

Of course, in all cases such changes are not attributable to mispronunciation or misspelling by recording clerks, or even to ignorance on the part of the descendants of those Irish immigrants who brought to America their historic old Clan names in all their purity. For indeed, it must be admitted that the descendants of some of the "Exiles from Erin" became "ashamed" of their names and deliberately changed them by cutting off all semblance of their Irish origin. I shall not make any attempt to

explain how or why this came about, for to do so would need the
services of a most acute psychologist, fortified by a complete
grasp of the historical facts. But this much is quite plain to any
ordinary observer, viz.: that occasionally in America the proud
and sensitive Irish spirit, in the early days, succumbed to the
taunts and jibes of those other racial elements who disliked the
Irish, some for political and some for religious reasons. In many
places the Irish were not strong enough to combat this, even if
they wished to, and their descendants having intermarried with
descendants of English, French, Dutch and other immigrants,
and nearly all having drifted away from the Catholic faith with
which their ancestors were identified for centuries, in time they
lost all traces of their Celtic characteristics. To understand this
thoroughly to-day, we should hark back to the time of the Penal
Laws when the English in Ireland "burned the schoolhouse and
hanged the schoolmaster," as Lord Byron so truly said at one time
in answer to an accusation by a member of the House of Lords, as
to the Irish being "rude and ignorant!"

Many such examples as those referred to are found in American
records and in old newspapers and genealogical works, and if
some one with a taste for that sort of research and the time to
devote to it would make a study of it, he could bring out a most
interesting and instructive work and one that would go a long
way to prove that Americans, far from being "of Anglo-Saxon
origin," are very largely Celtic. To try to prove this assertion by
merely pointing to the present make-up of the American people, as indicated by their names, would be impracticable, for the
obvious reason that so many American family names to-day are of
English sound and of apparent English origin.

O'Flannghaile, in the work already alluded to, explains that
"whilst the greater part of our Irish surnames have no doubt retained some trace of their Celtic origin, a good number also have
lost every sign of their Celtic nature by translation, half-transla-
tion and mis-translation; so that they are often cited as evidence
of English origin. How often do we find Irish families with such
names as 'Fox,' and 'Cox' and 'Wood' and 'Ford' and 'Smith'
and 'White,' names that would lead strangers, and do sometimes
lead their owners themselves, to think they are of English race.
Not, of course, that there are not many families of English name
and origin in Ireland; but there are hundreds of families who bear

such names who are well known to be pure Irish, and who themselves are well aware that their names are but translations, or quasi-translations of their Irish names. Others have not been translated at all, but assimilated to something of like sound in English, and in their new form look quite Saxon, as when Hardiman, Harrington, Sexton, Hart and Ward are made out of such Irish names as *Oh-Eireamhoin, Oh-Aireachtain, O Seascnain, Oh-Airt,* and *Mac-an-Bhaird.*

"To such a degree," continues O'Flannghaile, "have many Irish names been 'translated' or burlesqued into English that some of our people are led by their un-Irish names to think that like others around them they too are Cromwellians, when really they are of the ancient and noble stock of the *Clanna Gaedheal.*"

The study of Celtic patronymics, therefore, is seen to be one of absorbing interest and might well be taken up by Americans of Irish blood. I would advise any person interested in the subject to procure a copy of O'Flannghaile's work which can be had for the small sum of sixty cents from any Dublin publisher. Every American citizen of Irish blood who has any desire to learn something of this interesting subject should have a copy.

AN AUTHORITATIVE ACCOUNT OF THE EARLIEST IRISH PIONEERS IN NEW ENGLAND.

BY MICHAEL J. O'BRIEN.

Some New England historians claim that the most Anglo-Saxon community in the American Colonies was the city of Boston and its environs. In fact, Palfrey says that in ante-Revolutionary days Boston was "exclusively English," and another historian assigns this as the reason why that city has since been called "the home of culture and refinement!" They assert that the early settlements in the Colony were confined entirely to the English, and when some condescend to admit that there were intermittent immigrations from Ireland in the seventeenth and eighteenth centuries, as a rule they fall back on the theory that these people were "not Irish," but "Scotch-Irish." Indeed, in some cases they are referred to as "English." Unfortunately for their reputations as historians, the structure of falsehood that has been erected by these writers has been demolished, as at one blow, by the *Town Books* of Boston which were published by the Board of Record Commissioners of that city, and by numerous other colonial records which have been reproduced in their exact original form.

The fact that a great number of Celtic names appear in the records of the town of Boston and other places in New England, long before the opening of the eighteenth century, is readily proven, and when studying authentic records such as these one naturally wonders how certain writers of established probity and repute, not to speak at all of the minor historians who are but imitators of the others, can reconcile their statements that "the English were alone in the making of New England" and that no other people contributed to the laying of its foundations, or, in later years, to the maintenance and development of its institutions. It is admitted that the English were the predominant element in the Colony; that they controlled the business; that they owned the choicest lands and properties; that they made and administered the laws; that they filled the offices and enjoyed the emoluments and the privileges; that they erected social and political barriers against all who were not of their own class or of their own way of thinking; in short, in the vernacular of the day, they "cornered the market" on almost everything worth while and tried to keep everybody but themselves in the background.

It is perfectly natural that people of English birth or descent should figure most prominently in the early history of New England, and there can be no doubt that in the seventeenth century they were in the majority in the population. But, it is *not* true, as claimed, that at the time of the Revolution the English and their descendants constituted 85 per cent of the people of that territory, despite the figures that have been furnished to us by government statisticians in the publication entitled *A Century of Population Growth*, and any fair-minded person examining the figures in my book, *A Hidden Phase of American History*, will at once admit the truth of this assertion. And to say that none but English settled the Colony and that no other people are entitled to credit for performing the hard work of the pioneers, the erection of settlements and towns and their defence against the savages, the clearing of the forests, the making of roads and bridges, the cultivation of the land, and in numerous other ways clearing the way for the march of civilization, is about as true as if one said that none but English are allowed to enter the Kingdom of Heaven.

There are several New England historians who have made it a business to write history, and these people had infinitely greater facilities at their command for discovering the facts than are afforded to the ordinary delver among the records, who is usually pressed for time and opportunity. One cannot excuse them on the ground that the numerous references to Irishmen and Irishwomen in the colonial records escaped their attention when searching for historical material, and the natural conclusion is that their prejudices got the better of their sense of right and justice, and that the entire omission of any mention of the Irish was with deliberate intent. Where they did not actually falsify the events of history they suppressed certain facts, thus making it impossible for the American people to form a correct judgment of the racial character of the early inhabitants. Shakespeare wrote: "He who robs me of my good name taketh that which not enriches him, but makes me poor indeed." The early Irish in America have been "robbed of their good name"; Ireland and its people have been deprived of the credit to which they are justly entitled, and conscienceless historians have reaped pecuniary but unmerited rewards for their historical piracy.   But, all of this would have been rendered null and void if the Irish in America had themselves taken the trouble of searching the records and had seen to it that the "Irish Chapter in American History" was given to the public, instead of "sitting idly on their oars" all these years and permitting the historical driftwood to float by to clog the schools and libraries of America with a spurious and prejudiced "history."

In addition to the testimony already published in the JOURNALS of the Society and in *A Hidden Phase of American History*, in support of the claim that the Irish settled in New England in the seventeenth century, there are appended hereto some examples of the character of the material that is obtainable from Massachusetts records.   I have collected a great number of similar items which will furnish the basis for other papers on the subject, to be printed in the JOURNAL from time to time.   It should be borne in mind, however, that these fugitive references to the Irish by no means cover all people of our race who settled in New England in colonial times, and it would require a much more exhaustive search than I have been able to make to determine the full number of people who emigrated or were driven out of Ireland to the New England Colonies.   These are submitted merely as symptomatic of the presence of great numbers of Irish in the Colony at the period dealt with.

How do we account for the presence of so many Irishmen in New England at this early period, in view of the conditions then prevailing there?   We learn from authentic English and Irish records that in the year 1639 when the Scotch took up arms against Charles the First, the latter called upon the Earl of Strafford, then his Deputy in Ireland, to secure the fidelity of the Irish, as the king was apprehensive that the Scotch might derive aid from Ireland.   Strafford imposed on the Irish an oath of allegiance, which they refused to take, and in the attempts to enforce it numerous arrests were made and in many cases the captives were sent over to England, whence they were transported to the West Indies or the American plantations as "bond-servants" to their English masters.   Prendergast has shown that ten years later Cromwell began to transport many thousands of Irish men and women to the Colonies, and in the documents in the English archives reproduced by Hotten the names of these unfortunates are given, and these names clearly show that nearly all were of old Irish Catholic families.[1]

The majority of the Irish in New England at this time, therefore, were among these victims of English cruelty and while they were as much despised by their enemies in America as they were by the English at home, they proved themselves useful to the Puritan settlers, in whose service they were placed. It is evident, however, that in some cases, when their terms of service had expired and they had conformed to the established regulations of the Colony, they were able to embark in some business for themselves, which explains their independent ownership of lands and houses in the town of Boston. We find in the genealogies how some of these former Irish bond-servants in time rose above their lowly stations and became the progenitors of families who are mentioned in American history. To succeed in this way, of course, they had to renounce their faith and all ties of nationality, but in those days the transition was an easy matter. We have instances of this in the MacCarthy, Crehore, Dexter, O'Kelley, O'Brien, Sullivan and other families, all descended from Irish Catholic emigrants to New England.

That so many of the Irish immigrants and their descendants succeeded under the conditions in which they were forced to live is not only a remarkable fact in itself, but it is the best evidence that among them were a highly intelligent, persevering and determined class, a type of men most needed in the American Colonies. Indeed, this particular feature of their story is one of extraordinary interest, since it is so suggestive that the spirit and endurance of "the fighting race" must at times have been called into full play against the deep-rooted prejudices of the Puritans. Of the thousands of Irish immigrants and *redemptioners* of pre-Revolutionary times who "scattered like leaves by the ruthless winds of autumn" all over the American Colonies, among those who despised their country, hated their religion, ridiculed their speech, mocked their manners, caricatured their racial traits and scouted them as vagrants, those who settled in New England were particularly unfortunate.

[1] *The Original Lists of Persons of Quality, Emigrants, Religious Exiles, Political Rebels, Serving Men Sold for a Term of Years, etc., who went from Great Britain to the American Plantations between 1600 and 1700*, compiled by John Camden Hotten from the original records; London, 1874.

8

These Irish immigrants comprised chiefly the poor and the lowly who were driven from the homeland through poverty and political persecutions and who labored in the fields and the work-shops of New England; but in the eighteenth century there also came many voluntary exiles able to pay their own way, valuable colonists such as artisans, farmers, mechanics, shipbuilders, as well as numbers of proficient teachers to whom the children of the Puritans became indebted for their education. And of these the records bear witness that when the Revolutionary war came on, they were no less reluctant to join the patriot forces than were the boasted descendants of the Puritans. In some places in New England we find the children of Puritan families depending entirely for their early training upon schoolmasters bearing such old Irish names as Kelly, Sullivan, Fitzgerald, Hickey, Murphy, Mooney, Moloney, McMahon, Lynch, Reilly, O'Brien and so on, and we can say with a certainty that cannot be refuted, that they rivalled in every respect the native American and English teachers and that they inculcated in the minds of the children under their care a sound American patriotism, which stood the test when their country needed their services in her hour of trial.

The question was once put to me: "Why mortify us by the continued publication of the names of all those Irish apostates from the records of Baptist and Methodist churches?" And a writer in a New England Catholic paper criticized me severely for "exposing" the facts about "the lost Irish in the Colonies." These people don't think! Naturally, one has less respect for immature opinions hastily formed than he can for opinions based upon knowledge of the facts, and that is just the position in this case. As far back as I can recall, the Irish in America have been making certain claims as to "the rivers of Irish blood which flows through the veins of old American families," of "the great immigrations of our people to the American Colonies," which explain why so many Irish soldiers fought in the armies of Washington, and so on. But, the cold fact is, that we have been laughed at for our pains, because we have not submitted the *proof* that the Irish came to this country before the Revolution in any appreciable numbers. In only very few of the books, pamphlets, magazine and newspaper articles that have been written on the subject and in the oratorical outbursts of public speakers, has there been any *proof* offered substantiating these claims;

that is, the kind of proof that will convince Americans of other than Irish descent, especially those, and they are many, who have no love for the Irish. Repeated assertions of all kinds have been made, but we must produce something more tangible than mere assertions to prove the case. Where is this proof to be found, if not in the public records, and what better proof can there be than the Irish names appearing in these records? And since this Society began the publication of the evidence contained in these records, many of the anti-Irish critics have been silent and they will probably remain so. As far as I know, only one critic throughout the whole United States has taken exception to the statements and conclusions in *A Hidden Phase of American History*, simply because I have let the records "speak for themselves," and in the long run they will prove to be far more effective than unsupported statements, no matter how eloquently and plausibly they may be presented.

As an illustration of the attitude of the Puritans toward the Catholics and as showing what the Irish in Boston had to contend against, it was the custom in Boston for many years to hold a celebration called "Pope's Night" on November 5th of each year, and on these occasions processions paraded the streets which usually ended by burning the Pope in effigy.[1] In 1776, when Washington was in Boston, he denounced these practices in an address to the inhabitants and it was not until after the Revolution that reports of these annual processions disappeared from the newspapers. The earliest official recognition of the presence of Catholics in Boston was in the year 1746. A record of a town meeting held on September 22nd of that year contains an entry referring to "several persons Roman Catholics that now dwell and reside in the Town, and it may be very Dangerous to permit such persons to Reside here in Case we should be attack'd by an Enemy." At this meeting the selectmen appointed a committee, who were directed "to take Care and prevent any Danger the Town may be in from Roman Catholics residing here by making Strict Search and enquiry after all such and pursue such Methods relating to them as the Law directs." At a town meeting three days later this committee reported, that "they had found the Laws now in force relating to such persons to be insufficient

[1] See Boston *Town Books* for references to these "Pope's Nights"; 1765, p. 158; 1767, p. 224; and 1774, p. 194.

To Enable them to Effect the same and therefore could do nothing hereon although they suspected a considerable number of Roman Catholics to be now in Town." The number of Irish names in the town records indicate clearly who this "considerable number of Roman Catholics" were.

It was, of course, a terrible misfortune from any viewpoint we may consider it that the early Irish immigrants had to abandon their faith, and it is mortifying to see so many persons bearing the grand old Gaelic names figuring in the records of Baptist, Methodist and other churches alongside the Puritans who hated them. In the seventeenth century no one could acquire property or carry on business in New England unless he complied with certain conditions, the chief of these being that he should be an adherent of some Protestant church and take the "Test Oath" and "Oath of Allegiance." Catholics were debarred from every privilege and as such could not live among the Puritans. They were deprived of the civil rights accorded to those of other religious denominations. Religion was the standard by which all things, social and political, were regulated, and the man or woman who did not publicly join some one of the Protestant sects was ostracized from society and every possible obstacle placed in the way of their advancement in the world. When we find Irishmen recorded among the property owners, we know they must have complied with these conditions and that they abandoned the faith of their fathers soon after their settlement in the Colonies.

But, we must be charitable to their memory. There was no alternative for them; it was their only chance to succeed in life, unless they chose to remain in the condition of serfs, and it cannot be assumed that men who sprang from the ancient Catholic families of Ireland, as their names indicate, were other than Catholic in their own country. To-day, even considering the great lapse of time and the dearth of information, it requires but little imagination to visualize the sad condition of these unfortunate people. They had neither priests nor churches to commune with; they were compelled by law to attend religious services provided for them by the ruling element; marriages could be solemnized only by a minister of "the lawful church" or by an authorized civil officer; their children, to be recognized as "legitimate," had to be baptized in church; they had to attend schools where their race and religion were despised; and when these children grew up and married and scattered to other parts of the country, where they had to contend with the same racial and religious hostility, many of them soon lost all interest in their Irish forebears and in course of time their national characteristics! But, the fact still remains that Irish blood, brain and brawn were among the contributing factors which made for the advancement of the New England States.

DEEDS AND CONVEYANCES RECORDED AT THE REGISTRY OF DEEDS FOR SUFFOLK COUNTY, MASS., AT BOSTON.

All of the persons named are believed to have been residents of Boston.

Dates	Grantors	Grantees	Property Conveyed	Where Recorded
1645, October 11	John Coggan	William Goose	"Farm at the Rocks goeing to Lin"	Lib. 1
1649, March 24	John Roberts	William Healy	House and land in Roxbury	" 1
1650, October —	William Healie	Thomas Dudley	Land and barn in Roxbury	" 1
1652, March 18	John and Martha Coggan	Samuel Bennett	House and lands " belonging to the Township of Boston"	" 1
1652, March 31	Robert Starkweather	William Healy	House and land in Roxbury	" 1
1652, August 3	Thomas Foley, et al.	William Awbrey	Iron works in New England	" 1
1657, June 18	William Beamsley	David Kelly	Marsh on Hog Island	" 3
1659, June 16	William Healy	John Weld	Land in Roxbury	" 3
1657, December 28	John Moore	John Winchester	"Ronton farme in the town of Boston"	" 3
1660, April 2	John and Martha Coggan	Joseph Scottow	Land in Boston	" 3
1662, August 7	David Kelly	Elias Maverick	Marsh on Hog Island	" 4
1662, September 16	Nathaniel Gardner	John Corbett	"One half of the twelve shares of the two patents of Swampscott and Dover"	" 4
1666, January 18	David Kelly and David Kaly, Jr.	Samson Waters	House and land in Boston	" 2
1671, November 10	Tege and Mary Crohone	Robert Badcock	Lands in Milton	" 7
1672, May 23	Simon Pecke	John McGoune	House and land at Hingham	" 6
1674, June 10	John Bennett	Teague Barron	Land in Boston	" 8
Undated	Samuel Bennett	Teague Barrow	Land in Boston	" 8
1675, November 19	Elizabeth Smith	David Kelly	House and lot in Boston	" 9
1681, January 19	David Kelly	Thomas Harvey	Land in Boston	" 12
1682, November 2	William Stoughton	John Barrey	House and lot in Boston	" 12

Dates	Grantors	Grantees	Property Conveyed	Where Recorded
1686, August 18	William Ardell	Thaddeus MacKarty	Ketch, *Rose*, and one-half of the pink, *Blessing*	Lib. 14
1694, July 20	Thomas Brattle	Thaddeus MacCarty	House and lot in Boston	" 16
1697, July 23	William Mumford and wife	Thaddeus MacKarty	House and lot in Boston	" 14

RESIDENTS OF BOSTON WHO SIGNED AS WITNESSES TO DEEDS RECORDED IN SUFFOLK COUNTY.

Dates	Witnesses	Principals	Where Recorded
1659, February 16	Anna Mullins	?	Lib. 3
1662, December 8	Thomas Murphy	Josiah Loring of Hull to John and Thomas Loring of Hingham	" 8
1670, January 2	Thaddeus MacKarty	George and Elizabeth May to Thomas Thacher	" 7
1671, October 18	Miles Okely	Robert Penoyer to Jonathan Sellick	" 6
1674, October 3	Patrick Ohogan	Daniel Henchman to Edward Youring	" 9
1675, September 9	John Casey and Michael Martin	Bill of Sale by William Taylor	" 9
1676, October 6	John Casey	Nathl. Barnes to Lancelot Talbott	" 9
1676, November 17	Darby Maguire	Sir William Berkeley to Joshua Lamb	" 13
1676, July 7	Thaddeus MacCarty	Thomas Thacher to Sampson Sheafe	" 4
1679, December 16	William Dempsey	John Glover of Boston to John Glover of Dorchester	" 11
1681, November 7	John Kelley	Elizabeth Smith to Thomas Harvey	" 12
1682, June 6	David FitzGerald	William and Leah Towers to Joseph Lynde	" 12
1692, October 6	Florence MacKarty	Thomas Hamblin to Christopher Webb	" 14
1697, June 1	James Barree	?	" 14

OTHER LEGAL INSTRUMENTS ENTERED IN THE SAME RECORDS

Date	Parties Between	Instrument	Where Recorded
1664, ——— ?	Thaddeus MacKarty	Deposition as to assignment of mortgage	Lib. 4
1652, September 10	Thomas Foley, *et al.*, and William Tyng	Power of attorney	" -
1658, April 1	Roger Corbett	Deposition as to ownership of ship, *Oak Tree*	" 3
1658, May 25	Thomas Foley to John Becx	Power of attorney	"
1658, September 3	John Cosgrove, *et al.*, to John Fisher, *et al.*	Lease	"
1670, May 13	Patrick Calhoone to William Calhoone	Release	"
1672, February 12	John Kenny	Deposition	" 6
1676, October 3	John Casey	"	" 9
1692, December 26	Fergus McDowell and Ezekiel Cleasby	Power of attorney	" 14

It will be noted that several of those mentioned in these extracts from the Registry of Deeds for Suffolk County, Mass., were owners of lands and houses in Boston in the seventeenth century, and among the taxpayers of the town during that period there were men bearing such names as MacCarthy, Kelly, Barry, Healy, Foley, Cogan, Casey, Mulligan, O'Mahony, Carney, Carroll, Haley, Collins, Joyce, Mackdaniell, and so on. Yet, one searches in vain through the published works of most New England historians for any reference to such people! Of the MacCarthys, there were two brothers, Thaddeus and Florence, descended from the ancient and noble family of Clan Carthy of County Kerry, Ireland. In Massachusetts annals Thaddeus is the most frequently mentioned of the two. Besides holding office in Boston, he was a merchant and importer, and in the land, court, probate and church records of the Colony his name figures at various times, beginning as early as 1665 and down to the year of his death, 1705. So extensive was his business that he owned at least two vessels plying between the port of Boston and the islands of the West Indies. Side by side with some of the leading colonists of the time the name of Thaddeus MacCarthy appears, and as one instance of the prominent place occupied by this man, the Massachusetts records show that in the year 1691 he joined with Thomas Brindley of Boston as "surety for John Usher, treasurer of New England."[1] This fact, in itself, indicates that he was one of the substantial merchants of the town. Florence MacCarthy was a provision merchant and was the owner of a large tract of land on which he erected a "mansion," and down even to recent times this land is referred to in deeds and other legal instruments as "the Maccarty farm," and it now comprises part of the city of Boston. I have traced the descendants of these MacCarthys for several generations and find among them leading men in their respective localities, such as lawyers, physicians, clergymen, merchants, mariners and Revolutionary patriots, and their story furnishes a highly interesting account of pioneer days in New England.[2]

Kelly is a name that is met with almost everywhere in New

---

[1] See Massachusetts Historical Society *Collections;* Fourth Series, Vol. II, p. 304.

[2] A book entitled *The MacCarthys in Early American History* is now in course of preparation by the writer, this being intended as the first of a series to be devoted to colonial families of Irish descent.

England annals and it occurs more frequently than any other Irish name. That is to be expected, since the Kellys have always occupied the head of the list in Irish census returns and in statistics involving Irish names, and one of the things at which readers of *A Hidden Phase of American History* have expressed surprise is the list given in that book of the 695 Kellys who are recorded in the muster-rolls of the army and navy of the Revolution. I have often wondered why none of the numerous Kellys in the United States have thought of writing the history of people of this name in America. Certainly, there is no lack of material for a large volume on the subject and it would make an interesting and important contribution to American history. In Massachusetts we find one of the clan mentioned prominently only fifteen years after the coming of the *Mayflower*, in the person of John Kelly, who came from England in an English ship to Newbury with the first English settlers of the town in the year 1635 and at least two New England historians considered that sufficient authority for saying that he was "an Englishman," while another says that he was born in England of an Irish father. The David Kelly mentioned in the foregoing list from the Registry of Deeds of Suffolk County is thought to have been a son of John Kelly.

Among "Persons who took the Oath of Allegiance as administered by Governor Simon Bradstreet" of Massachusetts, on April 21, 1679, were Brian Murphy, John Gill, William Dempsey, John and Jonathan Casey, Samuel and William Garey, William Mackenny, and "Peter O'Kelly of Roxbury."[1] Five months before that time, or on November 11, 1678, Governor John Leverett administered the oath at Boston to Thaddeus MacKarty, Jeremiah Conoway, Richard Talley, Philip Mullen, John Mackemoryn, Michael Dalton, Samuel Kelly, John Dowgin, John Couney, Dennis Mackdaniel, Thomas Hearn, Thomas Sexton, Cornelius White and Matthew Collins, and I should not be surprised if the majority of these were Irishmen. Peter O'Kelly evidently removed to Dorchester, since the birth records of that town contain this entry: "Josiah, the son of Petar O'Kally, was borne Novembar the 3d 1688."[2] Peter O'Kelly, Teague Crehore and David Cremin are included in a list of persons who lived there prior to 1700, which appears in the *History of Dorchester* published

[1] Boston *Town Books*, Vol. XXIX.
[2] *Ibid.*, Vol. XXI.

by the Dorchester Antiquarian and Historical Society. On July 27, 1696, seven of Peter O'Kelly's children were baptized at the First Church of Dorchester, and in December of the same year Margaret, Hannah and Mehetabel O'Kelly and "Peter O'Kelly's wife," are included in a list of sixty persons who "publicly took hold of ye Covenant" and thereupon were "admitted to the Church."[1]

There are some interesting references to Peter O'Kelly in New England annals. About the year 1700 a number of people from Dorchester, Mass., left there to form a settlement in Berkeley County, South Carolina, which they called Dorchester, and the following is an exact copy of an entry taken from the records of the First Church of Dorchester, Mass.: "November 1, 1696. Deacon Sumn's wife and family and His Bro m' Samuel Sumn' with his wife and family, with Peter O'Kelley's wife and six children. Dismissed to y° Church of Christ near Newington in South Carolina" (since called Dorchester).[2]

Nowadays, it seems strange to find an O'Kelley associated with such an enterprise, but, as already pointed out, he had to belong to some church and no doubt attended the only religious body then in Dorchester. He and his associates received a grant of land on the Ashley River, South Carolina, about twenty-six miles from Charleston and here they located, but on consulting local histories of Berkeley County, I fail to find any reference to Peter O'Kelley beyond the fact that his name is mentioned among the Massachusetts emigrants. It is said "they were a band of religious enthusiasts bent on carrying the Gospel into the wilderness and they constructed at Dorchester, South Carolina, what is considered to have been the first church in that section of the Province."[3]

One of the interesting Irish pioneers met with in my researches was David O'Killia, who settled on Cape Cod about the year 1657, and who is mentioned in Old Yarmouth records as "an Irishman." There can be no doubt that he was an O'Kelly, and since he and his sons were engaged in the fishing industry it may be assumed that he came there from Galway, the original

---

[1] *The Records of the First Church of Dorchester in New England*, compiled by Rev. Charles Henry Pope; Boston, 1891.

[2] *Records of the First Church of Dorchester*, p. 148.

[3] *New England Historic and Genealogical Register*, Vol. II, p. 128.

home of the O'Kelly or Kelly family in Ireland. It is certain that at a very early period in the history of this country there was more or less intercourse between Ireland and Newfoundland and the New England coast. Irish fishermen from Galway and Waterford, and perhaps from other Irish ports, frequently visited these shores, and as shown in the last issue of the JOURNAL, there is a record of a settlement on the Isles of Shoals off the New Hampshire coast, of fishermen named Kelley, Haley and Mc-Kenna and their families, who are supposed to have come from Galway about the year 1653. The records of Old Yarmouth of the year 1676 contain a list of ninety-nine taxpayers of the town, each of whom was assessed his proportionate share of the expense of King Philip's War, and among these was "David O'Kelia" who was assessed £2 6s. 9d. Teague Jones was also included in this list and his given name warrants the assumption that he also was an Irishman. David O'Killia or O'Kelly had four sons, John, David, Jeremiah and Benjamin, and one daughter, Elizabeth, all of whom and many of their descendants are mentioned in the vital records of the town of Old Yarmouth.

John's marriage in the year 1690 is thus recorded: "John OKilly and Berusa Lewes marryd the 10th of August 90," and "David OKille Juny[r] and Anne Billes mary[d] the tenth of March 92," and from the Barnstable vital records we learn that "Benjamin OKilley and Mary Lambart marryd 2 August 1709." Elizabeth O'Killia became the wife of Silas Sears in 1707. While the name is spelled in the records in several curious ways, the descendants of the immigrant for three generations retained the "O'," except his son, Jeremiah, who seems to have been the first to drop the historic prefix.

Under the head of "John OKilley's Estate," there is an entry in the Barnstable County probate records of December 9, 1683, reading: "Bathsua OKilley *vid* Relict of John OKilley made oath to the inventory," and administration to her deceased husband's estate was granted to her on December 14, 1683. The records show that in 1710 the town of Old Yarmouth decided to distribute "the common lands" and "in February, 1711, the proprietors of the Common Lands met and agreed that one-third of the undivided lands be laid out to the individual proprietors." The division was made by lot and among those who drew lots of twenty acres each were Benjamin O'Kelley and Jeremiah Kelley, as well as John, Samuel and Thomas Joyce. Again, on January 21, 1739, the common lands in Crocket Neck were similarly divided and among those who received portions of these lands were Amos OKilley and the three Joyces. Jonathan O'Kelley and his sons retained the original name. Jonathan was a member of a militia company organized at Old Yarmouth in 1744 for the French-English war and took part in the capture of Louisbourg.[1] The following items, reproduced in *The Mayflower Descendant,*[2] illustrate how the name appears in the vital records of the town:

John OKelia, the Son of John an Bashrua Okelia was Borne the twelfe daye of october in the year 1692.

Ruben OKilley son of Baniaman and Mary OKilley he was borne on the 29th day of January in the year of our lord 1710/9.

abigail ye daughter of ye above mary okilley she was borne on ye 30th day of June in ye year of our lord 1714.

Susanah daughter of ye above mary she was borne in medfeild on ye 12 day of August 1717.

There are many other similar entries where the name is spelled "Ocelley," and I have no doubt also that the various persons recorded as "Oselley" were originally O'Kelleys. In the Chatham, Mass., vital records of August 14, 1762, there is an entry reading: "James Covel of Chatham entered his Intentions of Marriage with Ruth OKelley of Yarmouth." Some of the descendants of David, the immigrant, were important men on the Cape Cod Peninsula at various times during the eighteenth century. David Kelley was a representative to the Legislature in 1806 and Seth Kelley was a selectman at Old Yarmouth in 1817. David's three sons, John, David and Samuel, all born at Dennis, Mass., between 1779 and 1785, were engaged in the manufacture of salt in that town by a process known as "solar evaporation," and next to the fishing and shipbuilding, it was the most important and extensive industry carried on there for many years. The method was invented by John Sears in 1776, but in 1798 one of the Kelleys achieved considerable local fame by adopting some new methods of salt production from the sea, and in an account of it written by Dr. James Freeman in 1802 he said, "it is a subject of dispute which is the best invention, Sears's or Kelley's; experience can only decide the point."[3] Although

[1] *History of Old Yarmouth*, by Charles F. Swift; Yarmouthport, Mass., 1884.
[2] Vol. V.
[3] *History of Old Yarmouth*, by Charles F. Swift, Yarmouthport, Mass., 1884.

many of them removed to various places in New England, members of the Kelley family have remained on the peninsula and are still there, and the name is perpetuated in "Kelley's Bay" near the town of Dennis. Much interesting matter can be written of this family, and the foregoing items are mentioned here merely to show how readily information is obtainable from the records for a history of the numerous Kellys who are mentioned in New England records.

John Coggan, or Cogan as he himself spelled his name, was a merchant and is referred to as "The Father of Boston Merchants!"[1] He is generally regarded as an Irishman, and although I can find no authority for this statement, I have no doubt of its correctness, since Cogan is a purely Irish name derived from the original O'Cugain. John Cogan first appears at Dorchester in 1632 where he took the "Freeman's oath" on November 5, 1633. He was a man of considerable wealth and according to Washburn's *Judicial History of Massachusetts* he acted as "one of the attorneys under the old charter of the Colony of Massachusetts Bay." He died at Boston, in April, 1658. Henry Coggan, also an immigrant, was in Boston in 1634, whence he removed to Scituate, and in 1639 to Barnstable. His daughter, Mary, married Michael Long, on December 22, 1664. A great many of their descendants are mentioned in Massachusetts and Maine.

That William Healy, who executed a conveyance of land at Roxbury in 1659, was Irish, is shown by an entry in the town books of Cambridge of the year 1664, reading: "Willyam Heally, y⁰ Iershman." He was a resident of Roxbury and sometime of Cambridge, and as the town records of the year 1680 refer to the local school teacher as "our School Dame, Good Wife Healy," it is thought that this was either the wife of the Cambridge pioneer or of his son, William. The marriage of "William Healy, senior, and Sarah Brown, widow," is on record at Cambridge under date of November 29, 1677. Of Thomas Foley, I am unable to find any reference other than the entries appearing in the records of the Registry of Deeds for Suffolk County of the year 1652, one of which covered a conveyance to William Awbrey of "some iron works in New England." However, a Thomas Foley is mentioned in the records of the Salem Quarterly Court on

[1] See JOURNAL OF THE AMERICAN IRISH HISTORICAL SOCIETY, Vol. VII, p. 81.

December 26, 1654, in connection with some legal proceedings against one John Gifford.[1]

The "Tege Crohone" included in the appended list was an early settler at Milton, Mass. His real name was Teague Crehore, and a short account of his career, showing that he was kidnapped in Ireland and brought to the colonies about the year 1641, will be found in volume 17 of the JOURNAL of the Society. The John Barrey who is shown to have bought a house and lot in Boston in 1682 was a mariner in the service of the colonial government and is described as "an Irishman." In Essex County records "John Barry of Ipswich, aged about 28, 1669," is mentioned and another entry reads: "John Barry lived in Ipswich, sailor, 1670–1678; wife Hannah died May 29, 1676." It is probable that one of these was the John Barrey, the Boston mariner. Another John Barry married Mary Chapman at Ipswich on January 24, 1676,[2] and forty-one years after that time the name again occurs in Essex County records. "John Barrye, late of Ireland, now of Ipswich, appointed Administrator of the estate of his kinsman, William Bladen of Gloucester or Ireland, tailor, September 2, 1717,"[3] is an exact copy of an entry in the probate records of Essex County.

The John Moore who executed a conveyance to John Winchester seems to have been a native of the County of Cork, or possibly of the County of Wexford, Ireland. At the Registry of Deeds for Suffolk County,[4] under date of December 28, 1657, there is an entry showing that "John Moore late of Ballehonicke in the Countie of Corke in Ireland, Gentman, Eldest Sonne of the Late Ann Hibbins, the relict of William Hibbins of Boston," acting as executor under the will of his mother, conveyed to John Winchester "a farme of upland and meadow Comonly Called or knowne by yᵉ name of Ronton farme in the Towne of Boston." In the deed John Moore's brother, "Joseph Moore of Wexford in the Countie of Wexford in Ireland," is mentioned. Joseph was a legatee under his mother's will and gave his brother John power of attorney to act for him.

Of the other Irishmen appearing in seventeenth century records of Suffolk County deeds, there will be noted such surnames

[1] See *Essex Antiquarian*, Vol. VIII, p. 173.
[2] Essex County records.
[3] In *Essex Antiquarian*, Vol. VI, p. 184.
[4] Liber III, fol. 81.

as Casey, Corbett, Cosgrove, Kenny, McDowell, Ohogan, Mullins, Okely, Murfey, Fitzgerald, McGoune, Maguire and Dempsey. Of most of these there is no other mention. John Casey, doubtless, was the Boston "taylor" whose name will be noted further on among the taxpayers, but Darby Maguire and John Cosgrove possibly may not have been residents of Boston at all. Maguire was one of the witnesses to a deed recorded at Boston on December 20, 1676, by which Governor William Berkeley of Virginia conveyed Roanoke Island in North Carolina to Joshua Lamb of Boston, but it is not clear whether it was the grantor's or the grantee's signature that Maguire witnessed. In the case of Cosgrove, the instrument which he signed was a lease covering lands described as "part of the dissolved monastery at the Hogges, near Dublin, Ireland," and while the lease was recorded in Boston there is nothing to show that John Cosgrove was a resident of the town.

The case of Patrick O'Hogan furnishes a striking example of the way some Irish names became twisted into almost unrecognizable shape in early American records. Evidently, Patrick's education was neglected in so far as the meaning of the historic prefix to his name was concerned, so he carelessly signed his name "Patrick Ohogon," when witnessing a deed dated October 3, 1674, between Daniel Henchman and Edward Youring of Boston. The name, however, is entered in the Registry of Deeds "Patrick Chogon," and the explanation of the change is simple enough, namely, that in recording the deed either the scrivener or the registrar mistook the initial letter "O'" in O'Hogan's name for a "C," and thus easily transformed this pioneer Hibernian into "Chogon!" The fact that his name was O'Hogan is confirmed by the following entry among the death records: "Relict of Patrick Ohogan died at Boston June 5, 1694."[1]

The number of Irish names in the Boston land records admittedly is not very large, but the significance of the matter is not their numbers but the fact that any persons bearing such names are found at all. And since it is well known that only comparatively few persons, at any time and in any place, appear in public records, we have here a clear indication that many more Irishmen were residents of Boston and vicinity at that period. As a matter of fact, we do not have to rely upon conjecture for this

[1] In Boston *Town Books*, Vol. IX, p. 219.

information, for we know it to be the case from the researches made by Prendergast in the archives of Dublin Castle for his great work, *The Cromwellian Settlement of Ireland*. The records of the Registry of Deeds for Suffolk County[1] also furnish similar evidence, and a single instance is "A List of Passengers aboard the *John and Sarah* of London, John Greene, M^r, bound for New England." The ship sailed "for Boston in New England" on November 11, 1651, with "a mixed Irish and Scotch company," a number of whom bore unmistakable Irish names, and among them were no less than twenty bearing the prenomen Patrick, which is so often indicative of Irish origin.

Three years later there is a record of the arrival at Boston of "the ship, *Goodfellow*, George Dell, Master, from England" with a large number of Irish "redemptioners," who were parcelled out for service among New England planters. "By order of the 'State of England' many Irish people had been sent to New England, and on their arrival they were sold, by those at whose expense they had been brought over, to any of the inhabitants who were in want of slaves or servants," says Drake.[2] In 1654, Drake says that "a large number of emigrants of the above description" arrived in the ship, *Goodfellow*. Unlike other New England historians, he does not call them "Scotch-Irish"; in fact, he distinguishes between the Irish and Scotch emigrants, by his separate references to the Scotch who were brought over after the battle of Dunbar.

The "Tax Lists of Boston," reproduced in the *Report of the Record Commissioners*,[3] contain the following names of residents of the town who were assessed for taxes. The years given are the earliest under which these names appear:

Thaddeus Maccarty,	1674	Hugh Mallagan,	1681
"Dorman, ye Irishman,"	1674	Denis Mackdaniell,	1681
Denis Menan,	1674	Thomas Larkin,	1685
"Mr. Carroll,"	1674	John Barry,	1687
Thomas Collins,	1674	Teageo Barry,	1687
John Casey,	1676	Richard Talley,	1688
Florence Maccarty,	1676	William Joyce,	1687
Matthew Collins,	1681	Cornelius Collins,	1687
John Carney,	1681	Peter Bowden,	1687

[1] Liber I, fol. 5.
[2] *History of Boston*, by Samuel Gardiner Drake, p. 342.
[3] Vol. I.

Bryan Bradene,	1688	John Barry, "Tanner,"	1691
Edward Collins,	1688	Widow Barry,	1691
Edward Mortimore,	1688	Lawrence Driscow,	1691
William Gibbons,	1688	William Downey,	1691
William Macklaflin,	1688	Robert Moore,	1691
John Mulligan,	1691	Arther Haley,	1691

There were two John Barrys taxed, besides "Widow" Barry. One is described as a "Tanner" and the other I believe to have been the Boston mariner before mentioned. James Barry and his wife, Rachel, had a son James born to them at Boston on January 8, 1688, and James Barry son of James and Eliza Barry, was born there on June 14, 1692. A James Barry, probably one of these, is mentioned in the Boston town records of 1709 as "a huntsman." He kept a pack of hounds and complaint was made to the selectmen on June 27, 1707, that his dogs were "suffered to go at large in y⁰ Town and have done damage to the Inhabitants in their pastures and gardens," so James Barry was ordered "to shut them up" or else, "Rid the Town of such Hounds or Dogges wᶜʰ are by him So Kept."[1]

"Teageo" Barry, or Teage Barry as his name was spelled in the 1688 tax list, was assessed upon "Arable Lands and Meadow, Pasture Land, Oxen, Bulls and Cowes, Heyfers and Steers, Ewe Sheep, Wethers and Swine," and Bryan Bradene was assessed under the same heads in the same year. Two names, Peter Bowden and Edward Mortimore, will be noted on the list. Although these names are commonly found in Irish nomenclature, if I were to depend on the tax lists alone I would not have included these among the "Irish," but I do include them because of the following items secured from authentic sources: "Peter Bowden, protestant, Merchant of the City of Wexford, Ireland, now living at Salem, sold ship lately of Dublin, 1684–1686," this entry being taken from the Registry of Deeds of Essex County, Massachusetts. In the *Town Books* of Boston of the year 1678, "Edward Mortimer, an Irishman," is mentioned as a member of the fire-engine company in that year, and in the *Journal of John Dunton*, an Englishman who came to Massachusetts in 1685, he mentions several of the prominent persons of Boston whom he met, among them "Mr. Maccarty" and "Mr. Mortimer who came from Ireland, an accomplished merchant, a person of great

[1] *Town Books*, Vol. II.

modesty who could answer the most abstruse points in algebra, navigation and dialling." This *Journal* was reproduced in the *Collections* of the Massachusetts Historical Society.[1] Edward Mortimer's name also appears in the Boston tax lists of 1695 and he is referred to by Drake, in his *History of Boston*,[2] as an Irishman.

The Hugh "Mallagan" who paid taxes in 1681 appears in the 1685 tax list as Hugh "Mullagin" and in 1688 as Hugh "Mulligan," which was his correct name, and the fact that he was an Irishman is indicated clearly by the following interesting item concerning him, taken from the *Records of the Court of Assistants of the Colony of Massachusetts Bay*,[3] under the year 1685:

"Mulligan's sentenc[4] to return to Ireland under poenalty of 20ˡⁱ"

"Hugh Mulligan plaint on Appeale from the Judgement of the County Court in Boston After the Courts sentenc and evidences in the Case pduced were read Committed to the Jury and are on file wth the Records of this Court the Jury brought in their virdict they found a Confirmation of the County Courts sentenc and costs of Courts, *i. e.* defray ye charg of Tryall."

The fact that Hugh Mulligan was taxed in Boston in 1688 makes it appear that the sentence of the Court was not carried out for at least three years, if at all, and it is likely that he paid the penalty of twenty pounds. It is apparent from the vital records that there were three separate families named Mulligan in Boston at this time, namely those of Hugh, John and Thomas. The birth records in the *Town Books* contain the following entries:

Robert, son of Hugh and Elliner Mullegin, born August 9, 1681
John, son of John and Eliza Mullegan, born December 27, 1681
Thomas, son of Thomas and Eliza Muligan, born April 27, 1693
James, son of John and Elizabeth Mulligan, born December 4, 1694
Benjamin, son of John and Elizabeth Mulligin, born April 1, 1699

Mary Smith died at Boston on August 23, 1696, leaving a will dated May 13, 1696, in which she named as one of the benefici-

[1] Second Series, Vol. II.
[2] Page 463.
[3] Compiled from the original by John Noble, clerk of the Supreme Judicial Court; Vol. I, p. 280.
[4] Marginal notation endorsed on the docket by the Clerk of the Court.

9

aries her "granddaughter Elizabeth Mullegan." These are the only entries relative to people of this name in the Massachusetts records of this period. "John Moligan, Carpenter," is referred to in Boston records of 1685, and the name, John Mulligan, appears among a list of persons who received abatements of their taxes in 1701.[1] From the fact that "John Mullekin," one of Hugh Mulligan's descendants, is recorded as marrying Lydia Whiting of Boston about the close of the eighteenth century, it appears the name was changed to "Mullekin."

"Dorman yᵉ Irishman" is rather interesting. He paid taxes on "a house and garden in Boston." In one of the JOURNALS of the Society[2] will be noted an account of the career of Dermot or Diarmuid O'Mahony, who was exiled from Ireland about the year 1641 and who died in Boston in 1661. This New England pioneer is shown to have been recorded in various official documents under the names of "Dermont Mayhoone," "Dierman OMahonie" and "Dorman OMahone," and I have no doubt at all that the real Christian name of "Dorman yᵉ Irishman" was also Dermot or Diarmuid. This is the only reference to him I have been able to find. Matthew Collins, who appears first in the tax lists for 1681, was Matthew Colane or Cullane and was a cousin of the Dermot O'Mahony[3] just referred to. It was a common thing in Ireland to call the O'Cullanes or Cullanes, "Collins," and indeed people of the name are now generally known as Collins. The "Mr. Carroll" who was taxed in 1674 is down as "lodger at Mr. Mecarter's," that is, at Thaddeus Mac-Carty's house. His Christian name is not stated and the only other Carrolls mentioned in seventeenth century records of New England were: Thomas Carroll, who first appears at Salem, Mass., about 1688;[4] Katherine Carrol who, in 1685, was married to John Waite at Ipswich,[5] and Anthony Carroll of Topsfield, Mass., the birth records of whose children are as follows:

> Cathren, daughter of Anthony Carrell, born June 31 (?), 1658
> John, son of Anthony Carroll, born October 19, 1663
> Anthony, son of Anthony Carroll, born ———, 1666
> Mary, daughter of Anthony Carroll, born ———, 1666

[1] *Town Books*, Vol. X.
[2] Vol. XIV.
[3] *Ibid.*
[4] See *Genealogical Quarterly Magazine*, Vol. I, p. 71.
[5] *New England Historic and Genealogical Register;* Vol. II, p. 210.

I have no doubt that John Casey who was taxed in 1676 was the same John Casey, who fought in "King Philip's War," 1675–1676, and who is mentioned as a resident of Muddy River, a place that is now known by the more aristocratic name of Brookline. His name occurs three times in Suffolk County records;[1] on September 9, 1675, he and Michael Martin signed as witnesses to a bill of sale executed by William Tailer of Boston; on October 3, 1676, he made a deposition as to execution and delivery of a power of attorney from Sampson Chester to Thomas Bendish of Boston, and three days later he signed as witness to a release from Nathaniel Barnes to Lancelot Talbott.[2] On January 30, 1679, he was one of the sureties on a bond as indicated from the following extract from the *Town Books:* "We John Turner Vintner and John Casey Taylor both of Bostone doe bind ourselves to Capt. Thomas Brattle Treasurer of the towne of Boston in the Sum of ffortie pounds, that Alexander Hamilton confectioner Shall not be Chargeable to the towne, 30th day of January, 1679."[3]

William Macklaflin, taxed in 1688, was really William McLoughlin, and the following are exact copies of the entries in the *Town Books* covering the births of his children:

Sarah, daughter of William and Olive Mcloughlin, born October 29, 1689
Eliza, daughter of William and Olive Mcloughlin, born September 10, 1691
Mary, daughter of William and Olef McLoughlin, born March 23, 1694

I also find several other instances where McLoughlins were written down in Massachusetts records as "Macklaflin," and one of the early settlers at Wenham, Mass., was an Irishman named McLaughlin whose name was rendered in the records as "Macclaflin," and finally, "Claflin" by the dropping of the "Mac," and it has been shown in the genealogy of the family that the founder of the great dry-goods house of Claflin and Company of New York was one of his descendants.[4] In 1700, when William McLoughlin's widow was taxed, she was recorded "Widow Mackcloghlan," and other spellings of the name are "Mclaughflin," "McCloflin" and "McGlauflin."

Dennis Mackdaniell, taxed in 1681, probably was a MacDonnell, and one entry of his name in the *Town Books* was "Magdon-

<hr />

[1] *Suffolk Deeds*, Vol. IX, pp. 248, 387 and 391.
[2] *Town Books*, Vol. VII.
[3] *Ibid.*
[4] The writer of the Claflin family history, however, refers to the original McLaughlin as "a Scotchman."

iel." "Dennis, son of Dennis and Alice Magdoniel," is recorded as born at Boston on November 25, 1671, and "Michael, son of John and Isabel Magdaniel," was born there on July 26, 1666. There was another John of the same name, John Magdaniell, who was married by Governor John Endecott at Boston to Elizabeth Smith on May 15, 1658, and the births of whose children are on record between 1659 and 1674. One of them, "Daniel MackDaniel," was a police officer in Boston and was "added to ye North Watch" at a meeting of the selectmen on February 28, 1714. "Dennis Mackdaniel Dyed ye 20 Jan," is one of the entries in the *Town Books* of the year 1697.[1]

Among names not included in the foregoing list of taxpayers, because of the fact that I do not find them in the regular tax lists, are Joseph Burke and Mother, Thomas Higgins, Gilbert Crowley and Timothy Mackhue; yet, these are shown among "persons (at Boston) who had their taxes abated" in the year 1700.[2] Of the other taxpayers, with the exception of the MacCarthys, I have not found any mention. There are also other names in the tax lists, such as Barrett, Buckley, Butler, Bradley, Coleman, Cunningham, Foy, Ford, Flood, Gill, Griffin, Gwinn, Hayes, Reynolds, Shannon and Welch, who may possibly have been Irish, but I do not include these because we know there were people of such names of English or Scotch descent, and while all these names are now common enough in Irish family nomenclature, one cannot always be sure that they were Irish, especially at the period with which we are dealing. It will be noted that I have confined this list of taxpayers to the seventeenth century. Those of the eighteenth century would make a very much longer and more impressive list, which will be dealt with later. There is nothing said in the *Town Books* about the nationality of these people, but I hardly think that many will be inclined to dispute the correctness of the assumption that all were Irish. And in view of the attitude of our historians toward the Irish in omitting all mention of the fact that any such people came to New England in colonial times, it is really surprising to find so many old Irish names on record at this early period of our history.

The book reviewer of the *New York Evening Post* in a review of *A Hidden Phase of American History*, tried to cast ridicule on

[1] *Town Books*, Vols. IX and XI.
[2] *Ibid.*, Vol. X.

some of my statements as to the Irish in the Colonies, which were based partly on the names appearing in the Colonial records and the Revolutionary muster-rolls. If he had only quoted my statements, so that his readers could have a chance to form their own judgment on the question, I would not object so much, but when he not only failed to do so but ignored altogether the explanations offered for including certain names among the Irish, he betrayed his shallowness and dishonesty. Pretending to have knowledge of the subject, he claimed that "names are no assurance in determining nationality," and I agree with him fully on that proposition in so far as it relates to certain names commonly occurring among natives of England, Scotland, Wales and Ireland. But, when he intimates that persons bearing names of the most distinctive and ancient Gaelic origin may not have been Irish at all, he only makes a display of his ignorance of the subject, and his statement is really too absurd for serious discussion. Who can doubt that people bearing such names as the foregoing were Irish?

VESSELS REPORTED IN THE "BOSTON NEWS LETTER," 1714 TO 1725, AS "ENTERED INWARDS" AT THE CUSTOM HOUSE FROM IRISH PORTS, OR "OUTWARD BOUND" FOR IRELAND.

Date Announced in News Letter.	Name of Vessel.	Name of Master.	From or For.
1714, Apr. 19–26	*Gray Hound*	Benjamin Elson	From Ireland
May 31–June 7	*Elizabeth and Kathrin*	William Robinson	From Ireland
Aug. 2– 9	*Mary Anne*	John Macarell	From Ireland
Sept. 13–20	*York Merchant*	John Beach	From Cork
Oct. 4–11	*Thomas and Jane*	William Wilson	From Londonderry
1715, June 13–20	*Amity*	Nathaniel Breed	From Ireland
Nov. 28–Dec. 5	Not stated	James Hamilton	For Ireland
May 21–28	*Truth and Daylight*	Robert Campbell	From Cork
1716, May 28–June 4	*Truth and Daylight*	Robert Campbell	For Ireland
June 18–25	*Mary Anne*	Robert Maccarral	From Dublin
July 2– 9	Not stated	——— Montgomery	From Waterford
June 25–July 2	*Globe*	Nicholas Oursell	From Ireland
Oct. 8–15	*Princess Caroline*	Not stated	From Ireland
July 2– 9	Not stated	——— Montgomery	From Waterford
Aug. 12–19	*Globe*	Alexander Douglasse	From Dublin
Sept. 2– 9	Not stated	Robert Montgomery	From Ireland
Sept. 9–16	*Friends Goodwill*	Edward Gooding	From Dublin
Sept. 9–16	Not stated	——— Goodwin	From Dublin
Sept. 23–30	" "	Archibald MacPheaderis	From Ireland
Sept. 30–Oct. 7	" "	——— Mackarrel	For Dublin
1718, ?	"	Alexander Miller	From Ireland
Mar. 24–31	" "	——— Miller	For Ireland
May 12–19	" "	——— Gibbs	From Ireland
June 23–30	" "	——— Caldwell	From Ireland
July 21–28	*Willian and Mary*	James Montgomery	From Ireland
July 28–Aug. 4	Not stated	John Wilson	From Londonderry
Aug. 4–11	*Robert*	James Ferguson	From Ireland
Aug. 4–11	*William*	Archibald Hunter	From Coleraine

Date Announced in News Letter.	Name of Vessel.	Name of Master.	From or For.
Aug. 4–11	Mary and Anne	Andrew Watt	From Dublin
Aug. 25–Sept. 1	William	Not stated	For Ireland
Aug. 25–Sept. 1	Not stated	James Montgomery	For Dublin
Sept. 1– 8	Dolphin	John Mackay	From Dublin
Sept. 1– 8	Maccalum	James Law	From Londonderry
Sept. 15–22	Not stated	Archibald Hunter	For Ireland
Oct. 13–20	Maccalum	James Law	For Londonderry
Oct. 20–27	Mary and Elizabeth	Not stated	For Londonderry
Oct. 27–Nov. 3	Beginning	John Rogers	From Waterford
Nov. 17–24	Not stated	Alex. Miller	From Ireland
Nov. 17–24	" "	——— Remer	From Ireland
Dec. 8–15	Joseph and Mary	Eben Allen	From Ireland
1719, Dec. 29 (1718–			
Jan. 5)	George	——— Salter	For Ireland
May 11–18	Not stated	——— Yoa	From Waterford
June 8–15	Jane	John MacArthur	From Belfast
June 29–July 6	Not stated	John Jones	For Ireland
July 13–20	" "	Joseph Newell	From Dublin
Aug. 10–17	Globe	John Mackay	From Dublin
Aug. 17–24	Not stated	Philip Bass	From Londonderry
Aug. 31–Sept. 7	Joseph	Samuel Harris	From Ireland
Sept. 21–28	Mary	Philip Rawlings	From Dublin
Oct. 12–19	Amsterdam	John Wakefield	From Ireland
Nov. 2– 9	Joseph and Mary	Not stated	From Londonderry
Nov. 2– 9	Elizabeth	Robert Homes	From Ireland
Nov. 16–23	Gray Hound	William Lea	From Ireland
Nov. 30–Dec. 7	Mary and Abigail	Eben Allen	For Ireland
1720, Jan. 11–18	Not stated	Clifford Crowinshield	For Ireland
Apr. 4–11	" "	William Jarvis	For Ireland
Apr. 25–May 2	Amity	James Goodman	From Cork
May 9–16	Amity	James Goodman	For Ireland
May 9–16	Joseph	Philip Bass	For Ireland
Aug. 1– 8	Margaret	Lake Stafford	From Dublin
Aug. 22–29	Not stated	——— Marston	From Ireland
Aug. 29–Sept. 5	" "	Nathl. Jarvis	From Ireland
Sept. 5–12	Reburn	Joseph Newell	From Dublin
Sept. 21–28	Mary	Philip Rawlings	From Dublin
Oct. 17–24	Joseph	Philip Bass	From Ireland
Oct. 17–24	Essex	Robert Peat	From Ireland
Nov. 21–28	Prosperity	Josiah Carver	From Ireland
Dec. 5–12	Experiment	George Read	From Londonderry
Dec. 19–26	Experiment	George Read	For Ireland
1721,[1]Nov. 6–13	Not stated	Thomas Hendry	From Dublin
1722,[1]Nov. 5–12	" "	——— Handrey	From Ireland
1723,[1]Aug. 12–29	" "	Stephen Hall	From Ireland
Oct. 18–24	" "	Nathaniel Breed	From Dublin
Oct. 24–31	" "	Thomas Jones	From Ireland
Nov. 7–14	" "	Amos Breen	From Dublin
1724, Apr. 9–16	" "	Joseph Richards	For Ireland
Aug. 20–27	" "	——— Ward	From Ireland
Aug. 20–27	" "	Elias Bennet	From Dublin
Sept. 10–17	" "	Philip Bass	From Ireland
Sept. 24–Oct. 1	" "	Thomas Jones	From Ireland
1725, Mar. 4–11	" "	William Goodwin	For Ireland
Mar. 25–Apr. 2	" "	William Grubb	For Ireland
Mar. 25–Apr. 2	" "	Alex. McTyler	For Ireland
May 27–June 3	" "	Percival Farmer	From Ireland
June 17–24	" "	——— Grubb	For Ireland

[1] Only a few copies of these years' issues are in existence.

There are comparatively few copies of the *News Letter* of these years now in existence; for several intervals the files of the paper, both at Boston and New York, are missing for whole months at a stretch and for some years there are only two or three copies to be had. But even from the few items in the foregoing list we can readily see that vessels must have been trading regularly between Ireland and New England ports in the early years of the eighteenth century, and the occasional advertisements met with in the newspaper announcing Irish goods for sale fully confirm this conclusion. Moreover, instances are noted where no announcement would appear in the *News Letter* of a certain ship's arrival, yet a reference may be found in other records of the arrival of that ship at Boston with passengers. For example, in Chapter 52 of the Province Laws of 1716–1717, there is a record of an order issued in June, 1717, that "the passengers just arrived from Ireland be sent to Spectacle Island," in Boston harbor; but there is no mention in the *News Letter* of the arrival of any vessel from Ireland in that month. On the other hand, when the *News Letter* for the week, May 31–June 7, 1714, announced the arrival from Ireland of the ship, *Elizabeth and Kathrin*, at Boston it made no mention of passengers, yet the government ordered her captain "to place his sick passengers ashoar on Spectacle Island."[1]

Most, if not all, of these vessels carried passengers as well as merchandise, although in all cases the announcements of their arrival did not mention that fact. And it is also of some interest to note that, of the known arrivals of Irish vessels between 1714 and 1725, 44 per cent of them were reported as "from Ireland," without naming the ports of departure, 40 per cent were from Dublin, Cork and Waterford, and 16 per cent from Londonderry, Coleraine and Belfast, in which figures the "Scotch-Irish" advocates will hardly find very much confirmation of their pet theory! In case it should be thought that these proportions were unusual, I submit the figures obtained from an examination of the *Boston Gazette* of the year 1738, covering shipping with Irish ports. Of fifty-five vessels thus reported, twenty-two were from and for "Ireland," seventeen from and for Cork, fifteen from and for Dublin, two each from Belfast and Waterford, and one from Limerick.

So that the percentage recorded as from Ulster ports in that year was less than 4 per cent of all shipping from Ireland, and

[1] Chapter 45, Province Laws of 1714.

even if we should assume that all of the vessels recorded as from "Ireland," where the ports were not named, came from Ulster ports, the proportion would be only about 50 per cent of the whole!

These ships were of various sizes and capacities, ranging from the little vessel called a "Snow" to the large "brigantine," and the number of passengers were variously stated as anywhere from 6 to 250. From the *News Letter* we obtain occasional glimpses of the condition of these immigrants and of the hardships they suffered on the voyage across the Atlantic, and the following is an exact copy of an account published in that paper of September 9–16, 1717, of the arrival of a vessel at Boston: "Arrived here the ship, *Friends Goodwill*, from Dublin, Edward Gooding, Master, about Eighteen Weeks passage from Learn in Ireland, having on board two and fifty (250) who have sustained very great hardships in their Voyage by contrary Winds, being put to very short allowances, both of Bread, Water and Meat, that it is a Miracle they did not all perish; but God's good Providence has often been visibly seen in their preservation; first in meeting a Ship at sea that spared them some Provisions; and then by Dolphins and Sharks they catched, and by Rain Water saved on their Decks, and on the 26th of August last, all like to be swallowed up by a violent Storm, the Sailors being spent with hunger and thirst hardly able to Navigate the Vessel; one Man died on board and they had thoughts of casting Lots who should be killed to be eaten, which thro' mercy was prevented."

The *York Merchant* which arrived at Boston "from Cork, Ireland," in September, 1714, brought "Irish servants," and in the *Globe* from Dublin, which arrived at Boston during the week, August 12–19, 1717, came "sundry servants to serve for 4 to 9 years." But Boston was not the only port through which the Irish settlers entered New England, and from Marblehead and Salem, Mass., Piscataqua, Maine, and Providence, R. I., also came occasional reports of the arrival of vessels from Ireland. A dispatch from Marblehead to the *News Letter* dated May 16, 1718, said "Captain Gibbs has arrived here from Dublin with Irish and Scotch servants."[1] Piscataqua reported on June 27 that "Captain Caldwell is arrived here from Ireland with 178 Passengers,"[2] and under the head of "Entered Inwards at the (Boston) Custom

[1] *News Letter*, May 12–19, 1718.
[2] *Ibid.*, June 23–30, 1718.

House" there is an item reading: "Arrived, Captain James Montgomery in the Ship, *William and Mary* from Ireland."[1] During the next week "Captain John Wilson from Londonderry" arrived at Boston and brought with him "boys, young men and girls." The *News Letter* of August 4–11, 1718, reported the arrival at Boston of three ships from Ireland, viz.—"The *Robert* from Belfast, Captain James Montgomery"; "the *William* from Coleraine, Captain Archibald Hunter," and "the *Mary Anne* from Dublin, Captain Andrew Watt," and one vessel, the *William and Mary*, "outward bound" for Dublin under the command of Captain James Montgomery. There is no mention of passengers having come in these vessels, except that the *Mary Anne* from Dublin brought "servants."

"Captain John Mackay, ship *Dolphin* from Dublin," was reported as arriving at Boston during the week, September 1–8, 1718, and although there is no reference to passengers, the fact that the *Dolphin* brought passengers is made clear from the following advertisement printed in the *News Letter* of the week named: "Just arrived in the Pink, *Dolphin*, John Mackay, Master, with Servants, Boys, Tradesmen, Husbandmen and Maids, to be disposed of by Mr. John Walker at his Warehouse at the lower end of Woodmansy Wharff in Merchants Row, or at Mr. Benjamin Walker's House over against the Town House, Boston." From Casco, Maine, came the news that during the week ended September 29, 1718, "a vessel arrived at Casco Bay from Ireland with several passengers."[2] A despatch from Piscataqua in the issue of May 11–18, 1719, gave an account of the arrival there of "Captain Yoa, six weeks passage from Waterford," who "brought the news of the expected rising on behalf of the Pretender" and how "Irish Officers were raising forces in Ireland for him," etc. From the same port on August 21, 1719, came the news that "Captain Philip Bass is arrived at Kennebeck River from Londonderry with about 200 Passengers. A Passenger that came in him says that some Vessels with Arms that were going to the Spaniards and Rebels in Scotland were taken by our Cruisers, one whereof was brought into Derry, the Master, an Irish Man, and his Men made Prisoners."[3] The ship *Elizabeth* which arrived

---

[1] *News Letter*, July 21–28, 1718.
[2] *Ibid.*, September 22–29, 1718.
[3] *News Letter*, August 17–24, 1719.

at Boston "from Ireland" during the week, November 2–9, 1719, brought about "150 passengers," all evidently from Ulster, and at a meeting of the selectmen on November 3, 1719, "several persons who came passengers in the ship *Elizabeth*, Captain Robert Homes, Master," were "warned to depart."[1] There is also an entry in the *Town Books* of November 30, 1719, that "Sundry Passengers who came from Ireland with Captain Dennis and arrived here in November last," were "warned to depart."[2]

The *News Letter* of August 1–8, 1720, said: "By Letters from Ireland of the 14th of April last we are informed that the Briganteen, *Essex*, Robert Peat, Master, who sailed from this Port was safely arrived there, and that Mr. Benjamin Marston of Salem, the owner, was seized with the Small-Pox, whereof he died, and that his son, Mr. Benjamin Marston, was also taken with same, but recovered; and some Days ago we had a flying report that the said Briganteen was bound from Ireland for either this Port or to the West Indies, full of Passengers, and that they were all lost. But, by Captain Luke Stafford, Commander of the ship *Margaret* from Dublin, about nine Weeks passage from thence, who arrived at Marblehead the 4th instant, we are informed that the said Briganteen was stranded and is since safely arrived at London-Derry without any person being lost." The fact that the *Essex* again sailed from Ireland with her human freight, but was captured by pirates on the high seas, appears from an advertisement printed in the *News Letter* of October 10–17, 1720, in which "Daniel Starr of Boston, by Trade a Joyner, but lately a Mariner on board the Briganteen *Essex*, whereof Robert Peat was Commander," related that "in his Voyage from Ireland to Salem on the 17th of July last he was taken by one Captain Thomas Roberts, Commander of a Pirate ship and sloop of 150 men, and forced the said Starr to go along with him against his will." The owner of the *Essex* died in Dublin and after Captain Peat had taken the vessel on her second perilous voyage, Benjamin Marston, Junior, evidently secured another ship on which he sailed from Dublin for Salem. The *News Letter* of August 22–29, 1720, printed this account of the younger Marston's adventures:

---

[1] Boston *Town Books*, Vol. XIII, p. 63.

[2] *Ibid.*, p. 64. These warnings were of common occurrence in New England towns. There was constant fear that newcomers not well provided for would become a charge on the town, so they were "warned to depart."

"Last week arrived at Salem Captain Marston from Ireland
with several Passengers, both Men and Women, who was also
taken by Captain Roberts, the Pirate, about two Days after he
had parted from Captain Carey. The said Pirate had also taken
a Bristol vessel bound for Virginia from Bristol, out of whom the
Pirate took his goods and Forced some or most of his Men, and
put on board several of Captain Marston's Men or Passengers to
go with her for Bristol."

From time to time the Boston *News Letter* also published despatches from New York and Philadelphia relating to the arrival
of vessels from Ireland, some examples of which it may be of interest to quote here. In its issue of July 30–August 6, 1716, there is
an account from Philadelphia dated July 26, of the arrival of "the
ship *Cezer* of Whitehaven Matthew Cowman, Master, from Dublin, but last about seven weeks from Waterford, who brought
Seventy odd Passengers," and according to a despatch in that
paper of September 9–16, 1717, the same vessel and commander
arrived at Philadelphia on September 5th "from Dublin in eleven
weeks and brought about One Hundred Passengers." On October 24, 1717, "Captain Codd from Liverpool and Dublin with
150 Passengers, many whereof were Servants," arrived at Philadelphia, according to a despatch in the *News Letter* of November
4–11 of that year. It is a long account relating to the capture
of the vessel by the pirate sloop, *Revenge*, and Captain Codd also
reported that "the Pirate took two Snows outward bound, loaden
with staves for Ireland." From Philadelphia on November 7
came the news that "Joseph Travers of Liverpool is arrived here
from the North of Ireland with near 200 Passengers, about 12
Weeks Passage,"[1] and on November 14, "Gough in the ship *Dove*
is arrived here with Passengers from Ireland."[2]

A vessel "from Cork" arrived at Philadelphia in March, 1718,
with "fifty Passengers," and the *News Letter* of August 11–18,
1718, published an account from Philadelphia dated August 7,
stating: "This morning the ship *Elizabeth and Margaret*, John
Beeby, Commander, arrived in twelve weeks from Dublin with
160 Passengers; 9 or 10 Dyed at Sea," and on September 11, 1718,
"Captain Maclista (McAllister) in the ship *Brunswick* arrived
from Londonderry about 9 Weeks Passage, with Eighty Passen-

---

[1] *News Letter*, November 11–18, 1717.
[2] *Ibid.*, November 18–25, 1717.

gers." On August 20, 1719, Philadelphia reported: "Arrived this morning Captain Clark in a Snow from Londonderry, 12 weeks Passage, who has 149 Souls on board,"[1] and from New York came the news on November 9, 1719, that "a Pink arrived, said to be full of people, we suppose to be from Londonderry, for Amboy (N. J.) with Passengers."

Several other similar despatches appeared in the *News Letter* down through the years 1720 to 1725, all indicating that there were well-established commercial relations between Ireland and America during this period and that there were continuous immigrations of Irish people to the Colonies, where, in common with the English, Scotch and other colonists, they accepted a share of the burdens which fell to the lot of the pioneer settlers. That this statement is not made without authority, but is based on the public records of the time, can be shown in many ways. For example, at a meeting of the selectmen of the town of Boston on May 4, 1723, the following "order" was issued:

Whereas great numbers of Persons have very lately bin Transported from Ireland into this Province, many of which by Reason of the Present Indian War and other Accedents befalling them, Are now Resident in this Town whose Circumstances and Condition are not known, Some of which if due care be not taken may become a Town Charge or be otherwise prejuditial to the well fair and Prosperity of the Place, for Remady whereof Ordered That Every Person now Resident here, that hath within the Space of three years last past bin brought from Ireland or for the future Shal come from thence hither Shal come and Enter his name and Occupation with the Town Clerk, and if marryed the number and Age of his Children and Servants within the Space of five Dayes, on pain of forfeiting and paying the Sum of twenty Shillings for Each offence, and the Sum of ten Shillings for Every one that Shal Continue in the neglect or non-Observance of this Order, for and During the term of forty-Eight hours after the Expiration of the five dayes aforesaid So often as the Person offending Shal be Complained of and Convict before any Justice of the Peace within the Said County.

And be it further Ordered that whoever Shal Receive and Entertain and Keep in his family any Person or Persons Transported from Ireland as aforesaid Shal within the Space of forty-Eight hours after Such Receipt and Entertainment Return the Names of all Such Persons with their Circomstances as far as they are able to the Town Clerk.[2]

As already stated, the historians claim that the people who came from Ireland during this period and for many years thereafter were only those whom they call the "Scotch-Irish." It is

[1] *News Letter*, August 24–31, 1719.
[2] Boston *Town Books*, Vol. VIII, p. 177.

not always easy to determine what these writers mean by "Scotch-Irish." Mr. Lodge, for instance, once wrote me saying that "General John Sullivan was a Scotch-Irishman"; some historians place in that category all immigrants to the Colonies whose names bore the prefix "Mc" or "Mac," while others simply go ahead and seize upon every person who came from Ireland, no matter how ancient an Irish name he bore, and call him "Scotch-Irish!" Even O'Briens and Murphys, McCarthys and Flanagans and numerous others bearing obvious Irish names did not escape! While there is much confusion between them and they contradict each other right and left as to the origin of the "Scotch-Irish," there is one point upon which they seem to be generally agreed, namely, that the first requisite was to be a non-Catholic, and that fact being settled to their satisfaction, they then conferred upon every Irishman the privilege of being a "Scotch" Irishman! While they flounder around in their confusion seeking explanations, they never seem to strike the right idea. They don't know that the term, "Scotch-Irish," was first used in this country as one of contempt or reproach; when any one wanted to refer to an Irishman in a contemptuous way or to say he was of no account, they usually called him a "Scotch-Irishman!"

For one who has spent many years poring over old records such as the newspaper accounts herein referred to, records of land offices, Surrogates' Courts and Registrars of Wills and Deeds, church registers, and official lists and documents of all kinds of the Colonial and Revolutionary periods, which contain thousands of names of the oldest Irish origin, it is difficult to hold in check the indignation that arises at the palpably dishonest attempts of historical writers to color the facts to suit their own perconceived notions and ideas. The modern word, "camouflage," aptly applies to the work of these writers, because they make such feverish efforts to cover up the facts!

One of the historians who gave some attention to the early immigrations from Ireland to New England is Mr. Charles Knowles Bolton of Boston, author of a book entitled *Some Scotch-Irish Pioneers in Ulster and America.* One would think on reading this book that almost the entire population of Ireland sprang from the Scotch who were "planted" there by King James during the first decade of the seventeenth century, and that no one came from Ireland to America in the early days but the

"Scotch-Irish." Its author tries to support this idea by the reproduction of many names of evident Scotch origin appearing in eighteenth century records and documents in the Colonies, but he omits all reference to those bearing purely Irish names, with the result that he has created the impression that none of this class came to America. He quotes the letters of Thomas Lechmere, surveyor-general of Massachusetts, in which Lechmere refers to the "Irish Familys," and in the very letters and documents signed by the settlers from which Bolton quotes it is seen that the immigrants always referred to themselves as "Irish." Yet, Bolton fails to see the inconsistency of his now giving these people a new racial designation!

No one denies the fact that a good percentage of the people of the North of Ireland who emigrated to America were descended from the Scotchmen brought over in the "Ulster Plantation." These families lived in Ireland for many generations; in numerous instances they intermarried with the old Irish families; they were natives of Ireland; all their interests were in Ireland; their children grew up Irish, while yet, of course, retaining the religious beliefs brought by their ancestors from Scotland. But, religion by no means makes nationality, no matter how much certain writers may try to prove that it does. As natives of Ireland, they were *Irish* men, not *Scotch* Irishmen, for the same logical reason that the late Theodore Roosevelt, for instance, was an *American*, not a *Dutch* American, although of Dutch descent. If these immigrants were unworthy of mention, the historians never would have troubled themselves about them, but, because they exhibited qualities which redound to their credit and because they contributed something to the glory of America, they are dubbed "Scotch-Irish" in the effort to deprive Ireland of the credit that is her due!

Apart from the fact that the names so plainly demonstrate the racial origin of many of these immigrants, a little reflection on the part of historical writers would make it clear that the assumption that no "Irish" from the north of Ireland came to the Colonies, is erroneous. In the foregoing list there are six vessels which came from Londonderry, one from Coleraine and one from Belfast; but, what warrant is there for assuming that all persons who took ship at these ports were "Scotch-Irish?" Londonderry was and is the port from which passengers from Donegal, Derry and Tyrone embarked. Donegal is one of the most "Irish" counties of Ireland and the census figures show that Derry and Tyrone are about equally divided between the descendants of the ancient race and the Scotch planters. When we consider the primitive travelling facilities of the time, we know that the immigrants embarked at the nearest ports, so that, it is a fair inference that the majority of those who took ship at Londonderry were of the ancient Irish race.

All of the passengers arriving in these ships did not settle in Boston or vicinity, and it is evident that a large proportion of them went to New Hampshire and the present state of Maine, especially to the territory bordering on Merrymeeting Bay and along the Kennebec and Eastern rivers, where they located permanently. It was in this section of Maine that Robert Temple, in the year 1720, established the town of Cork, called after the city of that name in Ireland, and in the public records of this part of the state, especially in Lincoln County, down to the time of the Revolution, are found great numbers of Irish names. Of course, the names of all the immigrants from Ireland do not indicate old Irish origin, since some were evidently of English and Scotch descent; nevertheless, in nearly every available public record in which they are mentioned they are referred to as "Irish," as they were in fact. Robert Temple was of the Tipperary family of that name who intermarried with the famous Emmets, and two of the five ships which he chartered for his great enterprise sailed from the port of Cork bringing many immigrants from the Province of Munster, who, in all likelihood, were the people who settled on the Eastern River at the place which they called "Cork." A strange fact which historians gloss over is this, if these people were "Scotch-Irish" why did they name their settlement "Cork," and why, even to this day the bend of the Eastern River where the old town of Cork was located is known locally as "Cork Cove" and for more than a century the surrounding territory was familiarly known as "Ireland?" Bolton selects certain names among those who located in this section as showing they were of the "Scotch-Irish" element. The correctness of his lists is not disputed, but since it appears that he did actually examine the records for his information, he must necessarily have noticed the large number of old Irish names appearing in eighteenth century records of Lincoln and adjacent counties. Yet, he includes in his lists the "Scotch-Irish" names only! Among the surnames noted in these records are:

Barry	Duggan	McFadden	Noonan
Bourke	Flanagan	McGowan	O'Brien
Butler	Flynn	McCaffrey	O'Neill
Condon	Farrell	McBride	O'Murphy
Corbett	Foley	McKeowen	O'Dee
Carney	Fogerty	McGuire	Prendergast
Cassidy	Fitzgerald	McCarthy	Phelan
Connelly	Gahan	McGra	Powers
Clancy	Haley	McLaughlin	Quinnan
Costigan	Haggerty	McDonal	Quinlan
Connell	Hogan	McQuillan	Quinn
Cooney	Higgins	McManus	Ryan
Cleary	Hurley	McNamara	Riley
Conners	Hickey	Macgraw	Riordan
Connor	Hayley	McSweeney	Rourke
Carroll	Kenny	Madden	Roche
Connery	Kelliher	Meloney	Sullivan
Corcoran	Kelley	Murphy	Shea
Crowley	Kavanaugh	Malloy	Tobin
Daly	Leary	Maher	Tynan
Donnell	Lynch	Mahoney	Walsh
Dunn	McKenny	Mooney	Whelan
Doyle	McMahon	Mulligan	

SOME TRACES OF THE IRISH SETTLERS IN THE COLONY OF MASSACHUSETTS BAY.

COLLECTED BY MICHAEL J. O'BRIEN.

The vital records of many New England towns testify to the presence of a large number of Irish people in this section during the eighteenth century, and from these records, or from authentic copies of them published by historical societies, the following items are taken:

GLOUCESTER, MASS., MARRIAGE RECORDS.

Daniel McAfee and Hannah Denning, February 20, 1717
John Flinn and Mary Hammonds, October 20, 1719
Mary Flin and William Nelson, January 26, 1721
Mary Flinn and Rd. Tarr, January 1, 1740
Richard Tandy and Rachel Allen, March 17, 1725
William Moore and Lydia Parsons, January 22, 1732
James McCoy and Janet Fleming, December 19, 1732
James Brady and Jane Stevens, December 7, 1730
Timothy Higgins and Eliz. Hammonds, February 6, 1732
Jane Brady and John Carter, November 6, 1733
Thomas Kenneby and Lydia Riggs, November 2, 1726
Felix Doyle and Mary Goodridge, December 25, 1735
Catherine Connolly and Isaac Joslyn, September 9, 1744
Esther MacCarty and Epes Sargent, date omitted (she died July 1, 1743)
Richard McGuire and Abigail Bray, November 11, 1759
Michael Flanikin (alias Flanigan) and Martha Bishop, December 9, 1766
Nabby Cloughlin and Nathaniel Blatchford, October 2, 1790
Polly Brady and James Lane, December 16, 1792
David Donnehew and Rebecca Brown, December 22, 1796
Judith Garvin and Thomas Brown, February 12, 1797

Other names appearing in the Gloucester vital records in later years are Kelley, Collins, Hayes, McKean, Murphy, Shaw and Donahew. Four children of Felix Doyle, Daniel, Felix, Samuel and Mary, appear in the baptismal records between 1739 and 1747.

Malden, Mass., is a place which attracted several Irish families. Among the marriage entries in the vital records of the town are: Patrick Flinn and Mary Winsled, on July 16, 1713; James Hayes and Mehitable Sprague, on January 22, 1713; Patrick Cowen and Jean Crawford, on February 22, 1733; Charles Crouley and Mary

Marks, on October 1, 1745; and William Gill and Martha Flinn, on March 9, 1749; and in the ancient burying-ground at Malden there is a stone bearing the inscription: "Mary Flyn, wife of Patrick, in her 27th year, died May 24th, 1720." But, the earliest date in which an Irishman appears at Malden was in 1666. In the *New England Historic-Genealogical Register* (Vol. 2), are reproduced the "Lane Family Papers." The first of the family in Massachusetts was Job Lane, an Englishman, who settled at Malden early in the seventeenth century. He seems to have been an industrious recorder of events, if one is to judge from his voluminous papers, and among them is one dated "June 15th, 1666," reading: "John Quinne of the County of Cork in Ireland, binds himself to Job Lane. Witnesses, Thomas Rawlings and Thomas Rawlings, Jr."

In the seacoast towns Irish people are mentioned in the seventeenth century more often than at inland places. An entry in the town records at Salem reads: "John Garven, drowned 5: 12: 1661."[1] "Willm Obrien" appears under date of September 13, 1669, but in what connection is not clear. In the will of Walter Price of Salem dated May 21, 1674, the testator named among the legatees his "daughter Elizabeth Burke,"[2] and "Edward, son of Edward Burke," was baptised in the First Church at Salem on August 17, 1687. Bryant O'Dougherty who was at Salem in 1683[3] is another interesting individual, and an entry in the town records informs us that "Thomas Daley was married and his daughter borne 16th September, 1682; daughter Mary borne 6 July 1685."[4] Murphys also came early to Salem. William Murphy is mentioned among the "Early Settlers of Essex and Norfolk Counties" in 1669,[5] and it is probable that Captain William Murphy who commanded the ship, *Friendship*, trading between New England and the West Indies in 1679 was the same man.[6] "Thomas Murffee, Boatswain," was of the *Salem Galley*, and under date of August 16, 1696, he is mentioned as receiving part of some prize money earned by the crew of the boat.[7] "Francis

[1] *Essex Institute Historical Collections*, Vol. 2, p. 148.
[2] *Ibid.*, Vol. 41, p. 301.
[3] Historical and Genealogical Notes and Queries, by Eben Putnam of Salem.
[4] *Essex Institute Historical Collections*, Vol. 2, p. 42.
[5] *New Eng. Hist.-Geneal. Register*, Vol. 7.
[6] *Ibid.*, Vol. 8.
[7] *Essex Institute Historical Collections*, Vol. 41, p. 186.

Roache, shipmaster and chandler of Salem, a native of Ireland,"
is mentioned without date, and William Roache married Hannah
Potter at Salem and had children born there—William on "12th
6th mo. 1692"; Hannah, "October ye 12th, 1694"; Elizabeth on
May 16, 1697, and Mary on October 26, 1699.[1] There is a
"Roache's Point" at Winter Island opposite Salem, called after
William Roache, who, evidently, was a sea-captain.

The complete record of the "Mecartey" family of Salem, as it
appears in the Historical Collections of the Essex Institute,[2] is as
follows, but in other references to them the name is spelled variously "Mecarter," "Macarta" and "Maccartey": "John
Mecartey and Rebecka Meacham were maryed the 27th of
January, 1674; theire son John borne the 13th January, 1675;
Daughter, Rebecka, borne 4th 12 mo. 1677; Son Jeremiah borne
9th 7th mo. '79; Peter borne 1st 9th mo. '81; Andrew borne 6th
June, 1684; James born 17th 9th mo. 1686; Isaac born 3rd June,
1689; Rebecka born the second daughter 6th February, 1690."
The father of these children also appears in the Salem tax lists of
the year 1700 as "John Mackartee,"[3] and the probate records of
Newport, R. I., show that "John Mackartey of Salem" took out
letters of administration to the estate of his son, "Andrew Mackartey late of Salem, deceased," in the year 1703 or 1704. No
information as to these people seems to be obtainable, beyond the
bare references to them in the town records, but there is reason to
believe that they were engaged in the fishing industry and that
young Andrew and his father were masters of vessels plying out of
Salem. Another early McCarthy at Salem was "William Maccarty," who is mentioned among persons who owned land at
Salem prior to 1661. "John McCartey, a Dyer," came to
Salem from Warren, R. I., in 1699 and settled there, and "John
Mecarty," who probably was a son of the John and Rebecka
Mecartey above mentioned, is referred to in Salem records of
1702 as a "property owner."

On the town records of Brookline, Mass., under date of January
21, 1672, the name of "Bryan Merphew" is entered, with no
other reference to him. No doubt, this was the Brian Murphy

---

[1] *Essex Institute Historical Collections*, Vol. 3, p. 97.
[2] Vol. 2, p. 298.
[3] See *Genealogical Quarterly Magazine*, Vol. 4.

who, on July 22, 1661, married Margaret Mayhoone, widow of "Dermin Mahoone" or "Dermin OMahoine," whose real name was Dermot or Diarmuid O'Mahony. Bryan Murphy was awarded a plot of land in or near Boston for his services in King Philip's war in 1676. Another entry in the town records of the year 1686 which attracts attention is this: "Benjamin Sullivant, Clerke to ye Councill of Boston." At first glance, one would be apt to conclude that this man's name was Sullivan; yet that undoubtedly would be incorrect, for we could not expect to find a person of the name occupying such a position, and since there were people named Bullivant mentioned in Massachusetts records about this period, I assume this was simply a clerical error in writing down the initial letter of the surname. On the other hand, it is certain there were people named Sullivan in Massachusetts many years before Benjamin "Sullivant" or Bullivant is mentioned. On the Boston *Town Books* this entry appears: "Mackum Downing and Margaret Suleavan married June, 1653," and the births of their seven daughters and one son between 1655 and 1671 all appear in the vital records of the town of Boston.

The town records of Braintree contain this entry: "William Tosh and Jael Swillivan were united in marriage the 12th mo. 7th 1660, by Major Autherton."[1] That the bridegroom's proper name was McIntosh and the bride's name Sullivan is seen from the genealogy of the Mott family of New England,[2] wherein it is stated that "McIntosh was among the Scotch prisoners shipped to New England by Cromwell in 1651," and that "Jael Swillivan was evidently one of the ship-load of Irish captives sent to New England in 1654." "Tosh" and his wife settled at Braintree and when a company of men from that town set out to settle Block Island in 1661, Tosh was among the first settlers and became a man of prominence there. He was made a "Freeman" in 1664, Constable in 1676, and died in 1685. His wife's name is also given in the Mott genealogy as Sullivan. Other Irish names are also found in the vital records of the town of Braintree. A family named Hogan was there in 1715, since the birth of "Hannah, daughter of Daniel and Mary Hogin," is on record at Braintree on July 7, 1715, and among the marriage entries are noted:

[1] Braintree town records, p. 717.

[2] Nathaniel Mott of Scituate and his sons, in *New Eng. Hist.-Geneal. Register*, Vol. 67.

William Tosh and Jael Swillivan, "the 12th mo. 7th, 1660"
Denice Darley and Hannah Francis, "11th mo. 3rd, 1662"
Hannah Hogin and Clement Hayden, October 31, 1734
John Madden and Charity Silvester, July 6, 1765
David Kenney and Mary Tant, October 28, 1774
Mary Collins and Timothy Spear, May 18, 1777
Hannah Joyce and Isaac Thayer, May 4, 1782
John Maddin and Abigail Jones, September 13, 1789
Elizabeth Madden and Zebulon Randall, July 17, 1790
Betsey Barry and William Hooker, October 9, 1790

Speaking of Block Island, an interesting individual whose name appears in its early records was Timothy McCarthy. He was a mariner at Newport prior to 1700 and evidently was a man of some local prominence, since his marriage to Elizabeth Williams is on record at Block Island under date of November 21, 1700. Elizabeth Williams was a daughter of John Williams, a merchant of Boston and Newport and who, in 1687, was attorney-general of Rhode Island. Timothy and Elizabeth McCarthy had three sons, Daniel, Thomas and Joseph, and a daughter named Althea. Daniel dropped the prefix from his name, and the marriage register at New Shoreham, Block Island, contains an entry of his marriage to Elizabeth Trim on July 28, 1721, and the births of their children, Catherine and Daniel, are entered in the vital records on December 29, 1723, and May 26, 1726, respectively. The Cartys were residents of the Island up to 1742, when they removed to Westerly, R. I. Thomas and Joseph "Mecarty" inherited some property on the Island, left to them by John Williams and Robert Guttredge, but there is no trace of their names in the local records. During a visit to Block Island last Summer I examined the headstones over the graves in the ancient cemetery, but apparently the only descendant of the Irish mariner, Timothy McCarthy, buried there was Catherine Stafford, the above-mentioned daughter of Daniel Carty, wife of James Stafford. In the parish registers of Trinity Church at Newport there are recorded two marriages which attracted attention, namely, Eleanor McCarty and John Martin on March 21, 1744, and Judith McCarty and Edward Mitchell on October 28, 1744. It is entirely probable that Eleanor and Judith McCarty were granddaughters of Timothy, although there appears to be no record of their births in the Rhode Island vital records.

"Patrick Fassett, brother-in-law of John Reyley," is so mentioned in the vital records of Charlestown of the year 1671, and judging from the number of places where the former appears, I assume he was a mechanic who went from town to town in pursuit of his occupation. "Joseph, son of Patrick Fassett," was born at Malden in October, 1672, and in that year Patrick was taxed 3s. 6d. at Malden. In 1679 "Patrick ffacit" was taxed 6s. 6d. at Billerica, and it is evident that he and John Reyley moved back to Charlestown, on whose records appears the following entry: "John Reyley and his brother-in-law Patrick Fassett came with wife and two children from Eastward to town October 21, 1689." Fassett died at Charlestown on May 16, 1711. His wife's name was Sarah, and as there is an entry in the Charlestown vital records of the marriage of "Patrick Mackfassy and Sarah ———," it is probable that this was the man's real name, or a closer approach to it than "Fassett." No date is given for the marriage, but it was before 1670, since the record shows that "John, son of Patrick and Sarah Mackfassy," was born at Charlestown in that year. The large number of items containing Irish names in the town books of Charlestown indicate that many of the immigrants from Ireland located at this place. Thomas B. Wyman, a local historian, examined the original records and the following items are taken from his noted work, *Charlestown Genealogies and Estates:*

Persons and Estates Taxed and Periods.

Patrick Bowen } Patrick Boyn }	1732	William Lynch	1737–1742
		Daniel McLaren	1787
Patrick Carogan	1741–1748	James McCarty	1730–1734
Patrick Cowen	1760–1770	John Maccarty } John Maccardy }	1730–1737
John Connelly	1736–1737		
Thomas Flinn } Thomas Flynn }	1739, '48 and '56	Daniel McCarty	1782
		John McGrath	1761, '66, '70
Turner Daily	1771	Charles McKoone	1773
James Gallagher	1797	Lawrence McMinnis	1756
Thomas Garey } Thomas Gearie }	1688	Patrick McNamara	1773
		Patrick Maly	1732–1733
Joseph Gilmore	1737	John Moore, "formerly of Dublin"	
Thomas Gleason	1662		1680–1681
Matthew Griffin	1654	John Mouran	1734
Patrick Hay	1713	John Mullett	1745 to 1770
James Kellen	1688	William Quirk	1638
William Kelly	1756–1766	James Runey	1756 to 1773
James Kenney	1762	Darby Sullivan	1729, '34, '38
Joseph Killen	1720	Roger Tool	1771
John Larey	1742		

Marriages and "Intentions to Marry" at Charlestown.

Anna Callihan and John Nasson, November 30, 1658
Michael Callihan and Susanna Pierce, July 23, 1757
John Connelly and Rebecca Larrabee, November 15, 1737
Sally Connery and John Bennett, July 15, 1805
Nancy Conners and Charles Groves, August 14, 1808
Martin Conwell and Sally Baker, ———— (?) 1807
John Costigan and Jane ————, no date
Patrick Cowen and Abigail Halsey, January 5, 1759
Peter Roe Dalton and Anna Call, November 22, 1778
Sylvester Farrell and Dorothy Robinson, February 22, 1737
John Farrell and Catherine McNeil, ———— 1772
Michael Geohagen and Prudence Winship, May 10, 1744
Hannah Geohagen and Samuel Cooper, ———— 1763
Prudence Geohagen and Edward Goodwin, ———— 1772
Samuel Haley and Mary Reed, January 10, 1740
Daniel Haley and ———— Hunnewell, December 26, 1769
Christoper Hayes and Sarah King, October 2, 1669
William Healy and Sarah Brown, November 29, 1677
Owen Hendy and Martha Clark, August 25, 1670
Margaret Hennesey and Phineas Wheelock, April 8, 1804
Betsey Hennesey and Phineas Wheelock, November 24, 1809
Joseph Higgins and Polly Rand, February 19, 1786
Matthew Hogans (or Hogin) and Mary Wright, February 26, 1740
John Hogans (or Hogin) and Mary Davis, no date
Thomas Hoggin (or Hogin) and Rachel ————, May 27, 1759
Grace Healy and John Ireland, July 15, 1680
Oliver Keating and Sally Lyman, March 11, 1805
James Kellen and Hannah Trerice, December 12, 1679
David Kelley and Elizabeth ————, "prior to 1663"
William Kelley and Mary Powell, no date
John Kennedy and Jane Ferguson, August 14, 1735
James Kenney and Mary ————, no date
Edward Larkin and Joanna ————, ———— 1638
William Lynch and Hannah Howard, September 29, 1737
John Lennen and Martha Miller, August 30, 1785
Alexander Logan and Sussanna Burrage, January 15, 1679
Edward Murphy and Mary Gohen, ———— 1741
James Murphy and ———— Gohen, December 10, 1741
William Murpet (Murphy) and Susanna Bredrich, April 15, 1798
Patrick Mackfassy and Sarah ————, no date (their son John born in 1670)
Mary McCarty and Joseph Hunscot, ———— 1683
Dennis McClain and Mary Simpson, March 20, 1730
Timothy McDonel and Elizabeth Foster, no date (she died in 1766)
Margaret McKlennin and Francis Burns, ———— 1750
Hannah McSwain and Martin Cockrum, ———— 1735
Mary Mahonie and John Russell, ———— 1772

William Manning and Eliza Powers, November 8, 1733
Susanna Melony and William Gibson, —— 1763
Joseph Moore and Hannah Gellume, —— 1659
James Runey and Joanna Lane, October 18, 1753
Darby Sullivan and Margaret ——, February 8, 1729
Owen Sullivan and Hannah Newman, March 2, 1733

MISCELLANEOUS ITEMS OF HISTORIC INTEREST FROM CHARLESTOWN, MASS.,
RECORDS.

John Flinn, James Manning and Anderson Lynch joined a military company
at Charlestown in 1759.   John Flinn sailed on an expedition to Canada on
April 24, 1759.

Samuel Barry, also "John Barry, a native of Ireland," are on record in 1773.
Some of their descendants are said to spell the name "Barre."

—— Cadogan, "an indigent person," died at Charlestown on November 5,
1695.

Robert Calley was schoolmaster at Charlestown from 1748 to 1751.   He was
a son of Robert Kelley of Malden.

James Carey was in business as a draper in 1647 and on April 7, 1663, he was
chosen town clerk.

Edward Collins sold lands to Michael Gill at Charlestown in 1702.

John and James Conroy came there from Boston in July, 1788.

John Cunningham came on the ketch, *Mary and Elisabeth*, in 1680.   His
son, John, was drowned at Boston in 1757.   Had many descendants.

William Dadey was a butcher at Charlestown in 1630.   Testified before the
Legislature on August 11, 1679, that he "aided in building the battery with
bricks and sods."   He possessed much property.

William Daly bought lots at Charlestown from John Powers in 1812.

John Dunawen is mentioned in the town records of the year 1771.

Arthur Dunn, mariner.   Will filed November 2, 1767.

Eliza Fennecy of Cambridge, widow, executed a quit-claim deed to one
Carres in 1793.

Timothy Ford had a lot at Charlestown in 1637.   His son, Stephen, had a
servant "from Ireland."

James Gallagher was a "soap and candle manufacturer" in 1797.

Hugh Garrett was "admitted an inhabitant" in 1629.   Some of his descendants are "Garrards."

Daniel Hayley, wife and two sons, Daniel and Charles, came from Cambridge
in 1770.

Patrick Hartigan, "drowned at Surinam, August 17, 17—."

Patrick Hay bought lands at Charlestown in 1713.   Afterwards, he was a
physician and apothecary in Boston.

Sarah Larey was "admitted to Church" at Charlestown on February 7,
1639.

Edward Larkin, wheelmaker, "admitted as inhabitant" on May 30, 1638.

Luke Lennon was a merchant at Charlestown in 1809.

William Lynch was drowned and his widow was classified among "the town
poor" in 1781.

William McNeese was a ferryman in 1731.

Thomas McCarty is on record as "a stranger." His funeral was held on December 1, 1740, and "ordered to be paid for by the town."

Ann McCarty, widow, of Roxbury, mentioned in 1793.

Thomas McDonoghue is mentioned in the town records of 1798.

John McGrath, "leather breeches maker," is mentioned in 1761.

Dennis McInierney and wife came from Boston to Charlestown in 1723.

William McKeen came there from Halifax on January 26, 1764.

John McKown was a printer at Charlestown in 1816.

Robert McNeill, "of Londonderry or Antrim in Ireland," sold his estate in Ireland and came to America with his wife. Their son, Robert, married Mary Magee at Charlestown. No date is given. Many of their descendants appear in the genealogical records.

David Makloney, "servant to Edward Burt," is mentioned in 1655.

Dennis Monaane, "disallowed to be inhabitant, December 15, 1674."

John Moore, "formerly of Dublin, shipwright," appears on the tax lists in 1680. His estate was administered on January 15, 1683, to his widow, Mary Moore. Thomas Moore was also at Charlestown in 1680 and Francis Moore in 1706. There is a long line of Moores on the genealogical records.

Thomas Mullen and his wife, Mary, "in town, 1756." He was a soldier in 1757 and received a bounty of £6.

Arthur Mullen and wife mentioned in 1757.

Patrick Murray and wife, Sarah, and two children, Joseph and Molly, "notified," 1782.

Cornelius Rine from Marblehead, "notified" October 2, 1730.

Nicholas Roach came from Boston in 1715.

Dennis Ryan served in Lieutenant Whiting's company from Charlestown in 1762.

James Shahan's name appears in the census of 1789.

Mary Sullivan and John Sullivan, children of Darby and Margaret Sullivan, were born at Charlestown on May 8, 1731, and January 14, 1733, respectively.

A number of Reillys and Rileys are mentioned in early Massachusetts records. One "Henry Riley" was at Ipswich in 1670;[1] "John Reylie" served as a soldier in the Ipswich militia company raised for King Philip's war in 1675, and a "Jeremiah Reylay" was at Ipswich in 1678.[2] Henry Riley was the village blacksmith at Rowley. On August 12, 1656, he married Mary Elithorp, and her death is thus entered in the *Town Books:* "Good Reila, wife of Henry Reila, died October 10, 1700." Two months afterwards, Henry married Elizabeth Bennett and the death of "Henry Reiley, aged 82," is recorded under date of May 24, 1710, and the will of "Hennery Rylee," dated January 6, 1708,

[1] *New Eng. Hist. Geneal. Register*, Vol. 7, p. 86.
[2] Ipswich town records.

was probated in Essex County on June 19, 1710.[1]   People named
Kelley, Burke and Lynch also came to Rowley.   An entry in
the town records of October 17, 1714, reads: "Eujean Linch
and Martha Eliott declared their intentions"[2] (of marriage).
"Thomas, son of Thomas and Mary Burke," was born at Rowley
on May 25, 1719.   "Martha, daughter of Eugene and Martha
Lynch," and Mary of the same parents were born at Rowley
on April 2, 1721, and May 11, 1729, respectively.   Mary Lynch
appears in Beverly, Mass., death records "between September,
1736, and June, 1737"; "Widow Martha Lynch" died there in
1738 and the death of another Martha Lynch is recorded there
under "April or May, 1740."   Edward Fitzgerald and Elizabeth
Lynch of Rowley were married at Beverly on June 27, 1740.
In 1718 one Eugene Lynch was the local schoolmaster at Kittery,
Maine,[3] and as his wife's name was Martha, I believe the above-
mentioned was the Irish pedagogue, since it was customary for
many of the teachers in those days to travel from place to place
where they taught school for a few months of the year.

Beginning about the first quarter of the eighteenth century
and continuing down to within a few years of the outbreak of the
Revolution, many Irish families settled along the Merrimac
River on both the Massachusetts and New Hampshire sides, and
in the records of the towns of Newbury and Newburyport and
other towns in this vicinity are found the names of some of these
people or their descendants.   And as it is known that the fishing
industry along the New England coast, as far east as Newfoundland, attracted fishermen from Galway, there is not much doubt
that many of these people came from the west of Ireland.   In
fact, most of the Irish names which appear in these records are
indigenous to the Province of Connacht.   Coffin, in his *History
of Newbury*, quoting from the town records of March 10, 1719,
says: "This year potatoes were introduced by some emigrants
from Ireland.   They were raised in the garden of Mr. Nathaniel
Walker esquire of Andover."   The names of these Irish settlers
are not given, but, when the Irish names from the vital records
of Newbury and Newburyport are consulted, we can readily

---

[1] Essex Probate records, Vol. 10, p. 123.
[2] *Essex Institute Historical Collections*, Vol. 5.
[3] *Old Kittery and Her Families*, by Everett S. Stackpole, Lewiston, Me.,
1893.

imagine the racial origin of these early comers from Ireland and can point to them as justifying our criticisms of the "Scotch-Irish" historians.

EXTRACTS FROM THE RECORDS OF SAINT PAUL'S EPISCOPAL CHURCH, NEWBURYPORT, MASS.

MARRIAGES.

Michael Barry and Abigail Carr, July 8, 1781
Edward Burke and Jane Harris, August 22, 1789
Betsey Carroll and Jonathan Moulton, December 12, 1789
John Carroll and Mary Hidden, July 1, 1792
Sarah Carroll and John Reeves, August 8, 1783
Susannah Carroll and Samuel Greenleaf, August 13, 1787
John Carroll and Elizabeth Willet, December 24, 1778
Elizabeth Casey and Edward Jones, November 6, 1781
Henry Casey and Elizabeth Cooper, February 21, 1779
Susannah Cassaday and William Parsons, November 22, 1792
Timothy Cassaday and Abigail Wiley, May 29, 1796
Elizabeth Cassady and Samuel LeCourt, August 2, 1772
Mary Cassody and Nathaniel Mason, September 3, 1766
Michael Condon and Elizabeth Carr, July 8, 1781
Anne Conner and William Thomas, May 27, 1790
Sarah Conner and Samuel Weaver, June 4, 1796
William Conner and Nancy Harvey, October 4, 1791
Joseph Connor and Nancy Pierce, May 18, 1772
Polly Connor and Enoch Lunt, January 11, 1786
Humility Conway and William Gee, December 21, 1796
Mary W. Corbet and Richard Trusdel, April 13, 1799
Jeremiah Dalton and Anna Herbert, January 22, 1795
Mary Dalton and Patrick Tracy, March 24, 1773
William Delaney and Dolley Rolfe, October 20, 1796
Charles Doran and Sarah Stickney, July 27, 1780
Daniel Dougherty and Sally Carlton, June 30, 1785
Sarah Dougherty and Christopher Schorn, October 30, 1783
Mary Doyle and Thomas Smith, September 28, 1780
Owen Dunn and Hannah Bayley, December 9, 1781
John Dunn and Mary Bailey, January 12, 1773
Lawrence Dunn and Sarah Quimby, October 3, 1805
Mary Dwyer and William Hogan, November 8, 1789
Daniel Farley and Rebecca Noyes, December 2, 1792
Mary Farrell and Moses Pierce, August 6, 1787
Rebecca Fogarty and Joseph Chase, September 30, 1797
John Fogarty and Jane McDaniel, October 15, 1780
Michael Fogarty and Rebecca Stalks, November 7, 1781
Mary Henecy and Anthony Teucher, May 6, 1775
John Hogan and Ruth Salter, September 2, 1779

William Hogan and Mary Dwyer, November 8, 1789
Ruth Hogan and John Mills, July 6, 1783
Charles Kennedy and Patty Tappan, July 15, 1797
Abigail Kelly and Samuel Pike, September 19, 1791
Sarah Kenney and Joel Colton, November 20, 1781
Elizabeth Kenny and Enoch Coffin, October 29, 1772
Mary Kenny and Joseph Merrill, September 26, 1772
John Lannagan and Elizabeth Greenough, August 3, 1780
Gilbert Lyons and Anna Newhall, August 22, 1786
Joseph McClaren and Anne Blaney, August 31, 1739
Anne McClannin and Isaac Bowers, February 14, 1784
William McCleary and Mary Noyes, July 24, 1787
Elizabeth McClennen and William Smith, July 24, 1797
Daniel McCormack and Sarah Pettingal, July 12, 1786
Phillip McGuire and Lydia Ceoch, May 12, 1784
James McKeen and Priscilla Robinson, November 10, 1771
Priscilla McKeen and Anthony Devereaux, February 12, 1780
Robert McNeal and Margaret Beckman, September 12, 1772
Susannah Malligan and Zacheus Wellcome, July 12, 1770
William Maley and Mary Rolfe, March 25, 1784
Daniel Maley and Mary Pettingill, February 23, 1777
Mary Maley and Samuel Sellman, December 24, 1780
Alice Mayley and William Stickney, February 8, 1789
Benjamin Mayley and Lydia Mason, April 10, 1790
William Mayley and Lucy Bab, July 5, 1778
Daniel Moran and Eunice Jester, March 24, 1801
Martin Moran and Nancy Waiscoat, April 13, 1801
John Mullins and Mary Rearden, March 28, 1779
Eliza Mullens and Joseph Dearing, May 10, 1804
James Mulvaney and Sarah Clemens, October 3, 1778
John Murfy and Metabel Wells, January 13, 1765
James Murphy and Sally Letherby, June 20, 1806
Elizabeth Murphy and Isaac McKinney, October 8, 1796
John O'Brien and Hannah Tappan, September 12, 1779
Joseph O'Brien and Rebecca Moodey, November 7, 1786
Phebe O'Brien and Samuel Richardson, January 5, 1795
William O'Brien and Lydia Toppan, April 23, 1780
Hannah O'Bryant and Hugh Garland, November 11, 1784
Hugh O'Donnell and Abigail Smith, December 1, 1782
William O'Neil and Mercy Grove, June 6, 1781
Johanna O'Sullivan and John Choat, October 7, 1771
Francis Quin and Lydia Nowell, February 27, 1781
Michael Reddy and Abigail Woods, April 3, 1786
Mary Rearden and John Mullins, March 28, 1779
Joseph Riley and Anna Murray, June 22, 1805
Augustine Ryan and Betty Hale Pettigill, December 16, 1791
Elizabeth Ryan and Joseph Titcomb, January 17, 1788
Sarah Ryan and Jonathan Sayward, February 1, 1781

William Scallon and Mary Knight, December 17, 1780
Thomas Slattery and Mary Martin, January 28, 1793
Mary Tobin and John Gibson, February 16, 1789
Patrick Tobin and Mary Stanwood, August 29, 1779
Patrick Tobin of Salem and Elizabeth Coffin, May 20, 1804
Patrick Tracy and Mary Dalton, March 24, 1773
Peter Whealan and Lydia Straw, December 22, 1779
John Whaland and Nancy Livermore, September 13, 1795

SURNAMES APPEARING IN THE EIGHTEENTH CENTURY DEATH RECORDS OF
NEWBURYPORT.

Barry	Delaney	Kenna	McIntire
Carey	Donnell	Kenny	McKeen
Carroll	Dorrity	Kennedy	McKenna
Cavenaugh	Doyle	Kinnacan	McQuillen
Cassaty	Duggins	Lannigan	Magowan
Carty	Dunn	McAffee	Magriff
Connolly	Dwyer	McCarthy	Maley
Connor	Farrel	McCauley	Moran
Connel	Flannagan	McCaw	Murphy
Condry	Fogarty	McClary	O'Brien
Cremin	Geary	McCusker	O'Flannegan
Dacey	Garvin	McDonald	O'Lary
Daley	Haley	McGraw	O'Neal
Dalton	Kelly		

GREAT BARRINGTON, MASS.—From Records of Saint James' Episcopal Church.
BIRTHS.

Ann, daughter of Cornelius and Thankful Doud, January 3, 1771
Thomas, son of Thomas and Mary Garvey, July 14, 1771
Edmon, Daniel and Jemima, children of Edmon and Jemima Murphy, November 5, 1771
John, son of John and Rebecca Whalin, December 8, 1771
Hester, daughter of John and Esther O'Bryan, July 26, 1773
Mary, daughter of John and Esther O'Bryan, May 13, 1775
Joseph, son of Thomas and Ann McGraw, July 9, 1775
Elizabeth, daughter of John and Esther O'Bryan, February 1, 1777
Elizabeth, daughter of Thomas and Ann McGraw, December 25, 1777
Esther, daughter of John and Esther O'Brien, February 27, 1780
Mary, daughter of John and Esther O'Brian, December 30, 1781
John, son of John and Esther O'Brian, March 7, 1784
John, and Cate, children of William and Cate O'Hara, July 6, 1785
William, son of William and Catherine O'Hara, September 18, 1787

BURIALS.

Hester, daughter of John and Esther O'Brian, May 16, 1775
Mary, daughter of John and Esther O'Brian, May 18, 1775

MARRIAGE.

William O'Hara and Catherine Carr, May 8, 1782

BROOKFIELD, MASS.—From the Vital Records.

BIRTHS.

Abigail, daughter of Richard and Mary Burk, September 18, 1727
Jonathan, son of Jonathan and Thankful Burk, February 26, 1733
Mary, daughter of Richard and Mary Burke, May 6, 1729
Jesse, son of Jonathan and Thankful Burk, April 8, 1738
William, son of Charles and Hannah Doughorty, August 29, 1765
Mary, daughter of Charles and Hannah Doughorty, January 12, 1767
Anna, daughter of John and Anna Dunn, March 3, 1770
Jane, daughter of John and Anna Dunn, March 1, 1768
Lucy, daughter of John and Anna Dunn, August 10, 1772
Sarah, daughter of John and Anna Dunn, September 27, 1774
Mary, daughter of John and Anna Dunn, August 5, 1776
John, son of John and Anna Dunn, September 1, 1778
James, son of John and Anna Dunn, March 11, 1783
Patience, daughter of John and Anna Dunn, August 1, 1780
Minerva, daughter of John and Anna Dunn, April 2, 1793
John, son of John and Azubah Gleason, September 28, 1789
John, son of William and Mary McClenahan, March 9, 1795
Harriot, daughter of Elijah and Patience Carroll, March 11, 1796
Augustus, son of Elijah and Patience Carroll, November 10, 1798
Mary, daughter of William and Mary McClenahan, April 3, 1799
Thankful, daughter of William and Thankful Riley, May 8, 1806
Abigail, daughter of Pearley and Abigail Healey, December 28, 1807

MARRIAGES.

William McCoye and Tabath ———, November 22, 1744
William Dougherty and Hannah Gilbert, November 22, 1752
Rebecca Doughety and David Getchell, April 12, 1759
Elizabeth Doughety and Levi Kendall, June 12, 1760
Jesse Burk and Leah Rice, May —, 1761
Jonathan Burk and Sarah Gould, March 29, 1763
Charles Doroty and Hannah Hemmenway, November —, 1764
Jenne Dorety and Benjamin Felton, December 24, 1767
William Flahavan and Veronica Vanbibber, July 28, 1767
Violetty Kenney and Jonathan Gale, April 21, 1768
James Shay and Thankful Walker, September 21, 1768
John McMullin and Isabel Cobb, November 30, 1769
Michael Dougherty and Betty Pratt, October —, 1771
Daniel Shay and Abigail Gilbert, July 18, 1772
Edward Madden and Lois Goodale, May 7, 1775
Sarah Dougherty and Ezra Olds, May 9, 1776
John Flaherty and Silence Adams, May 2, 1776

Jeremiah Dwier and Mary Howard, February 11, 1775
Margaret Dunn and David Wood, November 15, 1779
Anna Kenney and Asa White, July 1, 1779
Benjamin Higgins and Mary Drury, January —, 1777
Margaret Ryan and Thomas Wedge, June 5, 1783

CHESTER, MASS.—From the Vital Records.

BIRTHS.

James Nooney, ——— 1777
Isabel, daughter of William and Thankful Quigley, March 17, 1779
Anna, daughter of William and Thankful Quigley, February 18, 1783
Betsey, daughter of William and Thankful Quigley, May 14, 1784
John, son of William and Thankful Quigley, May 5, 1795
Polly, daughter of James and Esther Quigley, March 31, 1796
Esther, daughter of James and Esther Quigley, December 27, 1789
James, son of James and Esther Quigley, May 27, 1791
Sally, daughter of James and Esther Quigley, February 19, 1795
Philip, son of James and Esther Quigley, March 31, 1796
———, child of Simon Mulhallen, ——— 1790
Abigail, daughter of Barney and Mary Higgins, August 27, 1793
John, son of John and Susanna Mahanny, May 7, 1797
William, son of John and Susanna Mahanna, August 22, 1796
Peggy, daughter of John and Susanna Mahanna, June 26, 1799
Barney, son of Barney and Mary Higgins, March 20, 1798
Daniel, son of Barney and Mary Higgins, November 11, 1802
William, son of John Mahon, January 18, 1802

MARRIAGES.

Eleanor Nooney and Elijah Churchill, March 10, 1777
Simon Mulhollen and Olive Fellows, December 25, 1783
Captain Hugh Quigley and Polly Mulhollen, June 12, 1789
Daniel Falley and Betsey Mulhollen, November 15, 1795
Dr. William Mulhollen and Clarry Moseley, October 8, 1797
Patrick Gray and Betsey Moore, September 12, 1799
Margaret Quigley and Lemuel Hamilton, October 24, 1799
Lois Riley and Rufus Black, February 24, 1802
Elizabeth Kelley and John Smith, June 4, 1804
Patty Kelley and Eliphalet Coleman, September 23, 1805

MEDFIELD, MASS.—From the Vital Records.

BIRTHS.

Margaret, daughter of Peter and Ruth Calley, March 4, 1674
Peter, son of Peter and Ruth Kalley, July 20, 1670
William, son of William and Deborah Higgins, September 1, 1739
Lucrecy, daughter of William and Deborah Higgins, March 20, 1740
John and William, sons of John and Elizabeth Connolly, December 24, 1745

James, son of John and Elizabeth Connolly, —— 1749
Mary, daughter of John and Elizabeth Connolly, October 18, 1751
Grace, daughter of John and Elizabeth Conole, February 8, 1755
Richard, son of John and Elizabeth Conole, March 11, 1759
Peggy, daughter of William and Margaret Connelly, February 13, 1772
John, son of William and Margaret Connelly, July 5, 1774
John, son of John[1] and Anna Foley, June 12, 1778
Elizabeth, daughter of William and Margaret Connelly, July 29, 1778
James, son of John and Anna Foley, July 10, 1781
William, son of William and Margeret Conoly, March 25, 1781
Silence, daughter of John and Anna Foley, May 25, 1780
Christopher, son of John and Anna Foley, July 18, 1784

MARRIAGES.

Mary Dailie and William Farrett, December 8, 1681
Sarah Maccany and Vincent Shetleworth, March 14, 1764
Grace Connelly and Zephaniah Hewes, March 11, 1778
Patrick Brown and Ruth Babrick, August 20, 1725

MEDFORD, MASS.—From the Vital Records.

BIRTHS.

Eleoner Macordy, "daughter of one Macordy, Irish," March 23, 1729
Mary, daughter of Daniel and Mary McCarthy, July 21, 1747
Margaret, daughter of Daniel and Mary McCarthy, July 11, 1749
John, son of John and Elinor Gill, February 12, 1738
Mary, daughter of Timothy and Mary Harraden, January 1, 1765
Mary, daughter of John and Mary Gill, June 4, 1765
Mary, daughter of John and Elizabeth Gill, July —, 1768
Isaac, son of Peter Connery and wife, March 7, 1785
Hannah, daughter of Joseph Barrett and wife, March 17, 1799
William, son of Patrick and Hannah Roach, March 13, 1809
Hannah B., daughter of Patrick and Hannah Roach, October 24, 1810
John P., son of Patrick and Hannah Roach, January 8, 1813

MARRIAGES.

Daniel McCarthy[2] and Mary Floyd, March 23, 1746
David Donahew and Abigail Hall, January 1, 1745
Abigail Donnahew and Timothy Fitch, August 18, 1746
Aaron McClinton and Martha Miller, December 12, 1749
Nicholas McDonald and Mary Ellis, December 5, 1754
Isac Conroy and Hannah Jackson, February 5, 1766

---

[1] John Foley was a soldier of the Revolution and served in the Lexington Alarm, April 19, 1775.
[2] Referred to as "Captain Daniel McCarthy" in the records of the First Parish, Unitarian Church at Medford.

Daniel Conry and Abigail Hadley, February 26, 1767
Hannah Connary and John Hadley, May 2, 1771
Peter Connary and Mary Fowle, October 13, 1774
Peter Connary and Elizabeth Wakefield, June 9, 1777
Nabby Connery and Moses Winship, April 19, 1796
Daniel McClister and Jane Hall, December 7, 1800
William Flanagan and Sarah Hall, May 7, 1805

HANOVER, MASS.—From the Vital Records.

BIRTHS.

Margaret, daughter of Richard and Margaret Fitzgerald, May 23, 1732
Katharine, daughter of Richard and Margaret Fitzgerald, March 16, 1735
Alice, daughter of Daniel Teague, July 10, 1763

MARRIAGES.

James MacCarty and Elizabeth Smith, August 9, 1732
Daniel Conner and Elizabeth Taylor, November 20, 1737
Dennis Carrie and Rachel Torrey, February 22, 1738
Edward Conoway and Elizabeth Cane, February 25, 1739

DEATHS.

Robert Mackerdy (McCarty?), July 6, 1729
Richard Fitzgerald,[1] February 11, 1746
Katharine Fitzgerald, June 8, 1762
Margaret Fitzgerald, March 22, 1763

CAMBRIDGE, MASS.—

From "List of soldiers, killed, wounded or taken prisoner, who were in Colonel Benedict Arnold's detachment from Cambridge, Mass., in the expedition against Quebec, September 13, 1775." In a "Journal kept by Joseph

---

[1] The record of Richard Fitzgerald's death on the *Town Books* of Hanover says "he had been schoolmaster in this town nearly 20 years." Fitzgerald also taught school at Scituate, Mass., and appears on the records of that town of the year 1729. Flanders, in his *Lives of the Justices of the Supreme Court of the United States*, says that "Justice William Cushing (who was a native of Scituate) was prepared for college by Mr. Richard Fitzgerald, a veteran Latin schoolmaster." Barry—(*Historical Sketches of the Town of Hanover*)—says "he seems to have been a man of talent, well skilled in the languages, especially Latin, and to have taught with good success. We consider the town highly favored in securing the services of so valuable a man early in its municipal career, and under his judicious training many were reared who afterwards became distinguished in town and state." Fitzgerald was a good type of the Irish schoolmasters who educated the youth of the country at a period when men of intellectual training were scarce in the American Colonies.

Ware of Needham, Mass," in *New England Historic-Genealogical Register*, Vol. 6.

Hugh Boyd
Tobias Burke
Roger Casey
John Conner
Edward Conner
Timothy Conner
John Cochran
Martin Clark
Robert Cunningham
Patrick Campbell
Edward Cavener
Michael Clansey
Daniel Doyle
Benjamin Dunphy
Paul Doran
Joseph Dockerty
Patrick Dooland
Michael Fitzpatrick
Solomon Fitzpatrick

Timothy Feely
William Flood
Henry Herrigan
Cornelius Hagerty
James Hayden
Patrick Harrington
Joseph Higgins
Peter Heady
Charles Harkins
John Kelley
Denis Kelley
Patrick Kelley
Joseph Kennyon
Richard Lynch
John McGuire
Barnabas McGuire
Charles McGuire
John Moore
Henry McAnalley

Alexander McCarter
Thomas McIntire
John McCalam
John McLin
William McCoy
Richard McCluer
Henry McGowan
William McLieu
Patrick Newgent
Charles Norris
Daniel O'Hara
William O'Hara
James Patten
Edward Roddin
William Rutlidge
Daniel Rice
Timothy Rice
William Shannon
Patrick Tracy

CHAPTER OF IRISH CHARITY IN THANKSGIVING HISTORY.

RECORDS DEALING WITH ORIGIN OF FEAST DAY SHOW HOW NEW ENGLAND COLONISTS RECEIVED RELIEF FROM IRELAND AND RECIPROCATED THE GIFT.

BY MICHAEL J. O'BRIEN.

This article, with the above headings, was displayed prominently in the columns of the *New York Sun* of November 23, 1919:

With each recurring November the President of the United States issues a proclamation reminding the country that the season has again arrived when the people are accustomed to unite in giving thanks to God for the blessings which He has conferred upon our country during the preceding twelve months. It is a beautiful and inspiring thing, when all the people cease their labors on Thanksgiving Day and join in the observance of the holiday, and I believe no other people but our own observe a similar festival.

From time to time inquiries are addressed to the newspapers as to the origin of Thanksgiving Day, and the reply usually is that it originated with the New England Puritans in the seventeenth century on an occasion after they had passed through a period of great distress, resulting from the failure of the crops. Some of the replies intimate that this event happened only a few years after the landing of the Pilgrims of the Mayflower (1620), and others ascribe it to the time of the Indian War in New England known as King Philip's War, which happened a little over half a century later.

It would appear that there is really no absolute knowledge as to the exact year the feast was begun, although there is no doubt that the origin of it was to celebrate the fact that the distresses of the people were relieved. In no case has any newspaper offered an explanation as to the agency whence the relief was received, and while I have no particular knowledge as to it, yet, since Ireland on two occasions had a hand in this godly work, it is appropriate that the story be related at this time.

163

In the year 1736 there was published in Boston a work for the Rev. Thomas Prince, a resident of that town, entitled *A Chronological History of New England in the Form of Annals*, and while it is a highly interesting and important book, it is generally known only to historical students. Mr. Prince was ordained in Boston in the year 1718, and an account of his work by the New England Historic-Genealogical Society says: "No man that has ever lived in New England can be said to have done more for its history than the Rev. Thomas Prince; his literary labors were constant for nearly half a century and his greatest literary work was his incomparable *New England Chronology*, which, for extreme accuracy, was probably never exceeded by any author in any similar work."

Under *Annals of the Year 1631* Prince relates in this book an account of the distress which prevailed in the Colony of Massachusetts Bay during the winter of 1630–31, and among other things he said:

"As the winter came on provisions are very scarce (in the Massachusetts Bay), and people necessitated to feed on clams and mussels and ground nuts and acorns, and those were got with much difficulty in the winter season. Upon which people grow much tired and discouraged, especially when they hear that the governor himself has his last batch of bread in the oven. And many are the fears of the people that Mr. Pierce, who was sent to Ireland for provisions, is either cast away or taken by the pirates. Upon this a day of fasting and prayer to God for relief is appointed (to be on the 6th of February). But God, who delights to appear in the greatest straits, works marvellously at this time; for on February 5, the very day before the appointed fast, in comes the ship *Lion*, Mr. William Pierce, master, now arriving at Nantasket laden with provisions. Upon which joyful occasion the day is changed and ordered to be kept (on the 22d) as a day of Thanksgiving. Upon the 8th the governor goes aboard the *Lion*, riding at Long Island; next day the ship comes to an anchor before Boston (to the great joy of the people), where she rides very well, notwithstanding the great drifts of ice. And the provisions are by the governor distributed to the people proportionable to their necessities."

It seems curious that the Puritans did not call upon the "mother country" for the much needed provisions, and we wonder why they selected Ireland, a country which, if we are to believe such historians as Palfrey, Lodge, Fiske, Bancroft and so on, was practically unknown to the New Englanders of the time! But, at any rate, here we have evidence upon which we can rely, since Prince quotes from the annals of the time that Ireland apparently was the only country in the world which sent relief to the suffering Colonists only eleven years after the landing of the Pilgrims!

In the absence of more definite knowledge of the subject, I submit this as the earliest record of a celebration of Thanksgiving Day in America. I have not seen this incident mentioned in the work of any other historians, and it is evident either that they considered it as of no importance or that they suppressed the facts for some ulterior purpose.

The war with King Philip, chief of the Narragansett Indians, was bloody and devastating in the extreme. It began in 1675 and continued throughout the year 1676. An account of it published by the New England Historic-Genealogical Society in 1848 says:

"The Colonies suffered more in proportion to their numbers and strength than was experienced during the Revolutionary struggle. The war was brief, but it had its havocs and its terrors, which many historians have tried to describe. Six hundred of the inhabitants, the greatest part of whom were the very flower of the country, fell in battle or were murdered, very often with circumstances of the most revolting cruelty.

"We may as well suppose that half as many more fell victims in the progress of the war. It was a loss to her children to New England not inferior to 20,000 at the present day (1848). Twelve towns in Massachusetts, Plymouth and Rhode Island were utterly destroyed and many more greatly injured. Six hundred dwelling houses were burned. One man in eleven of the arms bearing population was killed and one house in eleven laid in ashes."

In these times of distress and misery the people of Ireland promptly came to the relief of the sufferers, which event is known in New England annals as "The Irish Donation." No other country but Ireland is recorded as having come to the rescue of the famished Colonists, and whether or not the fact that there were natives of that country resident in the ravaged districts may have been the incentive to their humane action does not appear, but at any rate the question of nationality or religion did not interfere with the proper distribution of the charity.

The ship *Katherine*, of Dublin, brought the relief. It was directed that it be distributed "among the poor distressed by the late war with the Indians," and it was further directed that there was to be no distinction as to religious belief; all were to share according to their needs. "That it be divided between the three united Colonies of Plymouth, Massachusetts and Connecticut in such portions as the committee shall adjust."

The value of the consignment is uncertain, but from the fact that the Lord Mayor of Dublin appointed three men to come to Boston to supervise the distribution of the charity and that the cost of the freight alone was the very large sum, for those days, of four hundred and fifty pounds sterling, we may assume safely that, with traditional Irish generosity, it was liberal in the extreme. As a colonial historian remarks, "the donation at the time was as generous as its reception was welcome to the distressed ones in New England."

The *Katherine* sailed from Dublin on or about August 17, 1676, for Boston, which was designated as the place from which the distribution was to be made. A controversy arose between Massachusetts and Connecticut "on account of the Irish charity." The Council of Massachusetts, in a letter to Connecticut, dated January 4, 1677, "supposed the latter Colony had received its share." The letter stated that Massachusetts "had sent orders to the several towns of that Colony and found 660 families, consisting of 2,265 persons, in distress, besides thirteen towns from which returns had not been received," and they desired a similar account from Connecticut and Plymouth, "by which," they said, "we may proportion what is divisible among us." On February 28, Connecticut wrote Massachusetts desiring the latter to send them "our proportion of the Irish charity." The correspondence continued, and on May 10 Connecticut again wrote Massachusetts "justifying their conduct in regard to the late war," and stating that "a list of those in distress had been sent that they might receive their proportion of the Irish donation." Toward the close, however, they remarked: "But God has given supplies to our people; we remit to you our right in the Irish charity."

At a session of the General Court of Connecticut in the same month (May, 1677) the following act was recorded: "The court upon good reason moving them do remit their part in the Irish charity to the distressed persons in the Massachusetts and Plymouth Colonies." So it appears Connecticut received no part of "The Irish Donation," but relinquished her share to the two Colonies which had been much more distressed by the war. In this manner did Ireland exhibit her familiarity with things American and extend her sympathy to others when informed of their distress, one hundred years before the opening of the Revolution which emancipated the people of this land from the same tyranny under which she herself groaned.

It was a splendid mission on the part of Ireland, and a grateful acknowledgment of the event published by the New England Historic-Genealogical Society said: "One hundred and seventy-one years after this time the people of Massachusetts had an opportunity of reciprocating the gift of benevolence wafted to these shores by the good ship *Katherine* of Dublin when they organized a fund for the relief of the distressed people of Ireland suffering from the effects of the famine of 1847."

Thus we see that Thanksgiving Day in the year 1676 was an especially joyous one in New England, and it is of no little interest to note that the event probably was celebrated in the same month in which the annual festival is now held, since the vessel bearing the supplies sailed from Dublin in August and the transatlantic voyage at that time usually occupied about ten weeks. "The Irish Donation" is only one of the numerous "hidden phases of American history" concerning the connection of Ireland and her people with the American Colonies that are dealt with in my recent book, and the incident itself will serve to explain why that title was selected for the work.

"THE IRISH DONATION."[1]

By Rev. MICHAEL EARLS, S.J., Holy Cross College.

(In Worcester (Mass.) *Daily Telegraph*, November 27, 1919.)

God save old Ireland, say we all,
  God heal her woes, we pray;
What fitter time to bless her call
  Than here Thanksgiving day,
Than here where far-off echoes fall
  Of Massachusetts bay?

* * * * *

Oh, dreadful is the famine
  And the burning drought of tears,
When yesterdays walk ghostlike
  And fill tomorrow's fears.

[1] See *Annals of the Year 1631* by Prince.

Tomorrow's fears were plentiful,
  They clouded land and sea,
That year in Massachusetts bay
  And the starving colony.

For starving was the harvest,
  When autumn reaped a blight;
And winter looked to springtime
  With a blacker look than night.

Yet in the night are God's good stars,
  And across the sea a star;—
Distress will find the latchstring out
  On Irish hearts afar.

Afar the Irish hearts and hands
  Brought quick a valiant store,
And welcomed well good William Pierce,
  And filled his ship ashore.

The good ship *Lion* westward sailed
  To Nantasket of the bay,
And a colony blessed Ireland
  That first Thanksgiving day.

          *   *   *   *   *

Then God save Ireland, say we all,
  God heal her woes, we pray;
What fitter time to bless her call
  Than here Thanksgiving day,
Than here where far-off echoes fall
  Of Massachusetts bay?

EARLY IRISH SETTLERS AT WORCESTER, MASS.

Interesting Contributions on the Subject by W. HENRY TOWNE, City Clerk at Worcester, and by MICHAEL J. O'BRIEN.

The following article appeared in the *Worcester Sunday Telegram* of November 17, 1918:

Records at the city hall prove that the first Irish people came to Worcester long before the American Revolution, although the generally accepted belief was that no Irishmen came here until after the Irish Revolution in 1798.

The question when the first Irish people came to Worcester has been of interest to descendants of the inhabitants of the Emerald Isle for two generations. The accepted opinion has been held that there were no Irish in Worcester until about 1800. The earliest records do not mention men of Irish birth excepting those known as Scotch-Irish, who came to Worcester with their pastor, Rev. Edward Fitzgerald, and tried to found a Presbyterian Church on Ye Olde Poaste Roade, now Lincoln Street. There was tremendous ill feeling in Worcester against the very name of Irish and, although the newcomers were of Protestant faith, their church was torn down by an angry mob, and those who did not leave Worcester accepted things as they came and joined the First Parish of orthodox worshippers.

IRISH IN WORCESTER BEFORE THE REVOLUTION.

Recently, however, City Clerk W. Henry Towne has come across ancient records of the town that prove without a doubt that there were Irish people in Worcester long before the Revolution. Not only that, but the lists of soldiers who went from Worcester and Worcester County to join Gen. George Washington's Continental Army, included many men with names decidedly Irish. One historian says that every Irishman in the province eagerly took up arms against King George.

The accepted view has been that after the unsuccessful revolution in Ireland in 1798, when English soldiers were hanging every Irishman they could find who owned a pike, a few Irishmen escaped and came to Worcester. There were not many, although

there were some. Boston and New York received most of the
exiles, and those who came to Worcester married here and lost
their national identity in the melting pot of the new republic.
Such names as Bryant, Sherman, Prouty, Bemis and many others
were originally Irish.

It was later argued that the first Irish who came to Worcester
immigrated in 1824, when construction work started on the
Blackstone Canal, and it is true that several hundred members of
the ancient Celtic race did come here. In 1848, 1849, the famine
years, and 1850, and from then until the end of the Civil War,
Irishmen flocked to Worcester literally by thousands.

An O'Brien Paid Taxes in 1756.

City Clerk Towne has undeniable proof that Irishmen came to
Worcester and settled here many years before the Revolution.
On page 28 of the records of Worcester town for the year 1756,
mention is made of Dennis O'Brien as a taxpayer, and the name is
spelled elsewhere in the record as Briant. James O'Brien, or
Briant, is given credit for paying taxes of £1 10s. and 11d. In
1754, William Mahan, taxpayer, tried to buy some waste land
from the town, and the matter was threshed out at a town meeting, and Mahan's article was voted down. John McGuire and
John Hart were registered in Worcester many years before the
Revolution, and there are many others whose names indicate
that they were Irish.

A search of the old records for the actual first comers from Ireland will be made as all the ancient accounts are in excellent condition. City Clerk Towne prizes the old records more highly
than he would two tons of platinum at present prices. One of
the old records shows that David McCrahan, an Irishman, went
to war from Worcester in 1758, as a soldier in Worcester's quota,
and, the record closes by saying that McCrahan never came back,
"as he was killed or captivated."

In connection with the foregoing the following further data
have been furnished by Mr. Michael J. O'Brien, Historiographer
of the American Irish Historical Society.

It is assuredly a step in advance, since it is so unusual in American historical writings, to find a gentleman like Mr. Towne
bringing to light the fact that the Irish pioneers in America were

something of an acquisition to the new country, as is evidenced by the recording of their names as purchasers of lands at Worcester as early as the middle of the eighteenth century. The general impression as to the early Irish immigrants to this country is that they were all poor "redemptioners" and "servants," and that they seldom rose above their lowly station, yet those who have studied the records know that many of the Irish immigrants were men of substance and good social standing, who held their own in every way with their "Anglo-Saxon" compeers. City and town clerks, registrars of wills and deeds, court clerks, the custodians of the parish registers, of the land and colonial and other records, in all states of the Union comprising the original Thirteen Colonies, are in a like position to City Clerk Towne, but only very few of them have evinced any interest in the Irish pioneers of their respective localities.

Mr. Towne is quite correct in stating that the Irish settled at Worcester at an earlier period than is generally known to the public and probably to the historians, and while it is true to some extent, as he says, that "the newcomers (from Ireland) were of the Protestant faith," it is perfectly evident from the names of the settlers that many of them originally were of old Irish Catholic families. It is not to be supposed, for example that the Worcester pioneers whose names Mr. Towne mentions as appearing in the land records, were of the Protestant faith in Ireland, although it is true, since they had no means of practising their religion in America, which at that time was banned by the "tolerant" Puritans, they and their descendants attended the local Protestant churches. Because of that, in nearly all cases they were written down as "Scotch-Irish" by the historians, in an effort to deprive Ireland of any credit that might be given to that country for having furnished to America such valuable colonists.

AN IRISH SCHOOLMASTER.

The Rev. Edward Fitzgerald mentioned by Mr. Towne was the leader of an Irish colony who came to Worcester about the year 1720, and Mr. Fitzgerald was one of the first schoolmasters of the town. What a strange turn in the wheel of fate it was that the very man whom the Puritans tried to run out of town was the one on whom their children had to depend for their early education, and that man was of the proscribed Irish race! Among those who came with him from Ireland was James McClellan, the great-great-great-grandfather of Gen. George B. McClellan of Civil War fame, and in local annals besides those mentioned by Mr. Towne appear such names as McCarty, McKonkey, Moore, Gleason and Mahony, and it is of no little interest to note that among the memorials of the dead in the ancient burial ground on Worcester "Common" the oldest stone of all was erected to the memory of an Irishman, "John Young, born in the Isle of Bert, near Londonderry, in the Kingdom of Ireland. Died June 30, 1730, aged 107."

At Worcester we also find Rev. Thaddeus McCarty, grandson of Thaddeus McCarthy, who came to Boston from Kinsale, County Cork, some time during the last quarter of the seventeenth century and who, with his brother, Florence McCarty, is mentioned prominently in the *Town Books* of Boston. Rev. Thaddeus McCarty was a patriot of the Revolution and was a powerful factor in molding public opinion in the right direction in that section of New England, where so many were wavering in their allegiance to the patriot cause.

THE TEMPLES FROM TIPPERARY.

The vital records of Worcester contain many old Irish names, and among them I have found people named Daly, Fitzgerald, Larkin, McCain, McJerrald, McTroy, Murphy, Quigley, McGuire, McConaughy, Kelley, Conway, Keating, Donohue, Healy, Geary, McFadden, Mullen, Duffy, Sullivan, Lynch and Crowley, whose births, marriages or deaths or land transactions are recorded there as early as 1733 and down to the year 1781. The settlers of 1720 came to Boston in five ships in the year 1718. They were brought here by Robert Temple, of the Temple family of Tipperary, who intermarried with the Emmets, and I am informed by Dr. Thomas Addis Emmet that the tradition in his as well as in the Temple family is that they were chiefly from the counties of Cork and Kerry.

Indeed, circumstantial evidence in support of that tradition is found in the names of the immigrants, a large body of whom went from Boston to the district of Maine, where, at the junction of the Kennebec and Eastern rivers, in Lincoln County, they established the town of Cork, which, however, was destroyed by the Indians six years later. The names of a great number of these Irish immigrants which I have found in the probate and land records of Lincoln County read more like the parish registers of a town or city in the province of Munster or Connaught than of a New England town 3,000 miles away from their ancestral Irish homes, and it is an interesting fact that a bend of the Eastern River, near which the town of Cork was located, even to this day is known as "the Cove of Cork," and the surrounding district for more than a century was known by the familiar name of "Ireland."

ROBERT FARRELL, NEW ENGLAND COLONIZER.

The immigrants of 1718 scattered to various parts of New England. One contingent went to Derry, N. H., where an Irish settlement had already been established, and another went to Bedford, N. H., which place achieved everlasting fame in American history as the home town of the Revolutionary heroes who held the "rail fence" at Bunker Hill on the memorable 17th of June, 1775, and thus saved two battalions of Americans from annihilation or capture. And it is a remarkable fact that all of the officers of the Bedford company were Irishmen or sons of Irish immigrants. One contingent, under the leadership of Robert Farrell, went to Palmer, Mass. This Robert Farrell was the father of sixteen children, seven of whom were born in Ireland and many of whose descendants appear in the vital records of the town and some of whom are mentioned for their activity and prominence in laying out this flourishing settlement; while the genealogy of the family shows that descendants of the Irish pioneer fought in all the wars in which their country was engaged, and in all probability they are represented in the terrible struggle in Europe now drawing to a close. The Revolutionary muster rolls show enlistments from this town of Dennis O'Brient, Daniel Riordan, William Fitzgerald, Michael Dougherty, John McIlwaine, Daniel Moore, William Geary, William Roach, Timothy Murphy, Isaiah, Isaac and Timothy Farrell and others of Irish names. Patrick Smith, from Ireland, is mentioned in the town clerk's records as "one of the original proprietors of the town." The Shaws came there "from the Cove of Cork" in 1720. They were four brothers, all young men active in the early settlement of the town, and are said to have been the ancestors of the numerous Shaw families now in New England. A good-sized volume could be written on these early Irish settlers at Palmer.

DUBLIN AND COLRAIN, MASS.

Another portion of the Irish immigration of 1718 went to Shrewsbury, Mass.; still others to Spencer, Sturbridge, Oakham, Marlboro, Braintree, Auburn and so on, each of these places being only a short distance from Worcester, and in the vital records of these towns are to be found many Irish names. One of these Irish colonies located at Rutland, Mass., and it is strange that the historians failed to see the absurdity of the racial misnomer, "Scotch-Irish," by which they described them, since the records show that the pioneers gave the name of Dublin to the section of the town where they settled. Others of these immigrants from the valley of the Bann in Ireland established the present town of Colrain, Mass.

One company, which first settled at Worcester, went to a place called Leicester and from this town in 1756 were enlisted for the Colonial Wars soldiers named Larkin, Handy, Shaw, McDaniel, Gleason and Ryan, and in the Revolutionary companies from that district were many soldiers of Irish names. Three Ryan brothers—Anthony, John and Darby—came to Leicester from Ireland. They were sons of Sir Anthony Ryan, of Tipperary, who was the father of eleven other children, all born at Leicester between 1743 and 1756 and several of whom fought in the Revolution, and the name of his son Samuel appears in the baptismal records of the Congregational Church at Spencer, Mass., as the father of thirteen children.

IRISH HAD AN HONORABLE PART IN EVERY UPWARD AMERICAN MOVEMENT.

These Worcester County settlers came from many different parts of Ireland, and the names alone, to a student of Irish family nomenclature, are a sufficient indication of that fact. When the Revolutionary War came on the sons of these Irish families exhibited the same, if not greater, eagerness to join the forces fighting for independence as did any of the descendants of the Puritans; their blood dyed the same Revolutionary battlefields; they fought in the same trenches and for the same cause; Catholic Irishmen, Presbyterian Irishmen, Puritans and Pilgrims, all lie side by side, their dust mouldering in the same graves. While there may have been religious proscription in those days, the conscienceless historian had not yet been born, but although the pharisees of history like the Lodges, Fiskes and Palfreys, have withheld from Ireland the credit that is her due, thanks to the never-failing guidance of the records we are able to show that at all times, whether they came as voluntary exiles or were driven from their homes by the persecutions of government, her sons have had an honorable part in every upward movement in American life.

SOME IRISH NAMES CULLED FROM THE OFFICIAL RECORDS OF NEW HAMPSHIRE.

BY MICHAEL J. O'BRIEN.

The Provincial and State Papers of New Hampshire (which are comprised of 31 volumes, of about 20,000 pages), published by authority of the Legislature, contain a great number of references to petitions presented to the Legislature, usually in connection with land grants, but in many cases relating to boundary lines; public highways; improvements; the erection and repair of bridges and public buildings; the appointment of town officials; election contests; the encouragement of manufactures; fisheries, rivers and harbors; applying for rewards or payments for public services rendered, and many other reasons. The names of the signers of these petitions are given in nearly all cases and from the transcripts thereof contained in the published volumes of the Provincial and State Papers I have taken the following names, with the places where these people resided and the years in which the petitions were sent to the Legislature. The frequency with which Celtic names appear in these records serves as an indication of the large numbers of Irish people who emigrated to New Hampshire during the eighteenth century, although it must be said that these names alone afford no adequate idea of the extent of Irish immigration. Many people came from Ireland whose names had become so changed or twisted that it is now almost impossible to recognize them, except where the nationality is stated, which I find to have been the case in few instances only.

PERSONS WHO SIGNED PETITIONS TO THE NEW HAMPSHIRE LEGISLATURE.

Dates.	Names.	Where Located.
May 5, 1716	Timothy Connel	Oyster River
October 3, 1717	William Healy	Ware
	Nathaniel Healy	
March 14, 1727	William Doran	Not stated
	Cornelius Drisco (?)	
	Cornelius Connor	

Dates.	*Names.*	*Where Located.*
	Philip Connor	
—— 1725	William Barry	Rye
August 18, 1737	Jeremiah Larey	Portland
	Thomas Hart	
June 7, 1742	Timothy Dalton	Hampton
March 14, 1749	John Quin	Conatook
	Andrew McClary	
—— 1748	Daniel Kelley	Sanbornton
	Edward Kelly	
—— 1749	Jeremiah Driscol	Rochester
	James Driscol	
—— 1746	John Sullevant	Somersworth
	John Ferrall	
	James Foy	
—— 1748	Michael Martin	
	Daniel Halluran	
	Joseph Welsh	
	Benjamin Welsh	
	William Kennedy	
	Edward Kennedy	Immigrants who peti-
	Peter Greeley	tioned for a grant of
	Mauris Driskell	land on Merrimack
	Christopher Cullen	River in the year 1748.
	Jeames Hearn	
	Richard Fitzgerald	
	Michaell Madden	
	George Madden	
	Patrick Furlong	
January 11, 1748	John Carty	
	Jeremiah Connor	
	Moses Connor	
	Samuel Connor	Not stated
	David Connor	
	Neal McGaffey	
	Joseph Ceilley	
—— 1749	Patrick Manning	
	Hercules Mooney	
	John MacKelloy	
	Stephen Kelley	Cochecho Parish
	Daniel Mihaney	
	Joseph Connor	
	John Foye	
May 3, 1753	Matthew Heley	Nottingham
	James Kelley	
December 21, 1757	Edward Fitzgerald	Contoocook
—— 1752	James Lyons	Not stated
—— 1758	John McGaffey	Buckstreet

12

Dates.	Names.	Where Located.
—— 1758	David Connor	Buckstreet
April 4, 1754	Hugh McGinnis	Not stated
	James Kennedy	
July 20, 1756	Edward FissJarrel	Boscawen
April 12, 1769	Fergus Kennedy	
	John McKinney	
	Daniel McKinney	Bedford
	Matthew Patten	
	Thomas Murdough	
	John Goffe	
	John McLaughlin	
Undated	Matthew O'Brion	Society Land
	—— FitchGibbens	
March 13, 1762	Cornelius Danoly	Dunstable
—— 1769	John McMurphy	
	Robert McMurphy	Londonderry
	Maurice Lynch	
	Thomas McCleary	
	David McClearey	
	John McCarthney	
	Daniel McNeal	
—— 1769	Joseph Leary	Wolfborough
March 29, 1770	Edward Kelley	Sanbornton
April 10, 1769	Jeffrey Donough	Not stated
	Anthony Moran	
	Daniel MacMurphy	
April 7, 1774	Paul Hayes	
	Joseph Hayes	
	John Cotter	Barrington
	John McDaniel	
	William McDaniel	
April 12, 1774	James Gorman	Londonderry
	James McMurphy	
—— 1768	John Quigley	New Boston
February 22, 1775	Maurice Lynch	
	John McCleary	Camden
	John McCalley	
	John O'Nail	
August 21, 1775	Thomas Quigly	
	Thomas Quigly, Jr.	Francestown
	William Quigly	
	Thomas McLaughlin	
January 19, 1774	James Ryan	Plymouth
	William Nemens	
—— 1775	Daniel McAffee	Londonderry
—— 1775	Francis McAuley	Conway

Dates.	Names.	Where Located.
——— 1773	William Hierlihy	
	John McCarthy	
	Roger Magrath	Petition for changing
	Robert Gilmore	County lines,
	William Gilmore	various places
	John Gilmore	
	Matthew Thornton	
	James McKeen	
——— 1776	Richard Coughlan	Chesterfield
August 30, 1776	Maurice Lynch	Society Land
July 9, 1776	Garret Byrne	Wolfborough
——— 1776	John Danely	Richmond
August 25, 1777	John Donovan	
	Tobias Butler	New Boston
	Barnebas Magennis	
	Daniel McAllister	
August 27, 1777	Peter Kalley	
	Hugh Kalley	Londonderry
	Jeffrey Donohue	
	Richard Kelley	
	Dinis Haley	
May 19, 1778	Robert MacMurphy	
	William MacMurphy	
——— 1778	John Crowley	Tamworth
December —, 1777	James Monahan	
	Manes Burke	Goffstown
	Robert Kennedy	
	John O'Neill	
March —, 1779	Edward Kerwin	Lyndeborough
——— 1769	Richard Kelley	
	John Kelley	Salem
	Samuel Kelley	
	John Hulehon	
	David Nevins	
	Thomas Mackglathlon	
	James Dwyer	
——— 1780	Patrick Furness	
	Denis Pendergast	
	John Pendergast	Durham
	Edmond Pendergast	
	John Sullivan	
	Ebenezer Sullivan	
——— 1781	John Kenney	Chichester
December 23, 1788	Dennis Prendergast	
	Stephen Prendergast	Barnstead
	Cornelius Kirby	
February 23, 1783	Thomas Callahan	

Dates.	Names.	Where Located.
February 23, 1783	Jeremiah Bowin	Boscawen
	Henry Moore	
	Moses Kelly	
June 2, 1784	John Costelloe	Effingham
December 23, 1786	John Carney	Madbury
December 12, 1783	Jacob Flynn	Lyndeborough
December 12, 1783	Patrick Londergal (Lonergan)	Dunstable
December —, 1783	John O'Neill	Goffstown
March 31, 1784	Robert Burke	
	Daniel McAlvain	Windham
	James McIlvane	
	Robert McIlvaine	
June 1, 1785	Joseph Fitzgerald	Newmarket
	Joseph O'Shaw	
	Thomas Roach	
February 9, 1785	Daniel Fitzgerald	Rye
November 10, 1785	Philip Kelley	Northwood
February 1, 1785	Thomas Haley	Epping
	Samuel Haley	
June —, 1785	James Connor	Wolfborough
	John Lary	
	Joseph Lary	
———— 1783	Richard Kelley	Salem
	Richard Kiley	
	David Nevens	
	James Macglaughlon	
	Thomas Macglaughlon	
December —, 1789	Daniel Fitzgerald	Rye
June —, 1787	James Hickey	Lemster
January 7, 1789	Roger Dugan	Allenstown
	Gershon Dugan	
	Clement McCoy	
November 30, 1791	Daniel Leary	Conway
February 10, 1790	Joseph Larey	Middletown
	Joseph Larey, Jr.	
December 24, 1789	John Carroll	Newcastle
June 4, 1709	William Casey	Gilmanton
	Jacob Kelley	
	Thomas Hayes	
	Jeremiah Connor	
	Jeremy Connor	
December 23, 1789	John Mooney	New Holderness
	Bryan Sweeney	
	John Sweeney	
	Michael Dwyer	
	William Hogan	

Dates.	Names.	Where Located.
June —, 1795	Daniel Healy	Winchester
	John Higgons	
Undated	Robart Bryen	Greenland
	Joseph Melune	
	Henry Melune	
	Daniell Meloon	
	John Meloon	
Undated	Fargous Kennedy	Bedford
	Martha McQuaid	
April —, 1797	Philip Connor	Meredith
	John McDaniel	
	Jonathan Kelley	
June 13, 1792	Michael Ryan	Durham
	John Welch	
	Edmund Pendergast	
—— 1797	Patrick McLaughlin	
	James McLaughlin	
	Thomas Macloughlin	
	David McAllister	
—— 1797	Joseph Kenney	North East
	Stephen Kenney	
June 8, 1795	Thomas Burke	Eaton
	Hercules Mooney	
	John Mooney	
November 25, 1799	John Burke	Cockburn

STRAY HISTORICAL ITEMS FROM THE GREEN MOUNTAIN STATE.

PICKED UP BY MICHAEL J. O'BRIEN.

RUTLAND, VT.—"The Charter of Rutland was dated September 7th, 1761. The first named grantee is John Murray, an Irishman, the principal citizen of Rutland, Mass., and the man, probably, that named this Town."—(*Centennial History of Rutland, Vt.*, by Chauncy K. Williams.) "The first white child born in Rutland was William Powers."—(from same.)

DANBY, VT.—"The most numerous family in Danby were the Kelleys. They came from Rhode Island and were among its first settlers. Daniel Healey, who came from Rhode Island with Benjamin Kelley, married Lucy Kelley, and removed to Cherry Valley, N. Y."—(Genealogical Records, in Williams' *History of Danby, Vt.*)

ALBURGH, VT.—Captain Patrick Conroy and family are mentioned as at Alburgh. He acted as Justice of the Peace in 1792. The boundary lines between Vermont and Canada being in dispute, he was summoned before the Supreme Court at Burlington on May 16, 1792, "to show cause why he acted as Justice without authority." Several pages of the records of the Governor and Council are devoted to Patrick Conroy.—(*Council Records of Vermont*, Vol. 1.)

BETHEL, VT.—At a meeting of the Council held on June 11, 1785, it was "*Resolved*, That Michael Flynn of Bethel be and is hereby appointed a Justice of the Peace for the County of Windsor." Flynn was a member of the Council later in the year 1785 and at the Convention which adopted the Constitution of the United States, held at Bennington on June 10, 1791, he represented Windsor County.—(*Council Records*, Vol. 3.)

ARLINGTON, VT.—At a meeting of the Council held on October 11, 1781, a petition from Hugh McCarty of Arlington was read and referred to the General Assembly. In the Revolutionary War records of Vermont, there is a resolution of the Council of Safety, dated November 13, 1781, directing the Treasurer "to pay to Hugh McCartey or bearer ten pounds, which money was granted to him by the General Assembly at their session in October last, on account of his being a prisoner among the British in Canada the year past." Under the same date, there is a receipt for the ten pounds, "in full for the within order," signed Hugh McCarty.—(*Council Records*, Vol. 2.)

MILTON, VT.—"The Town of Milton, situated on the east shore of Lake Champlain, was first settled about the close of the Revolution. Among its original patentees under Charter from Governor Bennington Wentworth of New Hampshire, dated June 8th, 1763, were Timothy McCarty and Michael Duff."—(Rann's *History of Chittenden County, Vt.*)

SAINT GEORGE, VT.—Among the original grantees of this town, "chartered by the Royal Governor of the Province of New Hampshire on August 18th, 1763," were John Dervicos Murphy, Edward Ferrol Murphy and John Devereux Murphy, Junior.—(Rann's *History of Chittenden County.*)

VERGENNES and SHELBURNE, VT.—The earliest Methodist preacher mentioned at these places is Rev. Henry Ryan.—(Period not taken down.)

UNDERHILL, VT.—Among its "first settlers" are mentioned Louis Reiley, Carey Dunn, Michael Butler and Samuel Wall.—(Town History.)

TOPSHAM, VT.—"Daniel Keenan and his wife, Margaret McCowen, from Ireland," were among "the early settlers" at this place.—(*Gazetteer of Orange County*, compiled by Hamilton Child.)

BRADFORD, VT.—Daniel McDuffee and his wife, Margaret, came from Ireland in 1720 and located at Bradford. Five of their sons were in the French War (1757), three of them in the decisive battle of Quebec. Daniel McDuffee taught school several terms in Falmouth, Saco and Brunswick, Maine. His wife was the aunt of James Wilson, a native of Ireland, who is said to have been "the first maker of terrestrial and celestial globes in America." He was "a very talented man, whose genius and inclinations turned to the investigation of the science of astronomy." He "constructed the first globes, at Bradford, in 1799." His sister married John Cockran of Bradford, also a native of Ireland. Daniel Kelley is mentioned as at Bradford in 1797. He left many descendants.—(From Child's *Gazetteer of Orange County.*)

THETFORD, VT.—The grave of "Captain Ryley, a Revolutionary soldier," may be seen at this place.

WOODSTOCK, VT.—The most numerous family mentioned in local history was that of the Powers. Henry Swan Dana, in his *History of Woodstock, Vt.*, says of them: "Thomas and Walter Power, brothers, were born in Waterford, Ireland. They came to this country somewhere near 1680. They added an "s" to their name. The grandson of one of the brothers, Dr. Stephen Powers, was born at Old Hardwick, Mass., in 1735. His father was a farmer, but he decided to study for the profession and while thus engaged taught school for a livelihood. . . . He set up as a doctor at Middleborough, Mass. When the new state of Vermont began to be talked about, he removed from Massachusetts (in the year 1772), and settled at what is now Woodstock," where he purchased several tracts of land. He did not join any military company during the Revolutionary War, but, it is said, that "when he heard the guns roaring at Bunker Hill he was present on the battlefield while the engagement was going on and assisted in dressing the wounds of the wounded patriots." Dr. Stephen Powers' son, John D. Powers, was also a physician, as was John D.'s son, Dr. Thomas E. Powers. They were, in fact, a famous family of physicians and even to the present day there are physicians named Powers in Vermont and New Hampshire, descendants of the pioneers from County Waterford.

MOUNT HOLLY, VT.—A family named Crowley were early settlers at this place. Rev. Harvey Crowley, born at Mount Holly in 1805, taught school in Vermont with great success for many years. He is described as "a man of much ability and learning, who studied theology and joined the Baptist Church." —(Williams' *History of the Town of Danby.*)

CHARLOTTE, VT.—General John McNeil of Charlotte was one of the first settlers of Tinmouth, where he resided in 1777. He was the first town clerk of Charlotte in 1787; its first representative, in 1788; Judge of Probate of Chittenden County, 1787–1789, and County Judge for five years. He was a delegate to the Convention of 1791 which adopted the Constitution of the United States. McNeil's Ferry, between Charlotte and Essex, N. Y., perpetuates his name.—(*Records of the Governor and Council of Vermont*, Vol. I.)

PITTSFORD, VT.—"Jeremiah Powers from Ireland came very

early to Pittsford (date unknown). He settled first at Greenwich, Mass., where his son, Jeremiah, was born in 1735. His grandson, Jeremiah Powers, was also born at Greenwich. At the age of 16 he enlisted in the Revolutionary army and served during part of the war, after which he was employed as a surveyor in Vermont." Peter Powers, no relative of Jeremiah, is also mentioned at Pittsford. He was captain of a company of men from Hollis, N. H., who served at the capture of Ticonderoga and Crown Point in 1755.—(*History of Pittsford*, by Dr. A. M. Caverly.)

ITEMS EXTRACTED FROM THE "RECORDS OF THE COUNCIL OF SAFETY AND GOVERNOR AND COUNCIL OF THE STATE OF VERMONT."

"An Act empowering into and approving of a Sale of a Part of the real Estate of Simeon Burke, deceased," passed the House on October 23rd, 1783.—(Vol. 3, p. 30.)

The "Memorial of John Jay" and others to the New York Legislature, "in favour of Vermont," dated February 23, 1789, was signed by Daniel McCormick, John Kelly, Daniel Nevin, Hurcules Mulligan and Hugh Gaine, all citizens of New York.— (Vol. 3, p. 448.) McCormick was the first president of the Society of the Friendly Sons of Saint Patrick; Kelly was a noted New York lawyer and is on record as receiving a grant of 30,100 acres of land in Chittenden County, Vermont, for which he paid £903, according to a receipt of the state treasurer, dated October 22, 1791; Mulligan was a New York merchant, the personal friend of General George Washington and Alexander Hamilton; Gaine was the Belfastman who founded the *New York Mercury* in 1752.

John Burke is mentioned as captain of a company in the French War in 1757, and Jesse Burke was sheriff of Cumberland County in 1775. He was a captain in the Revolutionary army.

James McCormick was a member of the Vermont General Assembly in 1777, Michael Flynn in 1796, and John Crowley in 1806.

Among the petitions read in the Vermont General Assembly, I find the following:

> From Hugh McCarty on October 11, 1781
> From Simon Farrell on October 18, 1783
> From Daniel Burke on October 16, 1787
> From Andrew McGaffey on October 15, 1798

From Simeon Riley on October 15, 1801
From James Conner on October 22, 1804
From David McCoy and John Cummings on October 17, 1806
From John McMurphy on October 21, 1808
From John Barry on October 19, 1810
From James Murphy on October 18, 1810
From Daniel McCrillis on October 25, 1813
From Thomas Mooney on October 18, 1819
From Charles Sweeney on October 16, 1821

An Act empowering the executors of Daniel Ryan to sell certain lands, passed the House on November 2, 1814.

In the Council Records—(Vol. 6, p. 513)—there is an account of "the terrific night battle at Fort Erie on August 15th, 1814." In this battle Lieutenant Patrick MacDonough of the American artillery killed a number of the British with a handspike and after being severely wounded, was killed by the British Lieutenant-Colonel Drummond.   There is also an account of the fight in the *Northern Sentinel* of Vermont of August 26, 1814.

In the Council Records—(Vol. 1, p. 271)—there is a record of a very prominent Vermonter of the eighteenth century, named Crean Brush.   He was born in Dublin, Ireland, about 1725; was educated for the bar, but held a military office previous to coming to America.   He located in New York City in 1762, where he married Margaret Montezuman, who was the mother of the second wife of Ethan Allen.   He was licensed as an attorney in 1764 and is supposed to have been associated in his profession with John Kelly.   In 1771, he removed to Westminster, Vt., and in February, 1772, was appointed clerk of Cumberland County and surrogate in April, 1772.   He acquired many thousand acres of land in Vermont through New York grants and was a member of the Colonial Assembly from January 5, 1773, to April 5, 1775, when it dissolved.   In this body "he proved himself to be an able, eloquent and influential member."

IRISH PIONEERS IN DELAWARE.

Being Some Extracts from the Registers of Holy Trinity Church, Wilmington, and Other Records.

by michael j. o'brien.

The records from which the names in the accompanying lists are taken were kept by Israel Acrelius, the noted historian of the Swedish settlements on the Delaware, and by Rev. Isaac Acrelius, for many years the officiating clergyman of Holy Trinity Church at Wilmington. The originals are in the Swedish language and were translated by Mr. Horace Burr for the Historical Society of Delaware and were published in 1890 by that society.

The Swedish settlements were located in New Castle County and were known as "New Sweden." While the large majority of the names appearing on the church registers are Swedish and Dutch, it is interesting to note the number of people of Irish birth or descent who were married in this church, or whose children were baptized by the Swedish minister. Acrelius, in his *History of New Sweden*, writing of the state of education among the people in this territory about twenty-five years before the Revolution, remarks: "The first Swedish and Holland settlers were a poor, weak and ignorant people, who brought up their children in the same ignorance, which is the reason why natives of the country can neither write nor cipher and that very few of them are qualified for any office under the government. Forty years back our people scarcely knew what a school was. In the later times there have come over from Ireland some Presbyterians and some Roman Catholics, who commenced with school-keeping, but as soon as they saw better openings they gave that up." Unfortunately, the names of those Irish schoolmasters do not seem to have been preserved in the records of the time, with the exception of four, whose names I find in the public archives, published in 1911 by the Archives Commission of Delaware under the authority of the State Legislature. In the "Rosters of the Companies Enlisted for the Campaign (the Indian war) in the Lower Counties" in the year 1758, I find the names of:

"Richard Little, age 26, born in Ireland, occupation Schoolmaster."
"James Murphy, age 21, born in Ireland, occupation Schoolmaster."
"Arthur Simpson, born in Ireland, occupation Schoolmaster."
"John Bryan, age 20, born in Ireland, occupation Schoolmaster."

The first mention of an Irish name on the registers of Holy Trinity Church is that of the baptism, on April 18, 1714, of "Richard Whelan, son of Darby Whelan and his wife, Susa." It is probable they were the only Irish family in the parish at that time, for I note that the sponsors at the christening were: "Jacobus Van de Ver, Mathias Skagan, Olive Towassa's widow, Gertrude, and Peter Mayer's wife Sarah." Under date of January 7, 1719, appears an entry of the marriage of Edward Brennen and Mary Butcher, and in a later record of the baptism of their daughter, Annika, the name is spelled Brannin. It is probable that comparatively few Irish settlers located in this section prior to 1740, or thereabouts, as it is not until after that period that Irish names begin to appear on the records in any appreciable numbers.

Between 1745 and 1775 they were an important and aggressive element in the community, and from the "Delaware Archives" I have extracted a surprisingly large number of Irish names which appear in the muster rolls of the soldiers raised in New Castle County for the Indian, French and Revolutionary wars. In some of the company rosters the name, age, nativity and occupation of each soldier are given, and I find from the "Muster Roll of the Company of Foot commanded by Captain John Shannon," which was organized in New Castle County in September, 1746, that, of the full complement of 100 men, 51 are down as "born in Ireland!" In a "Return of a Full Company Enlisted for the Campaign in the Lower Counties by Captain McClughan, delivered Wednesday the 17th May, 1758," the total number of men is 98, of whom 43 are recorded as "born in Ireland," and of Captain James Armstrong's Company of 53 men, 27 were natives of Ireland. If we add to these figures the men with Irish names, who were born in America and evidently the sons of Irish immigrants, the proportion of Irish in these three companies would be 60 per cent! The complete rosters of these and other military companies raised in this vicinity for the defence of the colonists will make a highly interesting item for the JOURNAL, and will appear in a later issue. No better proof than this can be adduced in support of the assertion that the Irish settled in the American Colonies many years before the Revolution, and that they were not the type of Irish whom the historians are so fond of calling "Scotch-Irish," in their feeble attempts to deprive Ireland of the credit of having furnished such settlers to the Colonies.

MARRIAGES PERFORMED AT HOLY TRINITY CHURCH, WILMINGTON, DEL.

1719, January 7, Edward Brennen and Mary Butcher
1727, June 1, Edward Haley and Anna Cloud
1731, April 15, Daniel Moloughny and Margaret Starret
1731, May 30, Thomas Neal and Susanna Quin
1734, April 23, William Gavin and Briget Canady
1734, December 21, James Bryan and Mary McDaniel
1735, March 25, James Macgrau and Mary Dix
1735, July 15, James Mackmullen and Mary Mackloud
1735, August 10, Denis Mackginley and Elsa Mackkarty
1736, April 16, William Brown and Martha Dunn
1736, August 31, Johannas Springer and Mary Dempsey
1737, May 8, Francis O'Nayle and Anna Walker
1737, December 11, Michael Higgins and Frances Hendrickson
1738, January 17, John Mahafey and Jane Frey
1738, August 28, Bryan Macginnie and Sarah Jones
1738, October 12, Bryan Cullen and Sarah Kelly
1738, November 23, Michael Farlow and Mary White
1739, February 12, James Neally and Sarah MacMullin
1739, May 14, John Isac and Eleanor Connelly
1739, October 14, Hugh Kirgian and Catharine O'Nail
1740, April 21, Arthur Donnelly and Mary Macdade
1740, December 26, Christopher Flinn and Rebecca Hossey
1741, May 20, Myles Sweeney and Eleanor Campbell
1741, May 26, John Murphy and Catherine Spruce
1744, ———, John Reese and Marget McLaly
1744, ———, Patrick Monaghan and Sara Crafford
1744, ———, Edward Milligan and Mary Savage
1744, ———, Nail McGraney and Ann Docherty
1744, ———, Edward Carrell and Susanna Barker
1744, ———, Robert McCarthy and Elizabeth Plate
1744, ———, Cornelius Obragan and Mary Crockert
1744, ———, Thomas Cohens and Mary Gragan
1744, ———, Patrick Oreton and Rachel Reese
1745, February 28, David Kelly and Ann Royley
1745, May 6, Hugh Carrell and Mary Fips
1745, September —, Patrick Glason and Cicily Graves
1745, September —, John Steen and Jane McCoy
1745, October —, John Moore and Elizabeth McCarty
1745, November —, William Quighty and Jane Clansy
1745, November —, Martin Mac Gra and Judith Cory

1745, December —, Edward Duckerty and Elizabeth Carrel
1746, January —, William Griffy and Catharina Murphey
1746, February —, Cornelius Clark and Jane Conry
1746, February —, Samuel Hayes and Elizabeth Hearney
1746, February —, John Bodley and Ann Fitchgirl
1746, March —, Patrick Moore and Mary Brown
1746, May —, Cornelius McOllern and Christina Supingam
1746, October —, Cornelius McSweany and Ellinor Birk
1746, October —, John Sheals and Margaret Sarr
1746, October —, Dennis Sallovain and Mary Leat
1746, November —, James Bredin and Susannah Mullin
1746, December —, James Donn and Jean Farrell
1747, February —, William Smith and Ann McClare
1747, February —, Hugh McConnel and Elizabeth White
1747, May —, John McGinnis and Martha More
1747, May —, Thomas Flannegan and Mary Scoggen
1747, July —, Timothy Morphy and Ann Anderson
1747, August —, Niclas Fling and Sara Bettel
1747, August —, Patrick Cafford and Magdalen Dame
1747, November —, Francis McFall and Sara McGarvi
1747, December —, James Donally and Mary Morrow
1748, March —, Timothy Conners and Catharine Hays
1748, May —, Robert McGarrout and Agnes Kelly
1748, May —, John Tinn and Mary McGee
1748, June —, Patrick Burns and Rose Ingilsby
1748, July —, John Kelly and Sarah Welldon
1748, July —, John Mahan and Ellinor Caby
1748, July —, William Farniss and Mary Dowling
1748, October —, Hugh Laughlin and Mary Evans
1749, November 30, William Glinn and Mary Tool
1749, December 26, Thomas Corcoran and Prudence Foresides
1750, January 1, Andrew Beard and Elizabeth Connelly
1750, March 24, Matthew McLaughlin and Ann Han
1750, April 10, Cornelius Hart and Margaret Tuker
1750, June 14, Patrick Coyle and Jane Forquar
1750, October 1, William Odivans and Mary Egen
1750, October 8, James Rowan and Cathrine McGennis
1750, October 22, David Dalton and Joanna McCloskey
1750, December 5, Patrick Mullen and Mary Perkins
1750, December 27, Daniel Cashay and Ann Moore
1751, January 1, James Killen and Ann Duard
1751, March 11, Cain McKinni and Mary Hiery
1751, March 26, James McGarvey and Leane Pettecrow
1751, April 8, Harry McCloski and Margaret Monagle
1751, April 9, Phillip McGowen and Mary Preston
1751, April 17, Thomas McDonald and Mary McCorday
1751, May 4, Charles Cartay and Elizabeth Porter
1751, May 13, Patrick Fitch Patrick and Mary Patterson

1751, May 20, Patrick McMollholland and Sarah Baller
1751, June 6, Thomas Mahan and Martha Ball
1751, August 24, Daniel Finnin and Elinor Dougherty
1751, September 26, Edward Richards and Margaret Hogin
1751, October 24, Patrick Winters and Elinor Peril
1751, December 9, John McDerry and ——— Trussis
1751, December 21, Edward Dougherty and Anna Cassidy
1752, February 23, John Barber and Elizabeth Quinn
1752, April 5, John Smedt and Jane McNemee
1752, April 11, Peter Glansey and Mary McNail
1752, April 25, Thomas Williams and Mary Nealy
1752, May 10, James Allis and Elizabeth McMullon
1752, May 22, Michael Nelay and Else Flean
1752, July 14, John McCoy and Martha Ling
1752, August 3, Michael Robertsson and Mary Dougherty
1752, August 3, Thomas Fling and Mary Flower
1752, August 17, Edward McSorley and Mary Cauhoon
1752, November 29, Timothy Karenoss and Cathy Donnolly
1753, January 25, Philip Fits Simens and Mary McMolland
1753, February 28, Patrick Mooney and Jane Beard
1753, June 12, Matthew Kelly and Jane Stotts
1753, July 25, Edward Pilkinton and Margaret Casey
1753, August 21, James Donnerthy and Agnes Crosby
1753, August 12, Joseph Hayes and Joanna Pastmore
1753, August 20, Jeremiah Sulivane and Briget Welch
1753, November 23, Thomas McFadien and Susannah Kirk
1753, December 11, Joseph McCloskey and Agnes Huston
1754, January 14, James Tully and Nelly Holland
1754, January 27, Daniel McLonen and Dorcas McGhee
1754, February 18, John Hargrove and Catherine Gready
1754, May 9, William Tunkes and Catherine Cassidy
1754, June 29, Lin McDermott and Mary Wood
1754, July 20, Robert Few and Martha Conally
1754, December 26, Laurenz McKlayn and Sarah Griffith
1755, January 21, Barnabas Sweeney and Rebecca Massor
1755, February 24, John Standley and Bridget Collins
1755, March 4, James McCrady and Margaret Colluy
1755, March 6, John Henesey and Elizabeth Post
1755, July 6, Dennis McCassety and Susannah Kingkad
1755, July 6, Philip Cauvenah and Cathrine Moothy
1755, July 6, Patrick Boyd and Ann George
1755, August 3, James Donelly and Grace McLaughlin
1755, August 6, Isaac Adams and Marget Kelly
1755, October 10, John Goggin and Lathy McCollmay
1755, December 28, Timothy Mahoney and Hannah Reily
1756, January 3, Matthew Meloy and Anne Hansson
1756, February 9, Arthur Conolly and Jean Wench
1756, August 22, Joseph Clist and Mary McCahan

1756, August 22, Thomas Shannan and Johanna Carey
1756, October 16, William Crowley and Johanna Runnels
1756, October 18, James McBoyd and Elizabeth Buckley
1756, December 9, Patrick Duffee and Christian Barthelson
1757, February 1, Peter Murphy and Margreta O'Neil
1757, February 22, Edward Maghan and Margreta Welch
1757, March 17, James Doudle and Martha McCall
1757, March 29, Daniel Ragin and Mary Strong
1757, March 29, John McNamee and Martha Lea
1757, July 26, John Dayly and Elsa Voghan
1757, September 15, Dennis McKoy and Mary Davis
1757, September 15, Samuel McMullon and Agnes McVan
1757, November 5, John McCormack and Sara Hughs
1757, November 23, William Murphy and Jane Morrison
1757, November 23, Patrick McGlain and Elizabeth Lingin
1757, December 3, Solomon Springer and Margreta Kelly
1757, October 12, Lorance McManie and Catharina McCassily
1758, February 13, Joseph Perkins and Anne Dougherty
1758, April 25, John McEasie and Bridget McLean
1758, May 15, James Duggan and Cathrina Elliott
1758, July 8, Timothy Conley and Anna Gibson
1758, August 23, Philip McLaughlin and Cathrine O'Neal
1758, November 26, Roger McGally and Jane Rimson
1758, December 5, John O'Freel and Margret Farmer
1759, July 3, Francis McMullon and Margret Gallohur
1759, August 3, Patrick Kelly and Anne Hide
1759, August 5, Peter Gallorhon and Flora Hamel
1759, September 16, Barney Miles and Martha Moore
1759, November 5, Christopher Baril and Cathrine Farril
1760, March 6, Lawrence Flinn and Elizabeth Gordon
1760, March 29, Peter Gallohar and Mary Halom
1760, August 18, Cornelius McDonald and Cherry Dely
1760, October 10, Joseph Cloud and Margrite Brady
1760, November 24, George Donavan and Elizabeth Reese
1761, January 21, John Scarlet and Mary O'Neal
1761, June 20, John Ward and Elizabeth McMaghan
1762, February 9, Nathan Heald and Rebecca McBride
1762, February 24, John Fitz Jarel and Mary Hews
1762, March 17, James Meleehan and Mary Taylor
1762, August 7, John McGuier and Jane Bates
1762, September 13, Robert McDonnal and Eleonore Powel
1762, November 11, William Shay and Mary Latimore
1762, November 25, Cornelius Hines and Elizabeth Paterson
1762, December 22, Adam Ekman and Mary Ryan
1763, March 11, Peter Glancy and Jane King
1763, February 18, William Beats and Hannah McCafforty
1763, May 9, Roland Burke and Hannah Carter
1763, July 2, Jacob Brinton and Cathrine McCoy

1763, July 13, Martin Doyle and Rose Brogan
1763, July 3, John Karran and Hannah Miller
1763, August 29, Walter Welsh and Mary Rely
1763, November 20, Patrick McCloskey and Elizabeth Oversiller
1763, November 21, Patrick Brady and Mary Gore
1763, December 10, Abraham Flaharty and Rachel Ferris
1764, February 2, John Grow and Anne Danelly
1764, February 3, William Reath and Susannah Doyle
1764, March 13, Joseph Scott and Margaret Coughlan
1764, April 4, William Dennon and Elizabeth Hely
1764, August 7, James Moore and Mary Canely
1764, August 10, John Corkran and Mary Carr
1764, December 29, John Shee and Catherine Lawrence
1765, March 20, John Welch and Elinor Kildennin
1765, July 7, John McCafferty and Mary Prioer
1765, October 11, Thomas Mahaffey and Elizabeth Linsay
1765, December 24, Andrew Johnson and Mary Conelly
1766, February 26, Walter Sweeney and Susan Stewart
1766, April 7, Edmund Dougherty and ———— ————
1766, May 7, Cornelius Truax and Elizabeth Tobin
1766, December 22, Thomas Shannahan and Rebecca Wallace
1767, December 28, Joseph Mooney and Elizabeth Taylor
1768, February 9, Jacob Murfy and Elizabeth Welch
1768, June 13, Edward McCarty and Susannah Stedham
1768, August 14, Hugh Ferrill and Sarah Grime
1768, September 21, William Conner and Helena Lohnohill
1768, October 13, Owen Donnelly and Sarah Andrewood
1768, October 13, John Shay and Jean Manelly
1768, November 4, William Talley and Judith Fitzsimmons
1768, December 30, Tobias Peterson and Mary McCarty
1769, January 28, Cornelius McCashey and Cathrine Fisher
1769, March 21, John Stalkop and Cathrine Fitzgerald
1769, May 9, John Gackhagen (Geoghegan) and Cathrine Bryan
1769, October 2, Matthew Doile and Cathrine Grimes
1769, October 12, Thomas Kane and Elizabeth Elliott
1769, October 28, William Hatton and Mary Quinn
1769, November 3, John Frederick and Jean Maguire
1770, January 10, David Jenkins and Hannah O'Donel
1770, April 16, John Henley and Martha McKeever
1770, June 5, Brian Daily and Mary Murphy
1770, June 17, Jeremia Flemon and Ann Burns
1770, August 8, Dennis McGee and Susannah Roberson
1770, October 5, Evan Evans and Hannah Sullivan
1770, November 30, Robert Ryan and Mary Wilson
1770, December 18, William Login and Jane Way
1771, January 2, Lawrence Woods and Mary Kelly
1771, January 17, John McKellway and Jane McBride
1771, March 26, Nathaniel Maguire and Sara Collins

1771, March 27, John Flinn and Jeane Parker
1771, June 30, Edmund Dougherty and Leady Pyle
1771, September 3, Archibald McMurphy and Julianna Ricketts
1771, September 28, Christopher Gowing and Ann Murphy
1771, October 5, William Keeren and Rebecca Owen
1772, February 27, Charles McGonnigale and Elizabeth Lyle
1772, March 30, Daniel Dealy and Elizabeth Pitman
1772, May 11, James Murphey and Ann Zebley
1772, September 1, James McCallah and Hannah Evey
1772, November 5, John Dealy and Jean Gray
1772, November 12, Nathaniel Wilkinson and Elinor Dunihoo
1772, November 18, John McCarter and Margaret Thompson
1773, February 4, John White and Elinor Karney
1773, February 4, Michael McCrea and Mary Sullivan
1773, March 3, John Maguire and Margaret Shute
1773, June 9, Henry Cubbin and Christiana Dugen
1773, June 18, Daniel Kenney and Mary Alford
1773, August 10, James Sim and Margaret Calahan
1773, September 2, James McKean and Anne Wilson
1773, December 15, Thomas Treacey and Sarah Coplind
1774, January 6, James Dougherty and Livina Lawrence
1774, January 31, William Craig and Margaret Holahan
1774, February 14, Michael Higgins and Cathrine Menzener
1774, March 26, William Martin and Jean McCarty
1774, June 3, John Gold and Catherine McBride
1774, June 16, John Gritsie and Hannah Daly
1774, July 19, William Moore and Margaret McLouin
1774, July 31, Charles Bewgles and Margaret Byrnes
1774, October 24, Isaac Ryan and Hannah Townsend
1774, April 13, John McLaughlin and Jean Dunlap
1775, October 24, John Gars and Mary Mahane
1775, December 4, John Branan and Margaret Pingleton
1775, December 6, William Hanby and Elizabeth Konelly
1776, January 13, John Spenees and Mary Holahan
1776, April 6, James McKeever and Susannah McCafferty
1776, August 4, James Murphy and Mary Jackson
1776, September 9, John Cashedy and Mary Myers
1776, November 28, Peter Blankchaor and Martha McCann
1777, February 23, William Heagens and Margret Dougherty
1777, March 12, William Husbands and Margret Megarrough
1777, March 31, John McKaghnen and Hannah Moore
1777, May 14, Mathew McConnell and Margret Williams
1777, May 19, John Robinson and Alise McDermott
1777, June 27, John Tolan and Mary Laferty
1778, January 19, Patrick Burk and Susannah Fielding
1778, April 2, William McKee and Elizabeth Miles
1778, May 4, Joseph Burk and Eleanore McGinn
1778, May 12, Lawrence Conely and Rebecca Almond

1778, June 16, Edward Dunn and Anns Stalcops
1778, July 7, Hezekiel Kary and Elizabeth McCafferty
1778, October 23, Daniel Magennis and Catharine Mallen
1778, November 4, William McNail and Sarah Bailey
1778, December 20, Daniel Boyle and Elizabeth Ennis
1778, December 25, Peter McDonald and Margaret Fox
1779, March 3, Bryan McNally and Jane McFarland
1779, June 26, Thomas Morgan and Elizabeth Dougherty
1779, June 27, Arthur Dempsey and Johanna Riley
1779, August 30, Stephen Anderson and Elizabeth Farrell
1779, December 29, William Wood and Elizabeth McBride
1780, January 25, David Denny and Susannah O'Neile
1780, January 30, Nicholas Foss and Elenor Conolly
1780, April 9, William Hewes and Cathrine Connelly
1780, June 29, William McGlaughlin and Susannah Ford
1780, June 29, John Nowlin and Mary Gray
1780, July 29, Andrew Cunningham and Ann Farrel
1780, October 10, James Chalfont and Jane McCarty
1780, November 17, Philip Dwire and Margaret Sullivan
1782, March 28, Thomas Neilds and Mary Fling
1782, May 20, John Flin and Margarey Heagens
1782, October 8, Garrett McQuillen and Jane McGloien
1783, April 10, Archibald Philips and Elizabeth O'Donnelly
1783, June 9, John Fanrod and Martha Gallaher
1783, October 27, John Hewes and Hannah Connolly
1784, August 19, Edward McKeon and Ann Dougherty
1784, October 21, Hance Naff and Mary Colligan
1784, December 15, Owen McBraiherly and Ann Conner
1784, April 4, Daniel McBride and Rachel Bird
1784, May 19, Charles Savin and Mary McGinnis
1784, October 18, William Cassidy and Martha McHenry
1785, April 10, Patrick Rooney and Mary Ricket
1786, November 12, John McConnel and Mary Gissin
1787, September 4, Samuel Kelly and Margaret Gray
1787, October 17, Hugh Mclagan and Margaret McGaughey
1787, October 27, John Lary and Ann Combs
1788, April 24, Samuel Wallace and Ann Lafferty
1789, October 24, Neil Gallagher and Elizabeth Ball
1789, August 5, Michael Quinn and Elizabeth Runnels
1789, October 21, Charles Kelly and Deborah Cobbs
1789, October 25, John McConnaugh and Rachel McCarnaughie
1792, May 5, David Logan and Mary Long
1792, December 28, Charles Collins and Giles McNultey
1792, July 18, Thomas Mullin and Susan Readus
1794, April 6, Manasseh Dougherty and Cathrine Dougherty
1794, July 17, Thomas Dougherty and Mary Ford
1794, September 15, Michael Mullin and Mary Culbertson
1795, April 20, Cornelius McDade and Mary Carr

1795, June 25, Henry Barry and Elizabeth Rice
1795, October 16, James McMullin and Cathrine Bryans
1795, December 31, Patrick McNeil and Elizabeth Jeffries
1796, February 4, Francis ODaniel and Isabella French
1797, January 7, Patrick Nugent and Elianor Nugent
1797, October 12, James McConnal and Mary Harp
1797, November 1, Daniel McDaniel and Susanna Loone
1797, November 1, Adam Ayres and Sarah Larkin
1797, November 1, John Gallaher and Margaret Hedrick
1797, November 10, James Jack and Margaret McLarney
1797, December 9, Daniel Dingee and Mary Mooney

BAPTISMS PERFORMED AT HOLY TRINITY CHURCH, WILMINGTON, DEL.

1714, April 18, Richard, son of Darby and Susa Whelan
1719, May 15, Annika, daughter of Edward and Mary Branin
1722, April 28, Jane, daughter of Richard and Esther McCarey
1722, July 8, Mary, daughter of James and Eleonora Haley
1730, June 14, Susannah, daughter of Patrick and Elizabeth Done
1731, January 16, ———, child of John and Margaret Fitzsimmon
1732, April 23, Elizabeth, daughter of John and Elizabeth Fitzsimmons
1736, March 14, Maria, daughter of John and Helena Degnen
1749, February 12, Anne, daughter of James and Lady McGennis
1750, May 25, William, son of Philip and Margaret McBraid
1750, July 16, Jane, daughter of James and Rose (McLaughlin) Brochon
1750, December 16, James, son of James and Mary Conolly
1752, August 19, Peter, son of James and Lady McGinnis
1752, March 7, Rebecca, daughter of James and Catherine McDonald
1752, May 26, Anne, daughter of Cornelius and Rachel McWeyer (McGuire)
1752, February 25, Mary, daughter of Daniel and Mary Kain
1752, February 2, Elenor, daughter of Michael and Else Meloy
1752, August 21, Mary, daughter of John and Jane McKenny
1752, April 1, Mary, daughter of Robert and Elizabeth Dougherty
1752, November 7, William, son of John and Elizabeth Kary
1752, December 23, Anna, daughter of James and Lady McGennis
1752, February 12, Sarah, daughter of John and Bridget Collins
1753, June 30, Ezechiel, son of John and Elizabeth McKary
1753, March 17, William, son of Garret and Elizabeth Dougherty
1753, May 23, Elizabeth, daughter of George and Elizabeth Connel
1753, March 9, Else, daughter of Adam and Margaret Kelley
1754, April 8, Jane, daughter of Niclas and Sarah Fling
1755, January 8, Nail, son of Nail and Jane McCarty
1755, May 2, James, son of James and Lady McGinnis
1755, August 26, Mary, daughter of John and Elizabeth Carney
1755, April 8, James, son of Daniel and Anne Carney
1756, June 9, Anne, daughter of James and Margaret Maley
1759, December 11, Hugh, son of Arthur and Maria Murphey
1760, September 19, William, son of James and Maria McKeaver
1760, August 10, Sarah, daughter of Richard and Elizabeth McManneman

1761, November 4, Eleonora, daughter of Edward and Biggita McBride
1762, June 30, John, son of Daniel and Margaret Kildee
1762, June 16, Susannah, daughter of Richard and Eliz. McManaman
1764, January 10, Mary, daughter of James and Catherine Cavenau
1765, February 5, Cathrine, daughter of Patrick and Eliz. McCloskey
1767, October 11, Isaac, son of Thomas and Cathrine Quinn
1768, January 15, Mary, daughter of Patrick and Eliz. McCloskey
1768, April 30, Helena, daughter of John and Jeane Shay
1771, January 2, Thomas, son of John and Jeane Quinn
1771, July 13, Mary, daughter of Thomas and Elizabeth Kane
1772, March 20, James, son of Bryan and Mary Dailey
1773, September 19, John, son of Thomas and Cathrine Quin
1775, February 5, William, son of Brian and Mary Daily
1777, January 10, John, son of William and Margret Heagen
1777, October 12, Margret, daughter of Charles and Eloner McLaughlin
1777, December 15, Elizabeth, daughter of Patrick and Jane Mooney
1777, December 15, Mary, daughter of Patrick and Jane Mooney
1778, February 7, Elizabeth, daughter of Arthur and Johannah Dempsey
1778, November 30, Isabella, daughter of James and Elizabeth Murphy
1778, June 20, John, son of ———— Konolly
1779, December 23, James, son of William and Jane Flanagan
1780, August 6, William, son of William and Esther Kiley
1781, September 17, John, son of James and Elizabeth Murphy
1782, April 9, ————, child of Nail Dougherty
1782, February 11, James, son of William and Ester Kelley
1782, November 10, John, son of John and Hannah Flinn
1783, January 31, Thomas, son of John and Hannah Flinn
1783, October 23, Henry, son of John and Mary Nowlin
1784, November 23, Mary, daughter of Felix and Margaret Hanlon
1784, June 12, Elizabeth, daughter of John and Margaret McGlaughlin
1785, February 11, Peter, son of John and Anne Flinn
1792, November 17, John, son of Francis and ———— Lafferty
1793, October 18, Ann, daughter of John and Cathrine Duffy
1793, October 23, Hugh, son of Edward and Sarah McGonagill
1794, February 20, Marian, daughter of George and Mary Dunn
1795, February 12, James, son of John and Ann Gordon, "Irish people"
1795, March 11, Sarah, daughter of John and Margaret Welsh
1796, July 21, Martin, son of Martin and Mary Connor
1796, September 27, John, son of John and Hannah Fling
1797, July 22, William, son of Robert and Mary Lennon
1798, January 1, Sarah, daughter of John and Isabel McGloghlin
1799, February 10, James, son of Thomas and Isabel McCloskey

IRISH PIONEERS AND SCHOOLMASTERS IN BUTLER COUNTY, PENNSYLVANIA.

BY MICHAEL J. O'BRIEN.

Butler County took its name from the distinguished Major-General, Richard Butler, a native of Dublin, Ireland, who commanded a brigade of Pennsylvania troops in the War of the Revolution. Four of General Butler's brothers served as officers in the Revolutionary army. Three of them were born in Kilkenny and one in Pennsylvania. A great array of Irish names appears on the early records of this county. The names here mentioned by no means embrace the full numerical strength of early Irish immigration to this region, since I have extracted only such names as appear in the "survey lists," "lists of taxables," "freemen," etc., of the various places where Irish schoolmasters were located. Immigrants, principally Irish and German, began to come into what is now Butler County during the period of the Revolution and for many years afterwards the Irish continued to pour into this region in such numbers that about the beginning of the nineteenth century, some of the villages and settlements of Butler County were among the most populous rural communities in the state.

As in some other sections of Pennsylvania, during the first decade of their settlement but few teachers are located. The pioneer families could give little attention to education, for in the early stages of the settlements material wants took precedence over everything else. Not that they were unmindful of the desirability of furnishing educational opportunities to their children. They yielded simply to necessity in at first subordinating the cultivation of the mind to the taming of the soil, but, as soon as a fair start had been made and white settlements had begun to appear, scattered through the primeval forest, they usually installed a schoolmaster, who thenceforth became a man of influence in every community.

In a chapter on "Education" during the early years of the last century, in McKee's *History of Butler County*, the author says: "Some among the early teachers, especially the Scotch and Irish, were better educated and, as a rule, all did their work well, as is sufficiently attested by the great statesmen, writers and orators of the middle of the nineteenth century, many or most of them graduates of the pioneer schoolhouse." One of the earliest schoolmasters in the county was an Irishman, James Irvine, who, on coming to this country in 1770, located in Westmoreland County. He first appears in Adams Township in 1796, where he took up 100 acres of land by settler's right and was one of its foremost pioneers in other respects than chronological. He taught school in Adams Township for several years and was the progenitor of what might be called a family of teachers. Two of his sons, Mathew and Samuel Irvine, also school-teachers, were soldiers in the War of 1812.

In the same year that Irvine removed from Westmoreland County Archibald Kelly came from the same locality and settled in Parker Township. McKee says "he was a noted educator, his training both in Ireland and in Westmoreland and other counties having fitted him for far more exacting duties than he found in Parker Township." Another reference to him says: "he was the first teacher in Washington Township and attracted pupils from the surrounding country. Judge Bredin and other prominent citizens received their early training under the rigid discipline of Master Kelly." He had eleven children, some of whose descendants are now prominent people in Butler County. John Kelly also taught school in Washington Township. The historian of the county says: "Parker Township's early settlers were equally as good class as the Parkers, a large number of them being natives of the north of Ireland." Among them I find families named McMahon, Conley, Haggerty and McCafferty. In 1808, William Fleming, who participated in the Rebellion of 1798, settled in this locality.

In Winfield Township we are told "the pioneers who came first were natives of Ireland and, until 1836, the larger number of settlers were more or less of the same nationality, including a number of revolutionary veterans." It is said that "the first schoolhouse was built about 1799 near the Winfield-Clearfield Township line, those interested in its erection being Arthur O'Donnell, Andrew and Michael Dugan, James and John McLaughlin, Michael McCue and James Denny." The only teacher of Irish birth who seems to have conducted this school was James Denny, who came from County Donegal in 1793, locating in Clearfield Township on a tract of 400 acres. His wife was Mary O'Donnell, also a native of Donegal. They had a large family and their descendants still live on the original lands.

"John Kennedy, an Irishman, and a well-known schoolmaster in the early days, emigrated from Virginia to this county and was among the first settlers. He was wounded in the Revolutionary War. His son, James, was in the War of 1812 and four of his descendants were in the late (Civil) war. Kennedy taught school at Hannahstown as late as 1806. His scholarship was far above the attainments of most of the early teachers. He was a fine penman, was a very mild-mannered teacher for those days and was very popular"—(McKee). John Sweeney was also an early teacher at Hannahstown.

"The earliest of the pioneers in Clearfield Township, or the territory recognized as such since its organization in 1804, were almost entirely of Irish extraction and they came to this section as home-seekers, an entirely different class from the wandering and temporary residents. The early names include those of the McBrides, Connells, O'Donnells, Slators, Milligans, Coyles, Dugans, Dennys, McGinleys, Gallaghers, McCues, McLaughlins and others. The pioneer of them all was Patrick McBride from County Donegal, Ireland, who built his cabin and owned 400 acres of land there in 1798 and lived until 1848. County Donegal contributed a number of other pioneers, and some of these, after entering land, carried on the trades which they had learned in their native country"—(McKee). The first school in the township was erected in 1807 on Andrew Dugan's farm. The first teacher was John Smith, "all of whose pupils," we are told, "were Irish without exception." McKee adds: "Other teachers who taught at various times up to the period of the organization of the public schools were Michael Herron, Francis McBride, Daniel McLaughlin, Manassas Boyle, James Denny and Master Brandon," while, among "the first teachers of the public schools of the township" were Neal McBride, William Dougherty and Peter Fennell.

In the neighboring township of Donegal, Patrick McElroy, Charles Duffy, John Gillespie and Moses Hanlon settled in the year 1797, as well as others named Haggerty, Maloney, Breaden, Hunter, McFadden and O'Donnell, the majority from County

Donegal. Not only were those I have mentioned the earliest settlers, but, in everything pertaining to the civilization and improvement of this section they seem to have accepted all the responsibility. They subdued the wilderness, built comfortable homes, established mills and made roads and there is every evidence to show that they early concerned themselves about the education of their children and supplying them with religious influences. Nearly all were Roman Catholics and I find a reference to "a Catholic school conducted for some time in their interest" in Oakland Township, to where Dennis, Arthur and Cornelius O'Donnell, the Dugans, McGinleys and others removed from Clearfield. John O'Donnell seems to be the only teacher of this school on record.

In Venango Township, Michael Kelly, Hugh Murrin, John Logue, Robert Cochran and James and John Shields took up lands in the year 1796. "The first school-teacher was Robert Cunningham, who taught in 1802. He was an Irishman, as were the early teachers generally, a fine scholar and very strict in discipline"—(McKee). He taught for several terms in a log hut near the present town of Eau Claire. "An Irishman named Welsh, who taught with so much of a brogue that he could scarcely be understood, was among the early teachers of Venango Township"—(McKee). Prior to 1812, Hugh and John Murrin were teachers in Venango.

The first of the pioneers in Franklin Township were John McCandless and Aaron Moore, who came there in 1796, followed by the brothers James, George, William and Garrett Moore, John McGrew, William McCandless, Charles Sullivan and others. McKee says: "A number of these early settlers were natives of Ireland." They were not unmindful of their duties in regard to educating their children, for seven years after their arrival, "John Thompson fitted up a log cabin and conducted a subscription school for a term and was then succeeded by Charles Sullivan," who seems to have conducted the school until 1807. According to a genealogical record preserved by the Sullivan family, the schoolmaster was a grandson of Peter O'Sullivan who emigrated to Northumberland, Va., about the year 1700. Charles Sullivan, the schoolmaster, was born in Virginia in 1760 and "served under Washington at Valley Forge." His son, Charles

C. Sullivan, was one of the most prominent figures in public life in Butler County and a lawyer of high reputation.

"One of the first pioneers to venture into Clinton Township was Patrick Harvey of County Down, Ireland, who selected a tract of land as early as 1792. The only other settler at that time was John McKee. Robert McGinnis came in 1796. The Revolutionary soldiers were well represented in the years following and the majority of these early settlers were of Irish extraction"— (McKee). In 1800 came James Byrne, a Revolutionary veteran, his brother, Edward Byrne, and Daniel Lardin, the founder of the village of Lardintown. "The matter of educating the children of the township was early agitated and houses were utilized at first on the farms of the Riddle and Davis families. Among the early instructors may be noted the familiar names of Cunningham, Herron, Jack, Love, McCorkle and McGarry."

The first settler in Marion Township was probably Samuel McMurray from County Down, who reached this section with his wife in 1798. Hugh Gilmore and John Walsh came there in 1803. One of its first schools was taught by David Cunningham and among his immediate successors was John Walsh.

McKee says: "The first actual settlement in Buffalo Township was made in 1795 by a man of Irish birth, George Bell, after whom a hill and creek were named. He was followed in the same year by Robert Elliott, also a native of Ireland, who in 1796 brought out his wife and a large family." Among the "first teachers" were Michael Herron and Robert Cunningham, son of John Cunningham, a native of Ireland, who first settled at Greencastle, Pa. He is mentioned as "one of the earliest school-teachers of the county." A school was erected on the Elliott farm at the expense of Robert Elliott. We are told "it was a slight improvement over the old log structures which the scholars of this township had previously attended. Here Robert Hamilton, an Irishman, and a Yankee named Jones were early teachers. Hamilton was considered a good teacher in those days."

In referring to the pioneer schools in Penn Township, McKee says: "The early school-teachers were Irishmen and usually fond of showing their authority. Few are remembered who were noted for their mildness and none can be charged with sparing the rod unduly. Probably the first school in Penn Township was a small log building which stood on the Jacob Hartzell farm. Here Master Sterrett taught school and a little later John Boyle, a terror to evil-doers and little boys."

In Centre Township, "the first teacher was William Wallace in 1803. The building was constructed of logs and was as comfortable as most dwellings, rather a pretentious school for the time. Wallace came from Ireland in 1793 and settled on a tract of land with his brother, Benjamin, in Franklin County."—(McKee).

The earliest schoolmasters on record in Brady Township were Henry Evans and Thomas Gorley, whom McKee says were natives of Ireland. About 1806, a school was erected near where Karns City in Fairview Township now stands. John Brown was its first teacher and Morris Bredin the second. Thomas McCleary taught there in 1813. Bredin was a native of Stranorlar, County Donegal. He was a brother of Judge John Bredin, one of the most prominent early members of the Butler County bar and an ardent friend of the common school system and a very efficient factor in its success. He came to Butler County in 1802. It is of interest to note that at one period (1841) all three justices of the Seventeenth Judicial District, comprised of the counties of Butler, Beaver and Mercer, Judges Bredin, Duffy and Bovard, were natives of County Donegal, Ireland, and all three represented different religious denominations, Bredin the Episcopalian, Duffy the Roman Catholic and Bovard the Presbyterian.

In Mercer Township, "Major John Welsh, an Irishman and a land-jobber, settled near Harrisville in 1797. He was one of the pioneer schoolmasters. He was an excellent teacher, thorough and systematic in his methods"—(McKee). Among the early teachers at Harrisville was an old man named James Hardy who taught for many years. He was followed by "Master O'Hara" and David C. Cunningham.

The first of the pioneers of Jackson Township was James Magee, a native of County Down, Ireland, who made a settlement in 1797. He was a soldier in the War of 1812. William Martin, also from Ireland, located here in 1797. His brother, Michael, came in 1800, as did John Dunn and some time later, John O'Connor, Thomas McQuoil and Joseph McIlwain, all from Ireland. Mary Martin, daughter of Michael, taught school in Forward Township in 1812, as well as William McKenney, a

native of County Derry.   John Fleming was the local schoolmaster in 1815.   We are told "he possessed a good deal of the
schoolmaster's tact and managed his pupils well."

This is but a fleeting glance at the history of the Irish
pioneers and schoolmasters of this section of Pennsylvania.   I
have a vast amount of material on the subject of the contribution made by the early Irish immigrants to the education of
the youth in those times, which will appear from time to time
in the Journals of the Society.

EXTRACTS FROM VIRGINIA CHURCH RECORDS.

COPIED BY MICHAEL J. O'BRIEN.

FROM THE VESTRY BOOK AND REGISTER OF BRISTOL PARISH, VIRGINIA, 1720 TO 1784, AS TRANSCRIBED BY CHURCHILL G. CHAMBERLAYNE.

June 29, 1724. "It is ordered by the Vestry meeting that Dennis Daly be Allowed 400 pounds of tobb. for Support of himself and family, to be Allowed by the P'ish to be paid to him by the Church-Warden."

May 10, 1724. Birth records: "William, son of Patrick and Jane Doran."

October 9, 1724. "Richard Dearden is acquitted for paying Levies."

September 22, 1725. Baptismal records: "Mary, daughter of William and Mary Kally," and "Mary, daughter of William and Sarah Kelly."

————1726. Baptismal records: "Laughlin flyn."

June 29, 1724. At a meeting of the Vestry, it was "ordered that Jack Cook belonging to Mr. John Fizjarrell be Acquitted for paying P'ish Levies till he mends, he now being Ailing."

March 3, 1731. "Captain FitzGerrall for Barrett," mentioned, and also, "To John High for Farrell." The Vestry books contain a great number of entries relating to John Fitz Gerrald between 1738 and 1750. There was a place named Fitzgeralds in Prince George County and there is a record of court being held at that place on March 11, 1740.

July 25, 1741. Birth records: "John, son of John and Anne Fitz-Gareld."

July 9, 1745. Birth records: "Anne, daughter of Mr. John and Anne Gerralds, born June 17th, and baptised July 9, 1745."

November 11, 1723. "Margaret Moguire" appears on record, and on February 6, 1731, she is down as "Margaret McWire."

September 1, 1742. "To Mr. Thomas Field to be repaid by Brandon Parish, it being on Acct. of Joseph Barry, 70 lbs. of tobbacco."

January 5, 1760. At a Vestry meeting held at "the Brick Church of Bristol Parish" on this date, it was ordered that several persons "be appointed to Possision of the lands in this parish in their several Precincts," among them William Malone and Richard Geary.

The following appear on the birth records:

March 20, 1719, Mary, daughter of Daniel and Mary Mellone.
January 11, 1726, Lucrecee, daughter of William and Ann Mallone.
September 26, 1741, Reuben, son of William and Ann Meloney.
December 13, 1735, Jane, daughter of John and Ann Mooney.
February 27, 1744, Patrick Smith, son of Margaret Malone.
January 19, 1756, Thomas, son of Patrick and Sarah Roney.
October 8, 1757, John, son of Patrick and Sarah Roney.

Other names appearing on the Parish registers: Brannin, Carie, Cargill, Connell, Casey, Conway, Delahay, Delony, Dowley, Dunn, Finn, Gibbons, Garey, Garrett, Gill, Gilmore, Griffin, Hayes, Hiland, McNeil, McCarter, McConnico, McDearmon, McDonald, McDowell, McKenny, McLain, Kennedy, Kennon, Keown, Legan, and Sullivan.

Names appearing on the Vestry book of Henrico Parish between 1740 and 1760: Ann O'Brien, Eliza McCallum, Eliza Dalton, Mary Conway, Catherine McBarrett, Matthew and Martha Jordan, William Lawless, John McKean, Robert Moore, John Donlavie, Charles Sullivan, William Burk, Hugh McNemara, John Brion, William and George Kelley and Daniel Fitz Patrick.

At a meeting of the Vestry held on October 15, 1773, "Edward Conway, sexton of the Brick Church," was ordered to be paid five pounds, and on the same date "Dr. James McCartie was ordered to be paid £10 14s. 3d. for attending Elisha Lester." Dr. McCartie's name appears several times in the account books of the clerk of the Vestry in payment of fees.

October 26, 1792. Death records: "Edmund Ryan of the Town of Petersburg, died the 25th and was buried the 26th of October."

FROM THE PARISH REGISTER OF SAINT PETER'S CHURCH, NEW KENT COUNTY, VA., PUBLISHED BY THE NATIONAL SOCIETY OF COLONIAL DAMES OF AMERICA IN THE STATE OF VIRGINIA.

"Negro girl belonging to Mrs. Sarah Barry, born July 22, 1739."
"Ann, daughter of William and Amy Burk, born March 24, 1727."
"David, son of John Condon and Ann, his wife, born January 2, 1771."

"Nancy, daughter of John Condon and Ann, his wife, born June 7, 1774."

"Edward Coyle and Mary Brown married September 21, 1710."

"Thomas Cotterell and Martha Hacker married May 25, 1709."

"Thomas Butler and Catherine Maclagehe married April 2, 1713."

"Will, a negro girl of John Connors, born May 2, 1718."

"William Cotterell died, February 13, 1725."

"Elizabeth, daughter of Decinnah and Elizabeth Dalton, baptised February 19, 1734."

"Margaret, daughter of Henry Dillon, baptised March 15, 1690."

"Joseph, son of Danll Farell, born October 8, 1725."

"Richard, ye son of Danll and Elizabeth Farell, born November 28, 1727."

"Daniel Farele dy'd May 8, 1735."

"Joseph Kelly, child born the Beginning of March 1706–1707."

"David, son of William McCormick, born February 3, 1724."

"Martha, daughter of Grezel McCormick, born October 19, 1725."

"Mary, daughter of William McCormick, born October 18, 1727."

"Daniel MackDaniell departed this life Decemr ye 15, 1709."

"Sarah, Daugh of Danll Mackgert, baptised May 3, 1702."

"Susannah, ye Dar of Owen and Catherine O'Hern, born March 2, 1729–1730."

"Batt, a negro boy belonging to David McGill, born November 9, 1725."

"William, son of Daniel Mackhany, born July ye 15, 1712."

"Mary, Daughter of John Mackquery, Born May ye 30, 1716."

"Mark, son to John McCoy, bapt ye 7 Decembr 1690."

"James and William, sons of John and Ann McGehee, born March 31, 1756."

"John, son of John Murran, bapt ye 25, June 1699."

"Martin, son of John Reily Junr born Jany ye 30, 1716."

"Alice, dau to John Raylee, bapt ye 27th day of November, 1687."

"Jane Sullevan, a servt woman, Deceasd Augt 25, 1720."

IRISH IMMIGRANTS FROM ENGLISH PORTS IN THE EIGHTEENTH CENTURY.

BY MICHAEL J. O'BRIEN.

Under the caption, "Emigrants from England," the New England Historic-Genealogical Society published in its *Register*—(Vols. 62 to 66)—a list of names of persons who sailed from English ports for the American Colonies between December, 1773, and August, 1775, compiled for the Society by George Fothergill of London, from manuscript records discovered by him in the Public Record Office at London.

In these lists are recorded the names of the immigrants, their ages, occupations, the countries whence they came, their destinations in the American Provinces, the names of the ships and the dates when they sailed from London, Liverpool or Bristol, as the case may be. In no case does it appear that the vessels which brought these people came direct from an Irish port. I have copied the names of the immigrants from Ireland as they appear on this list, with other data relating to them. Besides these, there is a large number of names such as Moore, Hayes, Griffin, Bryan, Mead, Morrison, Curry, Lane, Blake, Farley, Dawson, Ford, Rohan, Reynolds, Strahan, Purcel, Gibbons, Grace, Gogin, Creedy, Clare, Long, Timmins, Burn, Millegan, Wall, Butler, Forrester, Hyland, Raney, McHean, Ward, Fox, Keene, Clarke, Manning, Hany, Boyle, Garrett, Miles, Hare, Fleming, Russell and Welch, all of whom are recorded as from English towns. Such names, as we know, have been common in Ireland for centuries and it is entirely probable that the majority of these people were Irish. Before embarking, all immigrants were required to furnish certain information to the Port officials, including the places whence they came, and while some gave their original home places in Ireland, others are known to have given their last places of residence or employment in England and were thus recorded as "from England."

Some of the names are spelled in such a way as to make it difficult to determine what the nationality may have been. For example, one would never take "John Flimaning, Clerk, from

London," who came to Maryland in the ship, *Jane*, which sailed from the port of London in the week between January 24, and January 30, 1775, to have been an Irishman. Yet, I learn from other sources that this man's correct name was "John Flanagin." It is also interesting to note that "40 emigrants from Baltimore in Ireland," whose names are not mentioned, sailed on the ship, *Adventure*, from the port of London in the week, April 19, to 26, 1774. The destination is not given, but, as the *Adventure* was bound for Baltimore, it is probable that these people went to some part of Maryland or Virginia.

From this list it will be observed that a large percentage of the Irish immigrants were sturdy young people whose ages ranged from 16 to 36, and among them were artisans, husbandmen, tradesmen and laborers, as well as two surgeons and six school-masters, a class of people then much needed in the American Colonies. The publication of such lists serves as an answer to those historical writers who assert—and have continued to assert because they have seldom been confronted with official data of this character—that the Irish who crossed the seas in colonial times comprised only the "bond-servant" class, who practically became slaves on the plantations, and for that reason were of "no account" and, therefore, unworthy of mention in early American history.

Name.	*Date and Port of Sailing.*	*Age.*	*Occupation.*	*From.*	*To.*
Thomas Gorman	London, Dec. 11 to Dec. 18, 1773	26	Schoolmaster	Ireland	Virginia
William Morgan	do.	31	Husbandman	Dublin	do.
Patrick Reiley	do.	25	do.	Ireland	do.
James Major	do.	27	Butcher	do.	do.
Terence McDonald	do.	30	Painter	London	do.
Thomas McKown	do.	28	Schoolmaster	do.	do.
James Demsey	do.	21	Husbandman	do.	do.
William Boyle	do.	26	do.	Ireland	do.
Archibald O'Brian	do.	24	Butcher	Dublin	do.
Arthur Raynells	do.	23	Husbandman	do.	do.
Patrick Redmond	London, Dec. 23, 1773 to Jan. 2, 1774	21	Laborer	Ireland	Maryland
John Ware	do.	23	do.	do.	do.
Patrick Allen	do.	25	Bricklayer	London	do.
John Collins	do.	39	Taylor	Ireland	do.
Thomas Carrol	do.	10	Shoemaker	do.	do.
Thomas Kenneday	do.	23	Husbandman	Essex	do.
John Farrell	do.	25	Groom	Worcester	do.

Name.	Date and Port of Sailing.	Age.	Occupation.	From.	To.
David Brennan	London, May 31 to June 7, 1774	22	Sawyer	Ireland	Maryland
Michael Conlon	do.	24	Husbandman	do.	do.
Francis Mountair	do.	25	Merchant	do.	New York
Dorothy Mountair	do.	26		do.	do.
John Lewis	Liverpool, June 14 to June 21, 1774	16	Farmer	· do.	Philadelphia
Charles Lewis	do.	17	do.	do.	do.
Joshua Lewis	do.	19	do.	do.	do.
Joseph Collins	London, July 3 to July 10, 1774	20	Currier	Dublin	Maryland
Darby Hogan	do.	22	Husbandman	Ireland	do.
Edward Kelly	do.	21	do.	London	do.
Michael Delaney	do.	18	Laborer	do.	do.
Alexander Hynes	do.	23	Peruke maker	do.	do.
Thomas Gillen	do.	17	Cordwainer	do.	do.
Michael Shields	London, July 10 to July 17, 1774	22	Plasterer	Ireland	do.
Patrick Tavlin	do.	23	Husbandman	do.	do.
Matthew Moor	do.	22	Farmer	do.	do.
John Connell	do.	39	Cordwainer	do.	do.
John Lynch	do.	37	Farmer	do.	Jamaica
John Birmingham	London, July 24 to July 31, 1774	20	Gentleman	do.	Philadelphia
Daniel Hurley	do.	21	Husbandman	London	Maryland
Charles Roach	do.	26	Tallow chandler	do.	do.
William Moland	do.	21	Tin plate worker	do.	do.
George Bolland	do.	21	Taylor	Ireland	Virginia
Daniel Hutchinson	London, July 31 to Aug. 7, 1774	21	Cordwainer	Dublin	do.
Gerald Byrne	London, Aug. 7 to Aug. 14, 1774	22	Carpenter and joiner	Kent	Pensacola
Michael Delaney	London, Aug. 14 to Aug. 21, 1774	21	Husbandman	Ireland	Carolina
Henry Havell	Bristol, Aug. 14 to Aug. 21, 1774	25	Cooper	Cork	Philadelphia
R. Seaton	do.	22	Shoemaker	do.	do.
Patrick Butler	do.	23	Seaman	do.	do.
Daniel Shiels	do.	21	Laborer	Kent	do.
William Cooley	London, Aug. 28 to Sept. 4, 1774	21	Founder	Dublin	Maryland
Matthew Branan	do.	21	Smith	London	do.
John Lynch	do.	16	Taylor	Bucks	do.
Mary Cormick	do.	24	Spinster	London	do.
John Byan	do.	18	Groom	Dublin	do.
John Carroll	do.	22	Husbandman	do.	do.
John Reilly	do.	26	Brass founder	London	do.
Martin Mullunly	do.	25	Groom	do.	do.
Edward Dunn	do.	21	Hatter	Stafford	do.
James Flanagan	London, Oct. 3 to Oct. 10, 1774	21	Husbandman	Scotland	do.
John Dunilton	do.	21	Baker	Dublin	Philadelphia
Joseph Doyle	do.	24	Cabinet maker	Warwick	do.
Richard Roily	do.	28	Breeches maker	London	do.
Patrick Boylan	do.	24	Cordwainer	Dublin	do.
Thomas Dailey	do.	24	Baker	London	do.
Lawrence Kamy	do.	23	Husbandman	Ireland	do.
Michael McDonald	do.	21	Plasterer	London	do.

Name.	Date and Port of Sailing.	Age.	Occupation.	From.	To.
Francis Sedley	London, Oct. 17 to Oct. 24, 1774	21	Carpenter and joiner	Ireland	Maryland
Elizabeth Maguire	do.	17	Spinster	Westminster	do.
William Kennedy	do.	35	Peruke maker	London	South Carolina
Charles Field	London, Oct. 21 to Oct. 31, 1774	21	Engraver	Ireland	Maryland
Nicholas Murray	Bristol, Oct. 31 to Nov. 7, 1774	30	Weaver	Cork	do.
B. Murphy	do.	30	Weaver	Dublin	do.
William Smith	London, Nov. 14 to Nov. 21, 1774	26	Clerk and book-keeper	Waterford	Virginia
Owen Keefe	do.	27	Husbandman	London	do.
John Cosgrove	do.	23	Laborer	Ireland	do.
Thomas Doyle	do.	22	do.	London	do.
Patrick Clarke	do.	21	Husbandman	Essex	Philadelphia
Patrick Rinney	London, Nov. 21 to Nov. 28, 1774	22	do.	London	Virginia
John Callaghan	do.	23	do.	Southwark	do.
Michael Nugent	do.	22	Paviour	Essex	do.
Jeremiah Murphy	do.	23	Gardener	London	do.
Luke Brady	do.	23	Laborer	do.	do.
James Fogerty	do.	27	Husbandman	Surry	do.
Cornelius Fogarty	do.	30	do.	do.	do.
Dennis Dowlin	do.	27	do.	Cork	do.
James Kelly	London, Dec. 12 to Dec. 19, 1774	25	do.	London	do.
Timothy Kennedy	do.	21	Schoolmaster	Westminster	do.
Edward Mahon	do.	23	Taylor	Ireland	do.
Joseph Mahoney	do.	23	Groom	do.	do.
Dennis Craigen	do.	27	Husbandman	London	do.
Martin Mealey	do.	25	Painter and glazier	Middlesex	do.
Morris Maney	do.	23	Bricklayer	London	do.
James Doyle	do.	28	Husbandman	do.	do.
Martin Doyle	do.	22	Laborer	do.	do.
William Doulan	do.	24	Peruke maker	Dublin	do.
Thomas Sullivan	Bristol, Dec. 19 to Dec. 26, 1774	17	Laborer	Somersetshire	Maryland
William Barry	do.	25	Butcher	do.	do.
Michael Tobin	Plymouth, Dec. 23 to Jan. 3, 1775	18	Laborer	Ireland	New York
Oliver Tate	do.	21	Husbandman	do.	do.
William Tear	do.	31	do.	do.	do.
James Butler	do.	24	Sawyer	do.	do.
John Lyons	do.	29	Clerk and bookkeeper	Dublin	Virginia
John Reiley	do.	19	Groom	London	New York
Daniel Finana	do.	36	Clerk and bookkeeper	Ireland	Virginia
Charles Murphy	London, Jan. 10 to Jan. 17, 1775	27	do.	do.	Maryland
Timothy Donovan	London, Jan. 17 to Jan. 24, 1775	23	Husbandman	London	do.
Andrew Conaly	do.	23	Footman	Dublin	do.
Patrick Collins	do.	25	Weaver	Ireland	do.
Michael Callan	do.	27	Coachman	London	do.
John Toole	do.	22	Buckle maker	do.	do.

Name.	Date and Port of Sailing.	Age.	Occupation.	From.	To.
James Doyley	London, Jan. 24 to Jan. 30, 1775	26	Clerk and book-keeper	Ireland	Maryland
David Connolly	do.	21	Bricklayer	do	do.
Jasper Mahony	do.	16	Laborer	London	do.
Edward Sutton	do.	16	Gentleman's servant	Ireland	do.
Redmond Roach	do.	18	do.	London	do.
James Connor	do.	24	Grocer	Norfolk	do.
Edward Dillon	do.	22	Clerk	Kent	do.
Patrick Connor	do.	35	Planter	London	do.
William Dashall	London, Jan. 30 to Feb. 6, 1775	24	Husbandman	Ireland	Virginia
James Roberts	do.	22	Cordwainer	do.	Maryland
James Mahar	do.	25	Husbandman	do.	do.
Anthony Byrne	do.	16	Laborer	London	do.
Jane Managan	do.	15	do.	do.	do.
Edward McFadding	do.	24	Husbandman	do.	do.
Daniel Linch	do.	22	Cordwainer	do.	do.
Arthur Morris	London, Feb. 13 to Feb. 20, 1775	36	Mariner	Ireland	do.
Thomas Ryley	do.	22	Gardener	Stafford	do.
Elizabeth Fitzgerald	London, Feb. 27 to Mar. 6, 1775	16	Spinster	Hull	do.
William Carroll	do.	29	Laborer	Bath	Philadelphia
Nicholas Linch	do.	26	Brazier	Bridgewater	do.
Edward McEnnis	do.	15	Laborer	London	Maryland
Michael Cockran	do.	22	do.	Bristol	do.
William Keaton	do.	25	Shoemaker	do.	Philadelphia
Matthew Keeling	London, Mar. 6 to Mar. 13, 1775	25	Husbandman	Cheshire	Maryland
John Malone	do.	30	Laborer	London	do.
John Bohannon	Liverpool, same date	30	Merchant	Ireland	Philadelphia
John McCunn	London, Mar. 13 to Mar. 20, 1775	22	Cabinet maker	do.	do.
William Bailay	do.	23	Clerk	do.	do.
John Logan	do.	19	Husbandman	Kent	do.
Paul Hurley	do.	48	Baker	London	Maryland
Dennis Sullivan	do.	26	Husbandman	do.	do.
William Power	do.	24	Gardener	Ireland	do.
Patrick Sheen	do.	21	do.	Essex	do.
Anthony Hopper	London, Mar. 27 to Apr. 3, 1775	19	Painter	Ireland	do.
Charles Connor	do.	24	Merchant	London	do.
Mary Dealy	do.	22	Servant	Middlesex	do.
John Connor	do.	21	Hairdresser	London	do.
George Ryan	do.	15	Laborer	do.	do.
John Madden	do.	17	Weaver	do.	do.
John Dealy	do.	21	Joiner	Buckingham	do.
James Little	do.	16	Husbandman	Wexford	Virginia
C. D. Fitzgerald	do.	30	Laborer	Suffolk	Maryland
James Hanlon	London, Apr. 3 to Apr. 10, 1775	29	Husbandman	London	Maryland
William Skelly	do.	29	do.	do.	do.
Jeremiah Regan	London, Apr. 10 to Apr. 17, 1775	23	Taylor	do.	do.
Robert Byrne	do.	22	Smith	do.	do.
William Higgins	do.	22	Waiter	do.	do.

Name.	Date and Port of Sailing.	Age.	Occupation.	From.	To.
Gilbert Cartey	London, Apr. 10 to Apr. 17, 1775	21	Farmer	Ireland	Maryland
William Walsh	do.	30	do.	Birmingham	do.
Charles Flynn	London, May 15 to May 22, 1775	24	Carpenter	London	do.
Brian O'Brian	London, May 22 to May 29, 1775	24	do.	do.	do.
Michael Carey	do.	23	do.	do.	do.
Cornelius Hagerty	London, June 5 to June 12, 1775	19	Gardener	Ireland	Baltimore
Christopher Morris	do.	22	Farmer	do.	do.
William Griffin	do.	24	Schoolmaster	do.	do.
Dennis Mahany	do.	27	Sailor	do.	do.
Thomas White	do.	24	Farmer	Dublin	do.
James Brooks	do.	22	Linen weaver	Cork	do.
James Dempsey	do.	22	Cooper	Middlesex	do.
Lawrence Kelly	London, June 12 to June 19, 1775	39	Mason	London	do.
William Moreran	do.	21	Servant	Surry	do.
Patrick McKernelly	do.	25	Laborer	London	do.
Martha McBride	do.	16	Servant	do.	do.
Anthony Dwyer	Bristol, June 26 to July 3, 1775	20	Taylor	Cork	do.
Peter Macquire	do.	17	Laborer	Ireland	do.
Roger Parke	do.	21	Clerk	Dublin	do.
Jordan Costallo	London, July 10 to July 17, 1775	31	do.	do.	do.
Roger Regan	do.	21	Cook	do.	do.
Michael Cottor	do.	30	Locksmith	do.	do.
Andrew Power	do.	15	Laborer	London	do.
Nicholas Morrough	do.	21	Dye and lace maker	Cork	do.
Michael Murphy	do.	22	Clerk	do.	do.
Bryan Burn	London, Aug. 14 to Aug. 21, 1775	22	Husbandman	Ireland	Philadelphia
Jeremiah Dowling	do.	30	Cordwainer	London	do.

HISTORICAL GLEANINGS FROM MASSACHUSETTS RECORDS.

CONTRIBUTED BY GEORGE F. O'DWYER.

Among the petitions presented to the Massachusetts General Court during the progress of the Revolutionary War were some relative to the allegiance of certain British soldiers and sailors. Many of the petitioners, dissatisfied with their treatment in the British service, and being desirous of settling down in Massachusetts, were granted permission to remain in the country and pursue their different trades. The following is an interesting example of these petitions:

To the Hon¹ the Council and Hon'l the House of Rep. of Mass. Bay in Genl Court assembled Nov. 30th, 1779:

The Petition of William O'Brien lately of the 9th Regiment and George Perkins lately of a Detachment of the 33 Regiment of General Burgoin's Convention Troops, humbly shews: That the said O'Brien and Perkins about fourteen months since, with a full design to become Inhabitants of this Country & not to return to the British Troops any more, and have ever since laboured with the good People of this State in a peaceable manner in the useful Business of nail-making, have each of us been rated & paid Taxes the year past. And that your humble Petitioners are very Desirous of being True and Loyal Subjects of this State, of taking the Oath of Allegiance & of fidelity & of paying & doing our part for the support of the War & and all other Taxes. Therefore pray your Hons to grant us the favours above and such protection as you Shall see meet and that we may not be taken up or sent to the British Troops to be punished for appearing in the Cause of American Liberty, and as in Duty bound ask leave to pray.

his
GEORGE X PERKINS,
mark

Witnesses:
  JOHN BLAIN,
  DANIEL CONNERS.

WILLIAM O'BRIEN.

These men settled at Oakham, Mass., where they followed their trade of nail-making. Thomas Mann, a merchant who employed them, certified to their good character and four of the selectmen of the town certified that they paid taxes for the year 1779. The petition was granted by the court, and at a session held on December 20, 1779, it was

Resolved, That the said George Perkins & William O'Brien, who have produced Certificates from the Select Men of the Town where they reside, that they appear attachd to the Government of this State and bid fair to be useful members of Society, have liberty to reside in this State during the Court's pleasure. JOHN HANCOCK, *Speaker*.

Another interesting instance is that of George McBride of Lancaster, Mass. His petition came up before the General Court on April 3, 1780, and reads as follows:

Humbly Shews George McBride that he was born in Ireland, and when only fifteen years of age was made a Soldier in the Army of Great Britain by force and fraud of the vilest kind; that in justice he could not be holden in that service and ever intended to leave the first opportunity; and accordingly when General Burgoin's Army lay at Saratoga and before the convention he did leave it and put himself under the protection of the American States with a determination ever after to remain a subject thereof, but has lately been arrested and in danger of being returned to the british Army and must there suffer death if America does not continue to protect him.

Wherefore he most humbly prays your Honours that he may be admitted to take the oath of allegiance to this State and be admitted a Subject thereof.

Lancaster, Mass., April 3, 1780.
his
GEORGE X McBRIDE.
mark

This petition was granted at the Council meeting on April 11, 1780.

PURITAN PIONEERS SAVED BY IRISH FOOD-SHIPS.

In Johnson's *Wonder-Working Providence*, a contemporary history of Puritan New England of the first years of the seventeenth century, are three interesting allusions to Ireland and the sending of food-ships from that country for the starving inhabitants in the settlements along the Massachusetts coast. The book is mainly a religious rhapsody in the strict Puritan style, but the historical interpolations are undoubtedly correct. In the first allusion to Ireland, the date is 1631, one year after the first settlement on Massachusetts bay. After commenting on the sore straits of the inhabitants, Johnson says:

And as they [the Puritans], were incouraging one another in Christ's carefull providing for them, they lift up their eyes and saw two Ships coming in and presently this newes came to their Eares that there were come from Jacland [Ireland][1] full of Victuals. Now their poore hearts were not so much refreshed in regards of the food they saw they were like to have, as their

---

[1] Dr. Jameson, editor of the reprinted edition, states that "Jacland" is probably a misprint for Ireland.

soules rejoyced in that Christ would now manifest himselfe to be the Commissary Generall of this, his Army, and that hee should honor them so far as to be poore Sutlers for his Camp.

Further on we read, on page 92 [Dr. Jameson's reprint] the following under date of 1633:

Feeling againe the scarcity of foode and being constrained to come to a small pittance daily, the Lord, to provide for them, causeth the Deputy of Ireland to set forth a great Ship unknowne to this people [the settlement at Cambridge] and indeed small reason in his own apprehensions why he should so do [but Christ will have it so] This Ship ariving, being filled with foode the godly Governors did so order it that each Town sent two men aboard of her (the ship) who tooke up their Townes allowance, it being appointed beforehand what this portion should be to this end that some might by [buy] all and others be left destitute of food.

Again, on page 108 of the work we find another mention of food-ships from Ireland. The date is 1635, the year that John Winthrop the younger, and his friend, Rev. John Wilson, made a visit to England and Ireland to recruit settlers for the Ipswich and Merrimack river settlements. Johnson says:

It pleased him [God] this yeare [1635] to visit them [the settlers around Massachusetts bay] and try them againe with a great scarcity of Bread, by reason of the multitudes that came brought somewhat shorter Provisions then ordinary, which caused them to be in some straites. But their Lord Christ gives out a Word of command to those who occupy their businesse in the great deepe to furnish from Ireland some Ships laden with food for his people.

Now an interesting fact about these allusions to food from Ireland at different intervals of the first years of the settlements of the Massachusetts Bay Colony is that the arrival of these food-ships precede by forty-one years the coming of the Irish donation (commented on exhaustively by Mr. Michael J. O'Brien) in the year, 1676, following the ravages of the King Philip war which told hard on the Colonists of both the Pilgrim as well as the Puritan settlements.

It also shows conclusively that the Irish and the Irish food-ships were depended on in the first years of the pioneer settlements of the two colonies.

IRISH SOLDIERS IN THE COLONIAL WARS.

During the war between England and France, in the middle of the eighteenth century, several regiments of New Englanders went to Nova Scotia and Quebec. One hundred and seventy-one prisoners, captured and imprisoned at Quebec and Louis-burg, were sent to Boston in the summer of 1747 in exchange for French prisoners. Among the Irish names noted in the list were the following:

Taken at sea 20th May, 1745: John Maddin (Ireland), Luke McNally, Ambrose Ryan, Samuel Deverix, belonging to the late Captain Donahew.

Taken by the *L'Aurora* and *Castor* April 4, 1746: Cornelius Mahaner of Ireland.

Captured by *L'Castor* at sea June 24, 1746: Dennis Field, Master, of New York.

Taken by *Albany* sloop July 19, 1746: Anthony Newgent (Boston).

Taken by Mons. Ramsay, January 30, 1746–47: John Kenny, John Dono-van and Thomas McCarthy (residence unknown).

Taken by the salvages [savages] August 20, 1746: Patrick Harrow, New York; October 12, Cornelius Farrol of Saratoga, and James Curry.

Taken at Saratoga June 19, 1747: Daniel and Philip Kelly of New York.

The following died during their captivity and·imprisonment: Thos. Magra, of Ireland (Boston); Timothy Cummings, of Georges; William Daily, of New York; Micah Dogan, of Ireland; James Doyl, of Philadelphia.

Those following "turned over" to the French and remained in Canada: Daniel Lary, of this Province (Mass.); —— Mallaly, of Boston; John Curren, of Boston; John M'Clure and Jane, his wife, of Saratoga; —— Tobin, of Ireland; Thos. M'Clathland and Katherine, his wife, of Philadelphia; William Lambert, of Ireland; John Macquire; David M'coo, Philadelphia; Jacob Con-noway, Philadelphia.

LETTER OF JOHN HAYNES TO J. WINTHROP, JR., 24TH OF MAY, 1653.

(Winthrop Papers, Massachusetts Historical Society.)

There are 3 ships come into the Baye (Boston) the first by the way of Ireland, that brought 90 passendgers for servants; the 2nd, one, of Charlestown is master; the 3rd, the *Addington*, who sett saile the 17th of May.

In a following letter to Winthrop, Haynes speaks of an Irish maid servant thus:

If this Irish woman is come upp to you, pray lett her by the first opportunity bee conveid [conveyed] to us, for I did soe order it, hoping to have pleasured, not to burthen you.

Evidently this Irish woman was an efficient maid servant as well as nurse in Haynes' family, for his wife was cared for by her while in the pains of childbirth. She was used later by the Win-throp and other prominent families of the Massachusetts and Connecticut colonies in a like capacity, and her skill was instrumental in saving offspring when a doctor or surgeon could not be brought in time. It is unfortunate that her name is unknown. Maybe in future researches the writer will come upon it. This useful woman is the first Irish nurse mentioned in the annals of the New England colonies, as far as is known.

THE FIRST KNOWN IRISH BRICKMAKER AND MASON IN AMERICAN HISTORY.

(From Records of Ancient Rehoboth, Mass.)

November 25, 1663.—"Voted, that Alexander, the Irishman, a brickmaker, should be freely approved among us for to make brick, and that he should have full liberty to make use of the clay and wood on the commons for that purpose."

SOME ADVERTISEMENTS AND NEWS ITEMS IN THE "BOSTON POST."

April 30, 1764—"Ran Away on the Night of the 17th Instant, March, five indented Servants viz.: Hugh Doyle, a tall, thin man, born in Ireland, much mark'd with the small pox; John Blake, a short, well-set Man, born in Ireland, both Servants to Capt. Abel Michener, of said Falmouth and had on blue jackets and home-dressed Moose skin breeches; John Attwell, a tall Man, born in New England; John Murphy, ditto, born in Ireland; James Sullivan, a lusty Man, born in Ireland. All these Servants to H. D. Denson, Esq. of Falmouth. Whosoever shall Cause these said Servants to be secured . . . will be paid a Reward of Twenty Shillings for each of the said servants and all charges repaid with many thanks!

"Falmouth, King's county, Nova Scotia, March 19th, 1764."

October 29, 1764—"New York Oct. 22, 1764—William O'Brien Esq. and the right hon. Lady Susannah O'Brien with Col. Croghan and Capt. M'Donald came passengers in the packet boat."

June 13, 1763—"All Persons having any Demand on the Estate of Capt. Patrick Connell of Boston, Mariner, Deceased, are desired to bring them to Margaret Connell, sole Executive to the last Will and Testament of the said Deceased."

The will of Capt. Patrick Connell, who was a Catholic Irish shipmaster, is of more than ordinary interest. It was dated 11th of June, 1760. It read:

"In the name of God Amen. I, Patrick Connell of Boston in New England, Mariner, being of sound, disposing mind and memory, thanks be to God, therefor, but considering the certainty of death & the uncertain time of Man's dissolution, Do, on this 11th day of June A. D. 1760, in the 33rd year of His Majesty's Reign, make & declare these presents to Contain my last will & Testament in manner following: That is to say, First, I commend my Soul into the hands of almighty God, hoping thro' His mercy & the merits of my ever blessed Redeemer, Jesus Christ, to Enjoy eternal life & touching & concerning my temporal Estate, I give & dispose thereof as follows [here follows the apportionment of the estate between his wife Margaret and his children, Mary, Peter and James Connell]. And I do appoint my wife [Margaret] sole Executrix of this my last Will."

PATRICK CONNELL.
(seal)

The will was witnessed by Richard Dana, Richard Jennys and Peter Barbour. It was probated in Boston July 15, 1763.

The inventory of the captain's estate, taken 26th July 1763, showed that he was worth £612. 5. 7, or $3100. Of this inventory £70 represented indigo and spices which the captain brought in his vessel from South America and the West Indies. His remains, with those of his wife, are interred in old Copp's Hill burying ground in Boston. He was born in the County of Kilkenny, Ireland.

June 13, 1763—"I do Hereby publickly advertize all People that I have legally revoked all Powers of attorney I ever gave to any Person and that no one has a right to act as my Attorney but Israel Daggett of Rehoboth, Cooper, whom I have since appointed." WILLIAM HEALY, JUN.
Rehoboth, June 4, 1763.

"A list of Strangers warned to Depart Accord^n to Law" from Boston in 1727, included: John White, an Irishman from Dedham; Robert Phenne (Feeney), an Irishman from Wells (Maine); Wm. Nugel, an Irishman from Philadelphia; Robt Sterling, an Irishman from Rutland (Mass.); James Dawley, an Irishman from Lisbon (Mass.?) and Joseph Doyle from Rhode Island.

IRISH AND SCOTCH BOND-SERVANTS TRANSPORTED BY CROMWELL.

On the 11th of November, 1651, one of the most unique deeds in the history of England or the world, was drawn up by one John Nottock, a notary public in London. It was a deed for the transfer of two hundred and fifty-six human parcels of property and they were conveyed to one Thomas Kemble of Charlestown in Massachusetts. On the 13th of May, 1652, these human parcels were received by Kemble in Boston Harbor and were attested by Edward Rawson, a recorder in the employ of the Massachusetts Bay Company. They were brought over in a freighter, the *John and Sara*, John Greene, master. The names of these human parcels and the deeds consigning them, can be found in one of the bound volumes of Suffolk Deeds, and this volume can be seen in Bates Hall in the central library in Boston or at the Suffolk County Court House.

They were Scotch and Irish prisoners, taken at the battle of Worcester, England, and were consigned directly to the pity of the Puritan slave-holders who, at that time, esteemed a good healthy parcel of white human property as a valuable asset to help run their plantations. One Oliver Cromwell, than whom there is, in the course of time, no ruler more execrated, was the original source of the above-mentioned deed. And the poor unfortunates sent over by his orders, were only the first of 6,400 deported by him and his hirelings during the following six years while he was in power.

History does not record what became of the two hundred and fifty-six Scotch and Irish hirelings. Some of their descendants may be still living in New England or in other parts of the country. For their blood was virile. They came of good old Celtic stock and the blood of this stock will never die. Witness the vital records of Maine, Massachusetts and other New England states in the seventeenth and eighteenth centuries, lately published. Some of their names and those of their descendants can be found in these records. Among these Celtic hirelings were the following:

James Moore	Patrick Morton
Michael ffossem	Patricke Mackatherne
Hugh Mackey	4 Patricks, last name missing
Daniel Mackannell	Patricke Crosshone
John Croome	Patrick Mann
——— Mackunnell	Patricke Mackneile
——— Moore	Rory Machy
John Macdonnell	John Mackane
Patrick Jones	Patricke Graunt
John Coehon	Patricke Harron
Edward dulen	Patricke Robertson
Patrick Timson	John Mann
John Hanoman	Patricke Mackane
James Jackson	John Shinne
Dani Mackayne	Jonas murrow
Dan Mackennell	Patricke Jacson
George Quenne	Patrick English
daniell Mackhan	Daniell oneale
dan Martyn	John murrow
John Morre	

IRISH GIRLS IMPRESSED AS SERVANTS IN BOSTON IN 1671.

In the seventeenth century, the early Irish living in and around Boston were forced to send their children abroad (meaning away from their own families and relations) to serve in the capacity of servants. In looking up the Boston *Town Records* of 1671, the writer came upon this interesting order, issued at a meeting in the state house of the governor, deputy governor, and their staff:

It is ordered that notice be given to the several psons under-written that they within one month after the date hereof dispose of their severall children (herein nominated or mentioned) abroad for servants to serve accordinge to theire age and capacities wch if they refuse or neglect to doe The Magistrates and Selectmen will take theire said Children from them and place them with such Masters as they shall provide accordinge as the law directs. And that they that doe accordinge to this ord^r dispose of their Children doe make returne of the names of Mast^rs & Children soe put out to service with their Indentures to the Selectmen at theire next monthly Meetinge beinge the last Monday in Aprill next:

John Glover's daught^r about 12 yrs. of age.
Bryan Morphew's Daught^r in law Martha Dorman about 12 yrs.
John Bohaman's Daught^r Mary about 14 yrs.
Robert Pegg's Daught^r Alice about 10 yrs.
John Griffen's Daught^r about 10 yrs.
Wm Spowell's Daught^r about 20 yrs.
Wm Browne's Daught^r about 15 yrs. unlesse she can excuse the service of a Nurse attendinge upon her weake Mother.

22 March, 1671.

went but the chief clerk stayed during many administrations, a bulwark of the department and an authority on all matters connected with the navy. There was no Assistant Secretary then, and whenever the secretary was absent the chief clerk became acting secretary. Often the office of Secretary of the Navy was vacant for a time or the incumbent was away from his duty beyond the time for which an acting secretary could be designated. In such cases John Boyle was appointed by the President Secretary of the Navy ad interim and such appointments by various Presidents aggregate a period of more than one year. Life was simpler then than now for when President Jackson wanted to confer with the head of the Navy Department he took his pen in hand and himself wrote a note asking him to call. A grandson, John Boyle of Washington, has in his possession a note which President Andrew Jackson wrote and signed asking John Boyle to call at the White House.

Mr. Boyle resigned from the Navy Department in 1839 after nearly thirty years of service. During his residence in Washington he had become an active participant in the life of the city. He was one of the leading laymen of St. Patrick's Church, the first Roman Catholic Church in Washington. He was a member of the Philosophical Society, the pioneer of the many scientific societies afterwards established in the national capital. He acquired large holdings of real estate, some parcels of which are now among the most valuable in the city. After his resignation he devoted himself chiefly to his business interests. He was a director of the predecessor of the Metropolitan National Bank, one of the leading financial institutions of the national capital. Among his local contemporaries were Thomas Corcoran, father of the philanthropist William W. Corcoran, and James Hoban, the architect of the White House—both Irishmen. He was on terms of intimacy with many naval officers and men prominent in official life. Among those he knew was a namesake John Boyle, a representative from Kentucky, a man who looms large in the early history of the state and who was the founder of a noted family. Both John Boyles, according to a tradition in the Washington family, believed they were of the same racial stock. Whether or not he was also related to the privateer Captain Thomas Boyle of Baltimore, whose exploits in the War of 1812 made him famous, and who was the bold man who caused to be affixed to the doors of the Parliament House in London a notice that he had placed the English Channel under blockade, and from whom is descended United States Senator France of Maryland; to Mayor Boyle of Annapolis who welcomed to the capital of Maryland Lafayette on his tour of the country he had helped to liberate; to Rev. Francis Boyle, for many years the beloved pastor of St. Matthews Roman Catholic Church—the church of diplomats—in Washington, is not known to the writer, but it is within the range of probability that all had a common ancestor in Ireland.

John Boyle was a personal and political friend of Andrew Jackson and when a meeting was called to form an organization to perpetuate the principles of General Jackson he was called upon to be the presiding officer. The Jackson Democratic Association of Washington, which was then organized, has been in continuous existence ever since and, with the exception of the Tammany Society is the oldest political organization in the United States. Dr. Cornelius Boyle, John Boyle's son, was the president of this association at the zenith of its influence in 1860, and the latter's son, John Boyle, has been chairman of the Democratic Central Committee of the District of Columbia, and was a delegate to the Democratic National Convention of 1896. Others of the family have been active and influential workers in Democratic party organizations. Before the Civil War the people of Washington were allowed a measure of self-government, which is now denied to them; they elected their mayors, and John Boyle was the candidate of the Democratic party at one election for the honorable office of mayor of Washington city. Although he received a larger proportion of the votes than the candidates of his party usually got, he did not succeed in overcoming the normal federalist majority and Mayor Bradley was elected.

John Boyle died March 23, 1849, aged seventy-two, and the newspapers of the city which gave brief notices of his career said the community had lost a valuable and esteemed citizen.

Five sons and two daughters of John and Catherine Boyle grew to maturity. The sons were Junius I., John F., Eugene, N. Burke and Cornelius; the daughters Lavinia and Catherine. Eugene, Burke and Lavinia never married; there are numerous descendants of the other children most of whom reside in or near Washington.

Junius I. Boyle died a commodore on the retired list of the United States Navy. As was the custom before the establishment of the Naval Academy he was put into the navy as a midshipman when about twelve years of age and learned practical seamanship in the old sailing war ships. During his long service he visited most of the ports of the world. In the Mexican War he was in the blockading squadron and took part in the bombardment and capture of Vera Cruz. In Commodore Perry's expedition to Japan he was commandant of the *Southampton*. As commander of the naval hospital at Philadelphia he had a turn of shore duty. He was a type of the old sea officer, a skilled seaman always ready for a fight and not averse to accepting a challenge to a duel. He was born in Baltimore and died at Norfolk, Va. Appleton's Cyclopedia of American Biography contains an outline of his career.

Junius Boyle married the daughter of his father's intimate friend, John McLeod, a native of Ireland, who was principal of an academy for boys in Washington, that was a noted school. Another daughter was the mother of Colonel John McLeod Turner, one of North Carolina's heroes of the Civil War, and grandmother of Captain John McLeod Page, U. S. A. retired, who served in the Philippine insurrection and on detailed duty in the late war. Junius Boyle had four daughters and one son. Of the daughters, Oceana married Colonel Thomas S. Sedgwick, an officer of the Union Army, and afterwards an official of the Atlantic and Pacific Railroad Company; Emily married Hon. Z. Poteet of Cockeysville, Md., and Rebecca, George Van Inwegen of Nebraska; all died without issue. Literature attracted Esmeralda Boyle and she became an authoress. A volume of poems received praise in America and abroad and her book, *Biographical Sketches of Distinguished Marylanders*, is a valuable contribution to American history. The only son, Juan, was born at Port Mahon, Minorca, while his father was stationed in Mediterranean waters and was christened in the Spanish form of the name John. He became an extensive operator in Washington real estate and failed when the Jay Cooke crash brought down his associates. He then moved to Kearney, Neb., was active in the politics of the state and died there. He married Mary Miles of an old Maryland family and left her a widow with six children. She has since lost two sons while serving in the army. Lieutenant

Juan Ashton Boyle won mention in reports and promotion for gallantry in Cuba during the Spanish-American War; he was transferred to the Philippines and lost his life by drowning under unusual circumstances. A lady's hat blew off her head and into the sea from a boat in which Lieutenant Boyle and a brother officer were sailing with two ladies. He jumped overboard to recover the hat, went down and did not come up; his companion jumped from the boat to his rescue; he, also, went down and did not come up. Both had been caught in seaweeds and held until drowned. This is one of the sad tragedies of the American Army in the Philippines. The other son, Lieutenant Junius I. Boyle, was killed in France in 1918, after a series of daring exploits in raiding the enemy's lines. Their sister, Eleanor Boyle, is the wife of Major General H. E. Ely, who commanded a fighting division of the American Expeditionary Force.

Eugene, the third son of John Boyle, also died while serving his country in the army. As a youth he had secured a commission as midshipman in the navy and made a cruise to the South Seas in the frigate *Potomac* and took part in the engagement of Quallah Batoo. Resigning he entered civil life but when the Mexican War broke out he volunteered, and was made a lieutenant of Company D of the Baltimore and Washington battalion. Four companies from Baltimore and two from Washington composed the battalion which was commanded by Colonel William H. Watson of Baltimore. Mustered in June 8, 1846, it sailed June 15 and reached Brazos Santiago July 2, was put in the division of General Twiggs, and was precipitated into a battle after the scantiest amount of training. On September 21, 1846, the battalion took part in the attempt to storm the fortified city of Monterey and the three days' battle that ensued was one of the fiercest American troops have ever been engaged in. The brigade to which the battalion was attached attacked a fort the first day and was repulsed with serious losses. On the second day the attack was renewed and continued on the third day when the city was captured. Colonel Watson, the popular commander, was killed in the battle. Lieutenant Boyle conducted himself in such a manner in this engagement that he was designated captain. He died, however, January 6, 1847, before he received his commission. His funeral and that of Lieutenant Graham was held at Washington on the same day and was an event long remembered by those who witnessed it. It was made the occasion for the gathering of a great number of patriotic people—to whom the funeral brought a realization of the seriousness of the war—who wished to do honor to the memories of two local heroes and to show sympathy for their families. The history of this organization is given in *Memoirs of a Maryland Volunteer in the War with Mexico*, by John R. Kenly.

John F. Boyle, another son, lived an uneventful life in Washington and resided for the greater part of it in the fine old home of his father's, adjacent to the Potomac river. He was a daring boy and a good swimmer and it is not improbable that he was one of the mischievous lads who, as the tradition runs, rudely splashed water on the head of President John Quincy Adams while he was taking one of his daily swims in the Potomac. He has numerous descendants, one of whom, Inspector Richard Burke Boyle of the Washington Police Force, has worked himself up by merit, through long service, from the lowest to the highest position one of the force may attain.

The daughter Catherine married William E. Stubbs, a son of Edward Stubbs, a native of Ireland. Both father and son held important clerkships in the State Department. The senior died before the Civil War occurred and, soon after it began, William E. Stubbs retired from office and made his home in Montgomery County, Maryland. He has numerous descendants, one of them being E. C. Stubbs, chief of the heating and ventilating department of the United States Senate, and in point of length of service one of the oldest employes. He entered the department at the lowest grade and worked up to the highest. When the late United States Senator Francis Kernan came as a youth to Washington to enter Georgetown College he bore a letter to Edward Stubbs. It is possible the families were acquainted in Ireland or may be distantly related.

Cornelius, one of the younger sons of John Boyle, was born in Washington in 1817 and died in that city in 1878. He was educated at McLeod's Academy and graduated in medicine from Columbian College, now George Washington University, Washington, and soon attained a large practice. He was a successful doctor, the beloved physician to a large circle of patients and friends; was a man of means and popularity, who was active in movements for the betterment of the community; was one of the organizers of the first street railway system in Washington; was the friend of many men prominent in official life, took an active interest in politics and was president of the Jackson Democratic Association. He held the southern view of the right of secession and when the Civil War broke out he did not falter for fear of consequences but cast his lot with the South. Abandoning his leading position in the professional life of Washington and large property interests—afterwards confiscated—he tendered his services to the state of Virginia, then according to the southern view of the rights of the matter about to be invaded, became a major in the Confederate Army, was made provost marshal general of the army of Northern Virginia, and also placed in command of the pivotal post of Gordonsville, Va. That he served well is attested by a letter written to him by his friend and commander, General Robert E. Lee, in his own hand, which is one of the most precious possessions of his children.

The Civil War broke into Dr. Boyle's career as a physician and caused him, after its conclusion, to be excluded from his native city for a number of years. It was not until 1871 that he was allowed to return, and he was getting back, in a city whose population had much changed, a leading position in the medical profession, when he died in 1878. A brief account of his career is contained in a book of biography of distinguished American physicians which was published in Philadelphia in 1878. Few men have died in the city of Washington whose death has been mourned by so many persons as a personal affliction. Many of these he had helped as a physician or as a friend for he was generous of money and services and they sorrowed for the loss of a knightly gentleman. The funeral was from St. Patrick's Church in which he had been christened sixty years before.

Dr. Boyle was twice married. His first wife was Fannie Reynolds Greene, who died in 1869, leaving six young children. His second wife was Cherry, daughter of General James N. Bethune, formerly of Georgia, to whom he was married a year before his death and who survived him and by whom there was no issue. Fannie Reynolds Greene was born in Fredericksburg, Va., and was the daughter of William Dabney Greene, a scion of the Greene family of Rhode Island, of which General Nathaniel Greene of the Revolutionary War was the most distinguished member. She was an accomplished woman of high social position, but above all a devoted wife and mother. Her mother was Fannie Johnston, whose father came to Warren County, Virginia, from the province of Connaught, Ireland, and married one of a family whose ancestors were among the first settlers in the colony of Virginia. Mrs. Boyle's ardent devotion to Virginia caused her to write in 1861 a poem that had much vogue in the south and which was included by Miss Emily Mason in the book *War Poetry of the South.* It was entitled "Hearts Victories," and presents from the woman's viewpoint and the southern viewpoint the theme that the northern poet Thomas Buchanan Read treats of in the well-known poem, beginning, "The maid that binds her warrior's sash." Mrs. Boyle died near Warrenton, Va., in 1869, leaving motherless six young children, five of whom are living.

John Boyle, the oldest son, namesake of the founder of the family in America, has been the head of the Washington office of the Wall Street *Journal* of New York, a position he reached after long service in the newspaper profession. He is one of the oldest in point of service of the Washington corps of correspondents and is recognized as an authority on financial matters. Two sons, Watson and Cornelius B., the latter a graduate in medicine as his father was of the medical school of Columbian College, reside in Montana.

One unmarried and one married daughter, Mrs. Frederick S. Hardesty, are residents of Washington. One daughter, Catherine Burke, married the eminent chemist Frank K. Cameron, Ph. D. She died more than ten years ago leaving one son and one daughter who live with their father at Salt Lake, Utah.

Of many citizens of America of the present generation was John Boyle, the Irish exile, the ancestor.

COLONEL JOHN FITZGERALD.

Aide-de-Camp and Secretary to General George Washington.

BY REV. THOMAS P. PHELAN, A. M., LL. D.

Professor of Church History in the Foreign Mission Seminary, Ossining, N. Y.

"The Geraldines! The Geraldines! 'tis full a thousand years
Since mid the Tuscan vineyards, bright flashed their battle spears;
When Capet seized the crown of France, their iron shields were known,
And their sabre dint struck terror on the banks of the Garonne;
Across the downs of Hastings they spurred hard by William's side,
And the grey sands of Palestine with Moslem blood they dyed;
But never then, nor thence, till now, has falsehood or disgrace
Been seen to soil Fitzgerald's plume or mantle in his face."[1]

The Fitzgerald family is of mixed Continental and Welsh origin. The founder of the Irish branch was Maurice Fitzgerald, who went to Ireland in 1169, at the invitation of King Dermot MacMorrough and assisted Strongbow in his campaigns. His great grandfather was Otho, a powerful baron of the house of Gherardini, Dukes of Tuscany, from which the name Geraldines was applied to the Fitzgeralds in after years. Otho migrated to Normandy, and during the reign of Edward the Confessor came to England. He obtained large grants of lands and became prominent in the social and political life of the time. The triumph of William the Conqueror strengthened his influence and power. His son, Walter, married Gladyss, a Welsh woman. Walter's son, Gerald, was confirmed in his rights by Henry I and was created Constable of Pembroke Castle in Wales, for his services against the Welsh chieftains. His son, Maurice, the first to settle in Ireland, adopted the surname Fitzgerald, son of Gerald, and in 1173 was appointed Chief Governor of Ireland. Large tracts in the present counties of Cork, Kerry, Kildare and Wicklow were bestowed on him. One branch of the family became Earls of Desmond, with the ancient patrimony of Cork, large estates in Kerry and smaller grants in Tipperary and Waterford. Another became Baron of Offaly, embracing large portions of King's county, with lands in Kildare and Queen's counties. The Fitz-

[1] Davis, Thomas, *Poems.*

geralds of Desmond were honored with many important offices, several serving as Lord Deputy during the fourteenth and fifteenth centuries. They held the rank of Prince Palatine, and were virtually kings in their own demesnes. The Fitzgeralds of Leincester boast of more than twenty earls, and in 1766, the reigning Earl was created Duke of Leincester. The descendants of this family to-day comprise many of the wealthiest and most prominent people in many parts of Ireland.[1]

At an early period, the Fitzgeralds adopted the manners and customs of the ancient Irish, spoke their language, practised their laws and used their war cries. The weakness of the English system, and the petty exactions of the foreign officials aroused their disgust and resentment, while the impulsive, warm-hearted, sympathetic, Irish character, with its kindly customs and poetic fancies, won their esteem and imitation. As the followers of Rollo had exchanged the harsh accents of the Northern climes for the musical cadence of French and Italian, as the enemies of religion and the foes of education became the patrons of learning and the bulwarks of Christianity, so these erstwhile conquerors of Ireland became "Ipsis Hibernicis Hiberniores,"—"more Irish than the Irish themselves,"—a phrase first applied to the Geraldines. Various laws were promulgated to arrest this dangerous tendency. The Statutes of Kilkenny, passed in 1367, enacted, that intermarriage with native women was high treason, that any Englishman adopting the Irish dress, languages or names, should forfeit his lands, and that no Irish postulants should be admitted into convents or monasteries.[2] These laws were ineffectual as the invaders gradually fell under the influence of the native customs and manners, and many of them became the bitterest enemies of England and staunch supporters of their adopted country. Thomas Fitzgerald, tenth Earl of Kildare, known affectionately in Irish history, as "Silken Thomas," refused allegiance to Henry VIII. After a long campaign against great odds, with treachery playing a prominent part, he was induced to surrender, with the promise of security for himself and his retainers. He was taken to London and executed with his five uncles. Gerald Fitzgerald, fifteenth Earl of Desmond, denied the spiritual supremacy of Elizabeth and refused to conform to the English church. He was

[1] Rooney, *Genealogical History of Irish Families.*
[2] D'Alton, *History of Ireland,* Vol. II.

slain in battle and his head was sent to London and impaled on a spike of London Bridge. During the revolution of 1688, various members of the family served in the army of King James. Col. John Fitzgerald, of the Desmond branch, fought at the siege of Limerick, and after the signing of the treaty sailed with his regiment and entered the French service. Lieut.-Col. Nicholas Fitzgerald also went to France after the fall of Limerick, and served with distinction in the campaigns against Marlborough in France and Flanders. Other members served in the Irish Brigade as officers in the regiments of Berwick, Clare, Dillon, O'Donnell and Walsh. Maj.-Gen. James Fitzgerald distinguished himself at Fontenoy, where the Irish exiles avenged the Broken Treaty. In the uprising of 1798, another illustrious scion of the family, Lord Edward Fitzgerald, laid down his life for the liberty of his country. For six centuries the Geraldines have been loyal to the country of their adoption, and have shown themselves,— "more Irish than the Irish themselves."[1]

The Irish emigration to the American Colonies began in the early years of the sixteenth century. The tyranny of the landowners, and the economic and political oppressions drove thousands of hardy settlers to the New World. The atrocities of Cromwell, the perfidy of William at Limerick, the penal enactments, the restrictions on trade and manufactures, the subservience and base corruption of the pseudo Irish parliament,—composed chiefly of bankrupt English nobles, place hunters and landlord appointees, representing only a small proportion of the Irish people, with the Catholics disfranchised and unrepresented,—sent many into exile, not only from Ulster but from every county. These immigrants settled in every colony from New Hampshire to Georgia.[2] Their industry and perseverance changed the wilderness into fertile farms and green pastures, their bravery and loyalty made the revolution successful and established the new republic. Virginia received Irish colonists as early as 1621.[3] Each subsequent year added its quota, until in the period of the war for independence, one fourth of the population was Irish by blood or descent.[4] Many of these pioneers journeyed to the wil-

[1] Rooney, *Genealogical History of Irish Families.*
[2] O'Brien, *A Hidden Phase of American History.*
[3] *Ibid.*
[4] Haltigan, *The Irish in the American Revolution.*

derness in the Blue Mountain region, others took up lands in the fertile valley of the Shenadoah. The natives were hostile, and frequent massacres occurred, yet these argonauts held their ground and protected the frontiers against the savages. When the struggle for freedom came, they entered the continental army, and served in the legislative halls. The muster rolls of the militia, the marriage and baptismal registers, the land records and will books contain a wealth of Irish names, attesting not only their presence in the colony, but their devotion to church and state.[1]

John Fitzgerald came to Virginia and settled in Alexandria in 1769 or 1770. He was born in the county Wicklow although the details of his early career are meagre. Tradition asserts he was a near relative of Lord Edward Fitzgerald, the Irish patriot.[2] He was cultured, educated, and refined and possessed means and business acumen, as he entered mercantile life and established a reputation in financial circles. He was a social favorite, and participated in the society events of the little town, and "became quite a favorite with the English maidens and Scotch lassies who made Alexandria, even then, true to its original name of Belle Haven."[3] In 1770, Washington was elected Burgess and the citizens of Alexandria tendered him a reception. Fitzgerald attended this function, and was introduced to his future friend and leader. He was an uncompromising Whig, and an inveterate enemy of Toryism, and during the agitations of those days always maintained that an appeal to arms was the only hope of the Colonies. "He was an officer of the old Buffs and Blues, the first volunteer regiment raised in the south in the dawn of the revolution, and commanded by Washington."[4] In April, 1774, he visited Mt. Vernon with his friends, Mr. Tilghman and Dr. Digges, to confer on the troubled state of public affairs. On Washington's return from the Richmond convention, where Patrick Henry sounded the slogan of armed resistance, he was visited by another delegation, among whom were Fitzgerald and his co-religionist, Daniel Carroll of Maryland. The people of Alexandria resolved: "If Boston submits, we will not."[5] In

[1] O'Brien, *A Hidden Phase of American History.*

[2] Griffin, *Researches*, 1909.

[3] *Ibid.*

[4] McGee, *Irish Settlers in North America.*

[5] Carne, *Washington's Catholic Aide-de-Camp.*

every movement looking towards independence, John Fitzgerald was a leader of his townsmen.

On April 19, 1775, the battle of Lexington was fought and the news of the conflict aroused every loyal heart to action. From city and hamlet troops hurried to Boston, congresses were organized in every colony, and committees of safety appointed, to recruit soldiers and provide munitions of war. Just as the news arrived that Ethan Allen and his "Green Mountain Boys" had captured Ticonderoga and Crown Point, the second Continental Congress met at Philadelphia, voted to raise twenty thousand men and chose George Washington, commander-in-chief. Fitzgerald had prospered in his business ventures and had lately bought property along the Potomac which he reclaimed, and which was long known as Fitzgerald's wharf. He married Jane Digges, daughter of Dr. Digges of Warburton Manor, a member of the ancient Maryland family. When the news of the hostilities came, Fitzgerald and eight others, the entire Catholic population of Alexandria, set out for Cambridge.[1] On his arrival he was designated aide-de-camp to the commander and occasionally acted as secretary.

"Aides-de-camp are persons in whom entire confidence must be placed. It requires men of ability to execute the duties with propriety and dispatch where there is a multiplicity of business as must attend the commander-in-chief of such an army as this, and persuaded as I am, that nothing but the zeal of these gentlemen who live with me and act in this capacity, for the great American cause and personal attachment to me, have induced them to undergo the troubles and confinement they have experienced since they became members of my family."[2]

In November, Fitzgerald was officially appointed secretary, sharing the duties with another Irish Catholic, Stephen Moylan. Tradition relates that Moylan met his future commander at a levee at Alexandria and was presented by Fitzgerald. Later research shows that he was introduced to Washington by John Dickinson, the sterling Philadelphia patriot.[3] After the evacuation of Boston, Fitzgerald accompanied the army to New York and during the disasters on Long Island, and the retreat through New Jersey, was continually at the side of his beloved chief. In the archives of the Continental Congress are various letters and

[1] Custis, *Recollections.*
[2] *Ibid.*
[3] Griffin, *Life of General Moylan.*

dispatches dealing with military and financial problems written in his well known style—enclosing a list of officers for the rifle battalion; a plan for forming a corps of continental artillery; a request for money to equip Moylan's dragoons; lengthy reports on skirmishes and raids.[1]

The darkest hour of the war had come. The victorious British and Hessians pursued Washington's naked and starving army through New Jersey and compelled it to cross into Pennsylvania. They awaited the freezing of the Delaware River to complete the rout of the patriotic forces. On Christmas night Washington crossed the river, surprised the Hessians at Trenton and killed or captured almost the entire detachment. Threatened by superior forces he outwitted Cornwallis, and during the darkness of night, marched to Princeton. Meeting the enemy emerging from the town, a sharp conflict began. The Continentals, lacking bayonets, gave way. Washington, disdaining danger, rallied his men and mounted on his white charger, plunged into the thickest of the fight.

"The discomfited Americans rallied on the instant, formed into line and the enemy halted, and dressed their lines; the American chief is between the adverse hosts, as though a target for both. The arms of both lines are leveled. Can escape be possible? Fitzgerald, horror struck at the danger of his beloved commander, dropped the reins on his horse's neck, drew his hat over his face, that he might not see him die. A roar of musketry succeeds and then a shout. The aide-de-camp ventures to raise his eyes. O Glorious sight. The enemy are broken and flying, while dimly, amidst the glimpses of smoke, is seen the chief, alive, unharmed, and without a wound, waving his hat and cheering his comrades to the pursuit. Colonel Fitzgerald, celebrated as the finest horseman of the American army, now dashed the rowels into his charger's flanks, and heedless of dead and dying, in his way, flew to the aid of the chief, exclaiming: "Thank God, your excellency is safe." The favorite aide, a gallant and warm-hearted son of Erin, a man of thews and and sinews, "albeit unused to the melting mood," gave loose rein to his feelings, and wept like a child for joy. Washington, ever calm amidst scenes of the greatest excitement, affectionately grasped the hand of his aide, and then ordered: "Away, dear Colonel, bring up the troops; the day is our own."[2]

After the return from Trenton and Princeton, Fitzgerald visited Alexandria and brought to Mrs. Washington at Mt. Vernon, the news of the victories. While at home, three British frigates sailed up the river, threatening to bombard the town. The

[1] Griffin, *Researches*, 1909.
[2] *Ibid.*

militia were called and Fitzgerald led a contingent to Jones' Point to repel the invaders. After firing a few shots, the flotilla dropped down the river without doing any damage. The militia captain frightened by the demands of the enemy had struck his colors in token of surrender. The Colonel was so exasperated that he inflicted bodily chastisement on the cowardly leader.[1]

The winter of 1778 brought fresh disaster to the American cause. The defeats at Brandywine and Germantown in the previous year, permitted Howe to place his army in winter quarters in Philadelphia, while Washington encamped at Valley Forge. It was the darkest hour of the revolution. The weather was severe, provisions and fuel hard to secure, tents and clothing lacking. Many of the soldiers were without shoes, leaving bloody footprints in the snow. Lafayette marvelled at the courage and endurance of the men. Hamilton writes that grim famine stalked through the camp. Washington labored incessantly to alleviate the sufferings of his gallant followers by appeals to Congress and the leading patriots for help. During these days another trial came to the great leader. He was unjustly accused of incompetence, his policy criticized, his leadership scorned, and Congress petitioned to choose a new general for the army. The capture of Burgoyne at Saratoga brought honors and renown to Horatio Gates, a sluggish and incompetent general, who had reaped the fruits of Schuyler's preparations and Arnold's and Morgan's bravery. A movement was launched to place the alleged hero of Bemis Heights at the head of the army to supersede Washington. Even such sterling patriots as John and Samuel Adams, Richard Henry Lee, James Lovell and Richard Rush protested against the Fabian policy of the general and advised his removal. The leaders in the scheme were given high positions; Gates was placed at the head of the Board of War with Mifflin as an assistant and Conway was named inspector general. Lovell of Massachusetts wrote to Gates:

"How different your conduct and fortune. This army will be totally lost unless you come down and collect the victorious band who wish to fight under your banner.[2]

Conway, an Irishman, educated in France and an officer in the French army was a leading figure in the conspiracy and from

[1] Griffin, *Researches*, 1909.
[2] *Ibid.*

him it has been called the "Conway Cabal." He wrote to Gates congratulating him on his coming promotion:

"Heaven has determined to save your country or a weak general and bad councillors would have ruined it."[1]

A copy of this letter in which the entire plot was disclosed was shown to Laurens, the President of Congress. While visiting York, Pennsylvania, where the seat of government had been transferred, Fitzgerald saw a copy and immediately wrote to the commander:

"Upon my arrival here . . . Mr. Laurens asked me to breakfast next morning . . . giving me to understand that he had something of importance to say to me. In the morning he asked me if you had ever seen the much talked of letter from General Conway to General Gates. I answered I was sure that you never had, unless since my departure from camp. He then said it was in the hands of Mr. Roberdeau. . . . Upon this I determined to demand it from Mr. Roberdeau in order to let you have a copy of it. I waited on him this morning. He was full of his assurance that the letter did not contain the paragraph alluded to, which gave him infinite satisfaction, as he entertained the highest respect for you and for General Gates. He added, however, that had the letter remained in his possession, he should not have thought himself at liberty to let a copy be taken without the consent of the gentleman who entrusted him with it. . . . I then returned to Mr. Laurens who gave me an extract he had taken from it which I take the liberty of enclosing to you. The whole of that letter I understand was couched in terms of the bitterest invective of which this is a small sample. . . . Mr. Laurens's sentiments upon the whole of this matter were exceedingly just and delivered with great candor."[2]

On receiving this letter, Washington immediately responded:

"I thank you sincerely for the part you acted at York respecting C——y and believe with you that matters have and will turn out different to what that party expected. G——s has involved himself in his letters to me in the most absurd contradictions. M—— has brought himself into a scrape that he does not know how to get out of with a gentleman of this state, and C——y as you know, is sent upon an expedition which all the world knew, and the event has proven not practicable."[3]

The plot was a failure. The invasion of Canada was abandoned, the commissariat broke down, and Baron Steuben was appointed inspector general. Charles Carroll of Carrollton with Samuel Chase and Robert Morris rallied Congress to the support of

[1] Griffin, *Researches*, 1909.
[2] *Ibid.*
[3] *Ibid.*

Washington. Mifflin was placed in a subordinate position; Conway, wounded in a duel with General Cadwallader, resigned; Gates was ordered to return to his command. The next year the much lauded hero was assigned to command the southern army. At the bloody battle of Camden his northern laurels changed to southern willows. Henceforth the hopes of the nation were reposed in the gallant commander who had been chosen to lead the hosts of democracy.

When Howe evacuated Philadelphia, Washington pursued him through New Jersey and at Monmouth engaged him in battle. The cowardice and treason of General Charles Lee discouraged the soldiers and defeat was imminent. Washington, riding to the front, found his men in full retreat. Rebuking the unworthy commander, he rallied the scattered forces and led them against the foe. Again the beloved chieftain's life was in jeopardy. At his side was his gallant aide and once more his tears of gratitude flowed as his leader was miraculously spared. The British retreated to New York and Washington and his ragged hosts held New Jersey and the Hudson Valley. The records of Congress show that Fitzgerald was with the army continuously during this period. Letters written to Philadelphia of a most confidential nature are in his handwriting, dictated by Washington, showing the character and extent of his services, and the confidence reposed in him by the great leader. At length the final act in the bloody tragedy was enacted. Cornwallis was hemmed in at Yorktown by the gallant Continentals and the fearless French while the ships of France commanded the sea. On October 19, 1781, the emblems of America and France were entwined in victory, the ensign of Britain was trailed in the dust of defeat. The independence of the Colonies was won, Washington, Rochambeau and De Grasse were saluted as heroes by two continents. Fitzgerald was present at the surrender and his joy was apparent to all. The crimes and insults that had driven him into exile were compensated by the glorious triumph, the broken treaty of Limerick avenged, his beloved country had taken her place among the nations of the earth.

When the last hostile soldier had left the shores of the new republic, Washington resigned his command and bade farewell to his faithful officers. His task was finished, and relinquishing the the sword, he returned to the peaceful scenes at Mt. Vernon.

16

Fitzgerald also retired to his old home at Alexandria and resumed his family and business relations. Residing only a few miles from his old comrade in arms, he maintained in a marked degree his former social and mercantile friendship with his neighbor. He was active in the newly organized Society of the Cincinnati, often acting unofficially in the secretarial work of the organization. During his visits to Alexandria, Washington frequently dined at the Colonel's table, and occasionally passed the night under his hospitable roof. Washington's diary contains many references to Fitzgerald, showing that their intimacy was close and cordial. They were associates in the Potomac Company, formed to improve the navigation of the river, Washington serving as president, Fitzgerald as a member of the board of directors. In politics the Colonel was a Federalist, and followed the political fortunes of his leader. He opposed the schemes of Jefferson and Madison, and frequently deplored their apparent radicalism. In 1787, Fitzgerald was elected mayor of Alexandria and filled the post with credit to himself and satisfaction to his constituents. In 1798 President Adams named him collector of the Port of Alexandria. His business, long neglected during his service in the army, did not prosper, and after his death, his country residence, "Federal Spring," was sold in the settlement of his encumbered estate. Yet in prosperity or adversity, he always retained the admiration and good will of his fellow citizens, who remembered his illustrious services and his friendship and loyalty with the great commander.

His married life was singularly happy. His wife, Jane Digges, was loving and devoted, and her home was the centre of the social activities of the little town. Her family, long settled in Maryland, was noted for its devotion to church and country, and her father, Doctor Digges of Warburton Manor, was honored as a loyal citizen and a learned practitioner. Two daughters came to bless their home, Elizabeth and Jane. The former married Francis Lightfoot Lee, son of Richard Henry Lee, the revolutionary patriot and member of Congress. She died childless, and the surviving sister, Jane, was also espoused by Mr. Lee. Five children were born from this union, three boys and two girls. One son became an admiral in the navy, another entered West Point and attained the grade of major in the army, a third embraced a mercantile career. One of the daughters died in young womanhood, the other survived until 1889. In his own state, and in Kentucky and Missouri, there are many collateral and direct descendents of the revolutionary Colonel.

Fitzgerald was a loyal and devoted Catholic. The Church of England was established by law in Virginia and all other sects were outlawed. Catholics were especially excluded. Penal laws were placed on the statute books to prevent them from settling in the Colony, and those who were already in the province were ineligible to vote or hold office, to give testimony in court and were fined twenty pounds for absenting themselves from the Episcopal service.[1] All priests were ordered to leave (1642), and henceforth only visited their scattered brethren secretly and in disguise. The Jesuits of Maryland, fearless and zealous, heedless of imprisonment, fine or death, came frequently into the Colony. Even in the period preceding the revolution, Catholic services were conducted secretly. In 1774, Rev. John Carroll returned from the Continent and his little chapel at Rock Creek gave the Catholics of Northern Virginia an opportunity of hearing Mass. After the war, the old enactments were abolished through the efforts of Jefferson, and divine service was held in the home of Colonel Fitzgerald. Rev. John Thayer, a Boston convert from Congregationalism, officiated as chaplain, and in a letter to Bishop Carroll, speaks of a certain gentleman, who was willing to donate a site for a Catholic church.[2] Through the influence of the Bishop and Colonel Fitzgerald, Mr. Alexander gave half an acre of land, and in 1796 the church was begun. For some years it served as the parish church for Alexandria and the immediate vicinity. In 1789, Georgetown College was founded. A committee to receive funds was appointed and Fitzgerald was named to represent Maryland. Other members were Charles Carroll of Carrollton and Thomas FitzSimons and George Meade of Philadelphia. The Colonel was ever true to the teachings of his church. He resisted the allurements which attracted many of his fellow religionists into forbidden societies and lived and died true to the teachings of the faith of his fathers.[3]

On the last day of the century, December 31, 1799, Washington died. A few months later, in the spring of 1800, Fitzgerald passed

---

[1] Shea, *History of Catholic Church in United States*, Vol. I.
[2] Shea, *History of Catholic Church in United States*, Vol. II.
[3] Griffin, *Researches*, 1909.

away. He was buried in the little Catholic Cemetery on the road to Mt. Vernon. The two friends were united in life, and when death came, neither time nor space separated them.

Secular historians rarely mention the name of Fitzgerald and seldom chronicle his honorable service. Lesser heroes have been immortalized in the hall of national fame. Even those of his own race and religion, frequently omit his name from the list of revolutionary giants. His achievements were not as splendid as the labors of Charles Carroll of Carrollton in the legislative councils, or the daring exploits of Stephen Moylan and his dashing dragoons, or the notable feats of John Barry on the quarter deck of his frigate. Yet his loyalty and devotion to Washington in the dark days of intrigue and warfare, his high and noble character, his honorable political career should entitle him to a niche in the pantheon of the republic. Loyalty to church and state was the distinguishing characteristic of the Geraldines for six centuries in Ireland. The American scion of that ancient stock was true to his family traditions.

"But never then nor thence, till now, has falsehood or disgrace,
  Been seen to soil Fitzgerald's plume or mantle in his face."

BIBLIOGRAPHY.

Bennett, William Harper—*Catholic Footsteps in Old New York.*
Carne, William F.—*Washington's Catholic Aide-de-Camp* (*Catholic World*, Jan., 1890.)
Condon, Edward O'Meagher—*The Irish Race in America.*
Cooke, John Esten—*Virginia.*
Custis, George Washington Parke—*Recollections.*
Davis, Thomas—*Poems.*
O'Alton, Rev. E. A.—*History of Ireland*, Vols. I–II.
Griffin, Martin I. J.—*American Catholic Historical Researches*, 1909–1911.
  The Life of General Stephen Moylan.
  Catholics in the American Revolution, Vol. II.
Haltigan, James—*The Irish in the American Revolution.*
Leonard, Lewis A.—*The Life of Charles Carroll of Carrollton.*
Lodge, Henry Cabot—*The Story of the American Revolution.*
McGee, Thomas D'Arcy—*A History of the Irish Settlers in North America.*
O'Brien, Michael J.—*A Hidden Phase of American History.*
Rooney, John—*Genealogical History of Irish Families.*
Shea, John Gilmary—*History of the Catholic Church in the United States.*
Sparks, Jared—*Writings of Washington.*

NECROLOGY

EDMUND J. CURRY

DR. FRANCIS J. QUINLAN

Edmund J. Curry, the subject of this sketch, was born at Temple, County Clare, Ireland, July 4th, 1846. When he was three years of age his parents came to this country and settled at Lewiston, Niagara County, New York. Sometime later the family moved to Niagara Falls where they had purchased a small farm. Here they remained until 1865. During this time Edmund attended the public schools. Later he took up a commercial course that subsequently enabled him to become a clerk in charge of the storerooms of the International Hotel in his home town.

His ambitious spirit was restless in this limited sphere and accordingly, in 1868, he came to the City of New York, where he sought a wider range for his progressive nature in fields that afforded a very broad scope in the post-bellum days. After a very brief residence here, we find him associated with his uncle, the late John J. Curry, whose numerous enterprises needed the quick moving spirit of his young partner. The partnership thrived, and the partners, through close attention to business and thrifty methods, soon realized notable returns upon investments made in the section known as Old Yorkville.

Later we find Edmund constructing one of the largest stables in that upper section and calling it the "Niagara Stables" after the town where he had spent the early years of his boyhood. His far-reaching mental vision saw future realty opportunities, and consequently he entered the real estate business. A keen appreciation of values and prudent judgment led him successfully into many avenues of commercial enterprise.

But Edmund Curry was not alone in these ventures, nor did the spur to his ambition come from himself alone. He married, and the fruit of this union was two children. One child was taken from him almost in its infancy. The other was spared to him for a period of twenty-two years. The loss of this boy was indeed a severe blow to his ambitious life. It seems that everything in the career of the father was centered in the future of the boy.   One can readily surmise the painfulness of the trial, but it fell upon a manly character, and the forbearance with which the trial was met was a preparation for a subsequent activity—interest in orphans—that characterized the later years of Edmund Curry's life.

But an ardent spirit cannot be circumscribed by domestic and business relations.   Hence, it is, that during many years of a successful life we find him identified with social organizations having for aim racial, civic and religious welfare.   Thus in 1890 he is the guest of honor at a complimentary dinner given at the Hoffman House of this City tendered to him by his admirers of the Irish Home Rule Club.   He manifested a rare civic pride in the land of his adoption.   He often said that he was more American than Irish, having been born on the birthday of our nation, a fact which perhaps added to his noble sentiments of unswerving loyalty to our great Republic.   As a citizen, he was enrolled under every banner of public utility, and the attention which he brought to such affairs was more than ordinary.   Conspicuous among his public performances, not too remote to be recalled, is the fact that he served as foreman of the Grand Jury during the November Term of 1913 and prior to that time he had been many times a member of that body.

Everything that blended race and creed appealed to his upright fiery soul.   He graced the meetings of the Catholic Historical Society, and his kind and genial countenance brightened the halls of the Catholic Club and the assembly rooms of the Knights of Columbus.   By birthright he possessed an artistic temperament and, accordingly, manifested unusual fondness for the great work of the Metropolitan Museum of Art where he frequently spent afternoons among the choice collections of that classic structure.

Worthy of note, and no less strong than his religious and social affiliations, was his political creed and his great admiration for Jeffersonian simplicity and the ideals of the Democratic party of which he was a true standard bearer.

Among the various organizations, philanthropic and educational, none appealed to his human nature as did the New York Catholic Protectory.   Here he was known to spend days among the many delinquent and destitute little ones, and his purse and time were at the command of the institution to further the welfare of those who were gathered under its sheltering arm.

The American Irish Historical Society has lost one of its faithful members and devoted friends; the St. John Guild, a worthy trustee and patron. His generous deeds will be recorded in the memories of those whom he earnestly sought to assist and to whom he gave lavishly. As a young man Mr. Curry took a deep interest in the work of St. Vincent De Paul, an interest which continued up to the time of his death. He was not only a generous contributor but a frequent and welcome attendant at the general meeting of the Society.

Edmund J. Curry occupied a peculiar position in our midst. Though not blessed with college training or social setting, nevertheless, he made unto himself a circle of friends and true companions that today mourn his loss and regret his absence. Although clouds overshadowed his life and keen sorrow wounded his heart, still, he was genial and cheerful, ever ready with a kind word and cheering response, so that we felt better that he had come into our lives.

He performed all his duties without break or falter in his march toward the goal. After a long and successful career he has gone to the reward that awaited him on the other side, where, most assuredly, joy and happiness greeted him. As to us, tonight, there is a yawning gap and painful rent in our hearts as we miss his genial smile and warm grasp. Of him, it may be truly said that a man has passed from our midst without fear or blemish, a man whose life is replete with affection, and whose memory is fraught with the sweetened burden of generous impulses and honorable deeds.

THOMAS ADDIS EMMET.

His Life and Triumphs and His Love of Ireland.

By Edward J. McGuire.

At a special meeting of the Executive Council of the American Irish Historical Society, held at its rooms, No. 35 West 39th Street, Manhattan, New York City, on March 10th, 1919, the following minute prepared by Edward J. McGuire on the occasion of the death of Doctor Thomas Addis Emmet was unanimously adopted:

Thomas Addis Emmet, who was the third to bear this illustrious name, died at his home at No. 95 Madison Avenue on March 1st, 1919 in his ninety-first year. He was born at the University of Virginia near Charlottesville, Virginia on May 29th, 1828. He spent his childhood and youth, except for short intervals, at that place. His father Doctor John Patten Emmet was one of the original professors of the University of Virginia, having been chosen by its founder Thomas Jefferson. He was the second son of Thomas Addis Emmet, the patriot of the Irish Revolution of 1798. He was the philosopher of the Emmet family and left behind him a distinguished name. Doctor Emmet's mother was Mary Tucker of the famous Tucker family of Virginia.

From his father who was born in Ireland in 1796 and who had vivid memories of the times of stress and storm that sent his uncle Robert Emmet to the scaffold and his family into exile, but even more particularly from his paternal grandmother the famous Jane Patten Emmet, the valiant woman whose name is dear to all who cherish the memories of '98 and who survived until 1846, Doctor Emmet got the intense love of Ireland and of the traditions of the Irish Race and the passion for religious and civil liberty that dominated his life. The memory of his grandmother with whom he had lived in closest intimacy was enshrined in his heart. He spoke of her with loving pride until the very end of his life.

After a short and disturbed period of collegiate life at the University of Virginia, when he was eighteen years old Doctor Emmet decided to follow the ancestral profession and entered Jefferson Medical College at Philadelphia in the year 1846. It is an interesting fact that he was in the fourth successive generation of physicians in his family, his grandfather having been a practicing physician in Ireland before he took up the profession of the law in which he won such great distinction.

In 1850 he was graduated as a doctor of medicine. He used to say that he then came to New York with $300 in his pocket and set up practice charging a quarter for a visit and glad when it was paid in cash. Through the kindness of friends, he was almost at once made physician to the Emigrant Refuge Hospital on Wards

Island, where he remained for some five years in most active practice. He gave large credit to these years of labor and even drudgery, for his subsequent success. In the year 1855 he met Doctor J. Marion Sims, a brilliant name in American medicine, who had invented methods of surgery in women's diseases that startled the world. The day of this meeting was a blessed one for womankind. He first became Doctor Sim's assistant, later his associate and finally his successor as surgeon in chief of the Woman's Hospital, which Doctor Sims founded in the year of their first meeting.

He leaped into fame at once. When Doctor Sims, who was a Southern sympathizer, left New York for Europe in 1861, Doctor Emmet took his place as the leading gynecologist in New York. He was then thirty-three years old. God had gifted him with genius in his chosen field of medicine. He had become a clinical lecturer to whom surgeons flocked from all over the world. He discovered facts and invented processes that saved the health and even the lives of multitudes of women. Before the days of Pasteur's and Lister's fame, when as he used to say he had never heard of them, he applied the principles of the antiseptic methods that they later developed and made famous. Through his genius and his industry, diseases which before his day had destroyed and invalided thousands of mothers every year, have now become medical curiosities. For forty-five years and until the year 1900, when he had reached his seventy-third year, he stayed in the harness at the Woman's Hospital. His fame grew with the years. It has been truly said of him that his discoveries were of truth and therefore they never became obsolete. In the field of surgery of the mucous membranes and of plastic surgery generally his name will never be forgotten. He was one of the very first American surgeons to become famous in Europe. His monumental book on "Principles and Practice of Gynecology" was published at Philadelphia in 1879 and was reprinted at once in England and translated into German, French and Spanish. When his day of final retirement came in 1900 he was undoubtedly the most famous gynecologist in the World. He estimated that between 90,000 and 100,000 women had been in his care.

Yet this, his great life work was done with the simplicity of a child. A great proof of the nobility of his soul is found in this, that he never knew avarice. He gave generously of his time and his means to the poor and the needy, and God rewarded him in the end with a large fortune.

When he retired from active practice in 1895 he gave himself to study and writing. His library was beautiful both in its books and their setting. He had as he called it, a hobby for collecting from his earliest years and his literary, artistic and historical treasures in prints, manuscripts and rare volumes were the envy of other collectors. He travelled widely in his vacation times and gathered his stores wisely and generously. In 1895 he sold his famous collection of "Americana" to Mr. John S. Kennedy who presented it to the Lenox Library as the "Emmet Collection." It is now preserved in the New York Public Library. In April 1912 a part of his remaining collection was sold for $72,000. One of his greatest pleasures was to show the many treasures that he retained and to point out their uniqueness and interest.

He wrote a great deal in the last twenty-five years and published much of it. Several of his volumes are of special interest. In 1903 he published the monumental book on Irish matters, "Ireland under English Rule" of which a second and revised edition appeared in 1909. Before this in 1898 he had published a limited edition of what many think to be the best history of a family written in English. It is entitled "The Emmet Family with some Incidents relative to Irish History." It is filled with treasures for the historical student and enriched with rare engravings and other illustrations. He received the "Lætare Medal" from Notre Dame University in that year, in recognition of its literary merit. In 1910 he had published by G. P. Putnam & Company a volume of autobiography called "Incidents of My Life" which is as interesting as a good romance and delightfully characteristic of the author whom nobody ever charged with being dull or lacking in wit and courage. In 1915 he published "Thomas Addis Emmet and Robert Emmet." The revised, enlarged edition of this work he finished just two weeks before he died.

In his retirement he had a host of friends. He loved to see them about him and up to the end he was glad to know that they thought of him. He disliked to be forgotten in his age. He remained in enjoyment of bodily health for many years afterwards. He never was of large frame or robust body. In the latter years he grew thin and stooped and used humorously to say that he had died below the waist but had kept vigorous and alive in the rest of his body. He was a remarkable figure then. He always sat in a large arm chair with a reading desk before him. His hands were as ready, his eyes as bright and his attention as alert as if he were fifty years old. He kept his sight and hearing wonderfully. He loved to talk about the events of his long lifetime and in which he had so great a part.

He particularly welcomed one who could speak to him of Irish things. He was the third generation in America and in his veins flowed streams of blood that were not Irish and yet he seemed to be dominated by the love of Ireland and the traditions of the Irish People. He was besides a man of abiding faith of the kind that can move mountains. In the year 1867 he left the Protestant Communion, in which he was born and raised, for the Catholic Church, when he was a man of 39 years. His wife was of that faith and his children had been baptized in it. When his mind was convinced after years of study and reflection he followed his conscience at once and without murmuring.

He was always an ardent Irish Nationalist. Sometimes he was criticised for holding what were called extreme views but he nevertheless persisted in them. But a few years ago, he declared to a group of his friends of this Society that he was sure that the good God had kept him alive into so great an old age so that he might see Ireland again a nation. He yearned to realize the dream of his great uncle Robert Emmet. He spoke these words with complete sincerity and abiding faith.

From 1871 when he first visited Ireland, he gave himself heartily to her cause. He expressly states his opinion in his autobiography that the Fenian movement accomplished more than all the others for the Irish cause. In 1879 he was a member of the Irish Famine Relief Committee of the United States. He was a wheel horse throughout the Home Rule movement of the late Seventies and the Eighties and Nineties of the last century and the trusted friend of its leaders. Parnell and Biggar relied upon him for their aid in America. He was President of the Irish National Federation of America founded in May 1891. John Dillon has testified in writing to the fact that the Committee of this Federation of which Doctor Emmet was chairman, saved the National party of Ireland from disaster in the general election of 1903 when eighty-two Irish Nationalists were returned to Parliament, by means of whom Gladstone passed through the House of Commons the first Irish Home Rule bill.

At his death he was probably the most advanced and scholarly student of Irish literature and history in America. He had in his library many rare works on the subject that he knew thoroughly. On no topic of this kind was he without knowledge. His conversation was brilliant and a visit to him ended with the gift to the visitor's mind of novelties and treasures of information on this difficult subject.

He cherished the American Irish Historical Society. He was one of its earliest members in New York. He took part in its activities until age crippled him. The Society specially honored him by making him the chief guest of honor at its annual dinner in 1916 and by electing him to honorary membership. He remembered it in his will. He has given to it generously of his rich stores of books for their preservation and access by the present and future generations.

He received so many public and professional honors in his lifetime that it would be almost impossible to set them down. He valued most highly of them all, the Knighthood of Saint Gregory which Pope Pius X conferred on him in 1906. The last tribute was given him in the Spring of 1917 when Bishop Shahan, President of the Catholic University of America, came to New York from Washington to confer on him the degree of Doctor of Letters. His response to the Bishop's address made, it will be remembered, in his ninetieth year will never be forgotten by his hearers. He spoke with the strength of one of forty and with the earnest words of one chosen of God.

He was married in 1854 to Catherine R. Duncan of Montgomery, Alabama. She lived a beautiful life of devotion and comradeship with him and celebrated with him their Golden Wedding. She died in 1905. She bore him five children, John Duncan Emmet, M. D., Annie Emmet Harris, Robert Emmet, Thomas Addis Emmet, Jr., and Katherine Erin Emmet of whom only Doctor John Duncan Emmet, Mr. Robert Emmet and Katherine Erin Emmet survive. During the last year his heart was wrung by the loss of his favorite grandson and namesake Thomas Addis Emmet Harris who died in France on the field of hono while leading his command as an officer of Field Artillery of the United States Army.

Doctor Emmet lived to a great age, more than twenty years beyond the Scriptural time. He wrote these lines of himself in closing his autobiography:

"To indicate my insignificant existence in connection with the affairs of the World, with yet form and being, my life is now as fragile as a bubble floating on the surface unbroken by a ripple and passing with the current down the great stream of Life and near its mouth where it is soon to discharge its contents into the boundless Ocean of Eternity."

To these beautiful words we ask leave to add this. When Doctor Emmet passed into the great beyond the World lost one of its gentlest souls, a Christian gentleman, a profound scholar, a lover of the right, a dear friend to multitudes, a benefactor of mankind of the unique sort and yet one who all the while kept the heart of a child and illustrated in his beautiful life the beatitude: "Blessed are the pure in heart for they shall see God."

JOHN P. HOPKINS.

AN APPRECIATION.

BY P. J. O'KEEFFE.

Seldom, indeed, even in the history of this great metropolis has there been given to Chicago a man of such parts as John F. Hopkins:

In any field he would have been a success; the elements were so mixed in him that the concrete expression was unusually great—here, indeed, might nature stand up and say to all the world, there is a man!

He was modest; humility is the handmaid of greatness. He was silent; charity never is effusive. He was brave; friendship is not the fibre of a coward.

He, above any one who ever graced the mayoralty chair, was of a type worth while to Chicago—from his pen came the endorsement of the first track elevation ordinance; he gave the people more than they thanked him for then, but he looked not for public applause when he knew what he ought to do, to protect life especially.

John P. Hopkins in political life had and held more *individual* friends than any one man Illinois ever had, with the possible exceptions of Lincoln and Grant; in the case of Hopkins, too, the friends needed no purchase price save the affection they held and the loyalty they knew reposed in the man they loved.

John P. Hopkins was not vindictive; that so-called quality belongs to small bore individuals—Hopkins was a giant in principle and he never hit below the belt. He may not forget but he freely forgave; he was a benefactor to some who reviled him.

John Hopkins was an ideal man in physique; he was more ideal in his kindly way. The Creator moulded him majestically and handsomely, but the greater mould was the heart; therein John Hopkins was a masterpiece. In truth, indeed, his impress was stupendous and it will live long as it should and until the friends once more foregather in the softer sward beyond the broad river, where we pray and hope and believe our beloved friend has found peace.

John P. Hopkins, a member of this society since November 12, 1909 and former mayor and secretary of the Illinois state council of defense, died October 13, 1918 in Chicago, Illinois.

Mr. Hopkins was 60 years of age. He was born in Buffalo, N. Y., in 1858, coming to Chicago in 1880. He began as a machinist for the Pullman Palace Car Company, remaining there until 1888, when he went into business for himself as secretary of the Arcade Trading Company, which later became the Secord & Hopkins Company. He became a director of the Aurora Automatic Machine Company, the Chicago and Great Lakes Dredge and Dock Company, the Independent Pneumatic Tool Company and the Consumers Company. Every one of his business enterprises was successful.

In politics, Mr. Hopkins was a national figure. Aside from being chosen to fill out the term of the senior Carter H. Harrison as mayor after the latter was assassinated, he was from 1890 to 1892 chairman of the democratic campaign committee, served as vice-chairman of the national gold democratic committee in 1896 and was chairman of the democratic state committee from 1901 to 1904. He was delegate to the democratic national convention of 1892, 1900 and 1904.

As mayor of Chicago during part of 1894 and 1895, Mr. Hopkins built a monument to his memory in starting the agitation that made grade crossing elevation a fixture for Chicago.

He was chairman of the campaign committee that secured the annexation to Chicago of Hyde Park, Lake, Cicero, Jefferson and Lake View. He was a member of the Knights of Columbus, the Art Institute, the Chicago Historical society, the Chicago Athletic association, the Midday club, the South Shore Country club, the Field Museum of Natural History and the Bibliophile Society of Boston.

Mr. Hopkins had served upon the executive council of this society since 1917.

It is requested that notice of the death of members of the Society be sent to the Secretary-General with published or other account of the deceased.

To the Secretary-General of the American Irish Historical Society.

———

Dear Sir:

    I hereby apply for membership in the American Irish Historical Society and enclose check (or P. O. Money Order) for

        { $5.00 for Initiation Fee and Dues for current year.
        { $50.00 Initiation Fee and Life Membership.

Name..

Occupation..

Address...

Date of Application.....................................

*Proposed by..

      Initiation fee and dues for current year $5.00.
      Annual dues $5.00.   Life membership fee $50.00.

   *Where an applicant is unacquainted with a member it is not necessary to fill this line.

To the Secretary-General of the American Irish Historical Society.

———

Dear Sir:

    I hereby apply for membership in the American Irish Historial Society and enclose check (or P. O. Money Order) for

        { $5.00 for Initiation Fee and Dues for current year.
        { $50.00 Initiation Fee and Life Membership.

Name..

Occupation..

Address...

Date of Application.....................................

*Proposed by..

      Initiation fee and dues for current year $5.00.
      Annual dues $5.00.   Life membership fee $50.00.

   *Where an applicant is unacquainted with a member it is not necessary to fill this line.

MEMBERSHIP ROLL OF THE AMERICAN IRISH HISTORICAL SOCIETY.

HONORARY MEMBERS.

His Excellency, Woodrow Wilson, President of the United States; Washington, D. C.

Hon. Edward D. White, Chief Justice of the United States Supreme Court; Washington, D. C.

Hon. William Howard Taft, New Haven, Conn.

Most Rev. Dr. Daniel Mannix, D.D., LL.D., St. Patrick's Cathedral, Melbourne, Australia.
(Vice-President of the Society for Australia.)

W. C. Durant, 1764 Broadway, New York City.

LIFE MEMBERS.

Barry, Hon. Patrick T., Western Newspaper Union, Chicago, Ill.
(Member of the Executive Council.)

Bolger, Miss Sallie, 2411 West Walnut St., Louisville, Ky.

Blake, Thomas M., 640 West 34th St., New York City.

Brann, Rt. Rev. Henry A., D.D., LL.D., 141 East 43d St., New York City.

Brennan, Edward, Shamokin, Pa.

Brennan, George E., 134 LaSalle St., Chicago, Ill.

Butler, James, 230 West 72d St., New York City.

Campbell, Hon. John M., Lafayette Bldg., Philadelphia, Pa.

Carter, Patrick, 32 Westminster St., Providence, R. I.

Carton, Rev. James J., St. Coleman's Church, Ardmore, Pa.

Clune, Frank R., 185 Dundaff St., Carbondale, Pa.

Cockran, Hon. W. Bourke, 100 Broadway, New York City.

Corbett, Cornelius, 663 E. Jefferson Ave., Detroit, Mich.
(Vice-President of the Society for Michigan.)

Corbett, Michael J., Wilmington, N. C.
(Vice-President of the Society for North Carolina.)

Colihan, William J., 141 East 95th St., New York City.

Collins, Maj.-Gen. Dennis F., 637 Pearl St., Elizabeth, N. J.

Conley, Col. Louis D., 541 W. 25th St., New York City.
(Member of the Executive Council.)

Corcoran, William J., 512 Barristers Hall, Boston, Mass.

Cox, The Rt. Hon. Michael F., P.C., M.D., 26 Merrion Sq., Dublin, Ireland.
(Vice-President of the Society for Ireland.)

Crimmins, Cyril, 624 Madison Ave., New York City.
(Ex-Librarian and Archivist of the Society.)

CUDAHY, EDWARD A., 111 W. Monroe St., Chicago, Ill.

DEVINE, THOMAS J., Rochester, N. Y.

DEVLIN, THOMAS, 3d and Lehigh Aves., Philadelphia, Pa.

DOHERTY, JOSEPH E., 115 Bay State Road, Boston, Mass.

DONOHUE, HON. MICHAEL, 2613 East Lehigh Ave., Philadelphia, Pa.

DONOVAN, E. I., M.D., Langdon, No. Dak.
   (Vice-President of the Society for North Dakota.)

DOOLEY, HON. MICHAEL F., National Exchange Bank, Providence, R. I.
   (Ex-Treasurer-General and Vice-President of the Society for Rhode
   Island.)

DOOLEY, WILLIAM J., 17 Gaston St., Boston, Mass.

DOONER, EDWARD J., Dooner's Hotel, Philadelphia, Pa.

DONOVAN, BRIG.-GEN. WILLIAM H., 155 Franklin St., Lawrence, Mass.

DUFFY, REV. FRANCIS P., 2317 Washington Ave., New York, N. Y.

DU PONT, GENERAL COLEMAN, Wilmington, Del.

DWYER, THOMAS, 601 West End Ave., New York City.

EGAN, JAMES F., 162 West 20th St., New York City.

FARLEY, JOHN F., Mutual Bldg. & Invst. Co., Cleveland, Ohio.

FARRELL, WILLIAM J., 115 Maiden Lane, New York City.

FARRELLY, STEPHEN, 9–15 Park Pl., New York City.

FITZGERALD, HON. JOHN F., 39 Welles Ave., Dorchester, Mass.

FERGUSON, THOMAS D., 520 Walnut St., Philadelphia, Pa.

FLYNN, COLONEL DAVID M., First National Bank, Princeton, N. J.
   (Vice-President of the Society for New Jersey.)

GALLAGHER, JOHN J., 21 E. 40th St., New York City.

GALLAGHER, M.D., 402 N. 146th St., New York City.

GALLAGHER, PATRICK, 1181 Broadway, New York City.

GAYNOR, PHILIP B., 165 Broadway, New York City.

GEOGHEGAN, JOSEPH G., 537 West Broadway, New York City.

GIBBONS, JOHN T., Cor. Poydras and South Peters Sts., New Orleans, La.

GILLESPIE, GEORGE J., 20 Vesey St., New York City.

HASSETT, HON. THOMAS, 730 Riverside Drive, New York City.

HENRY, CAPT. DOMINICK, 325 Central Park West, New York City.

HERBERT, PRESTON, 176 Broadway S, New York City.

HICKEY, JAMES G., United States Hotel, Boston, Mass.

HIGGINS, ROBERT, 4642 Lancaster Ave., Philadelphia, Pa.

JENKINS, HON. THEODORE F., 1100–1102 Franklin Bank Bldg., Philadelphia,
   Pa.

JOYCE, HENRY L., Pier 11, N. R., New York City.
   (Member of the Executive Council.)

KEARNS, PHILIP J., 2311 Concourse, New York City.

KEHOE, JOHN F., 2 Rector St., New York City.

KELLY, THOMAS HUGHES, 5 Beekman St.

KENNEDY, JEREMIAH JOSEPH, 52 Broadway, New York City.

KINNEY, TIMOTHY, Cokeville, Wyoming.

KNIGHTS OF ST. PATRICK, care of John Mulhern, Secretary, 182 Second St.,
   San Francisco, Cal.

KUSER, MRS. JOHN LOUIS, Fernbrook, Bordentown, N. J.

LEE, HON. THOMAS ZANSLAUR, LL.B., LL.D., 49 Westminster St., Providence, R. I.
> (Ex-President-General and Member of the Executive Council.) ·

LENEHAN, JOHN J., 192 Broadway, New York City.
> (Vice-President-General of the Society and Member of the Executive Council.)

LEVINS, ANNA FRANCES, 53 W. 39th St., New York City.
> (Official Photographer of the Society and Member of the Executive Council.)

LONERGAN, JOHN E., 211 Race St., Philadelphia, Pa.

McCAFFREY, WALTER A., 1711 North 4th St., Philadelphia, Pa.

McCAFFREY, WILLIAM A., 1836 North 4th St., Philadelphia, Pa.

McCALL, HON. EDWARD E., 165 Broadway, New York City.

McCLATCHEY, JOHN H., Merion, Pa.

McCONWAY, WILLIAM, Pittsburgh, Pa.

McDONNELL, PETER, 2 Battery Pl., New York City.

McGILLEN, JOHN, 105 South LaSalle St., Chicago, Ill.
> (Vice-President of the Society for Illinois.)

McGOWAN, FRANCIS P. A., 724 E. 12th St., New York City.

McGRAW, JAMES J., Ponca City, Okla.

McINTYRE, REV. WM. P., O.P., Editor *Rosary Magazine,* Somerset, Ohio.

McLOUGHLIN, JOSEPH F., 27 William St., New York City.

MAGRATH, PATRICK F., 244 Front St., Binghamton, N. Y.
> (Member of the Executive Council.)

MAHONEY, WILLIAM H., 1118 Broad St., Newark, N. J.

MALONEY, PETER J., 74 Broadway, New York City.

MEHAN, WILLIAM A., Ballston Spa, N. Y.

MITCHELL, HON. RICHARD H., 394 East 150th St., New York City.

MULCAHY, JOHN H., 623 West 34th St., New York City.

MULHERN, JOHN, 182 Second St., San Francisco, Cal.

MURPHY, COL. ERNEST VAN D., General Staff School, Ft. Leavenworth, Kans.

MURPHY, REV. TIMOTHY J., St. Michael's R. C. Church, Flint, Mich.

NEWELL, MRS. M. ALIDA, 438 Hope St., Providence, R. I.

NOLAN, JAMES J., 751 Columbus Ave., New York City.

O'BRIEN, WILLIAM J., M.D., 1765 Frankford Ave., Philadelphia, Pa.

O'CONNOR, MAJ. DANIEL, Wilmington, N. C.

O'CONNOR, MICHAEL P., Box 59, Narrowsburg, N. Y.

O'DONOHUE, CAPT. LOUIS V., 25 West 42d St., New York City.

O'FARRELL, HON. PATRICK ALOYSIUS, Vanderbilt Hotel, New York City.

OLCOTT, CHAUNCEY, 437 Fifth Ave., New York City.

O'NEIL, FRANK S., O'Neil Bldg., Binghamton, N. Y.

O'NEIL, HON. GEORGE F., Binghamton, N. Y.

O'NEILL, EUGENE M., Pittsburgh, Pa.

PHELAN, JAMES J., 50 Congress St., Boston, Mass.

PIGOTT, WILLIAM, Alaska Bldg., Seattle, Wash.
> (Vice-President of the Society for Washington.)

QUINLAN, FRANCIS J., A.M., M.D., LL.D., 66 West 52d St., New York City.
> (Ex-President-General and Member of the Executive Council.)

REILLY, THOMAS F., Bala, Pa.
ROGERS, REV. JOHN, 756 Mission St., San Francisco, Cal.
RYAN, JAMES J., 1130 North 40th St., Philadelphia, Pa.
RYAN, JAMES T., P. O. Box 1010, New York City.
RYAN, JOHN D., 3 East 78th St., New York City.
RYAN, MICHAEL P., 18 Boulevard, Rochelle Park, New Rochelle, N. Y.
RYAN, HON. THOMAS F., 858 Fifth Ave., New York City.
SASSEEN, ROBERT A., 165 Broadway, New York City.
SOMERS, PATRICK E., 35 Lagrange St., Worcester, Mass.
SPROULE, WILLIAM, Flood Bldg., San Francisco, Cal.
SULLIVAN, HON. MARK A., 23 Duncan Ave., Jersey City, N. J.
SULLIVAN, PATRICK, Casper, Wyo.
THOMPSON, FRANK BARTON, 127 West Main St., Louisville, Ky.
THOMPSON, JAMES PITKIN, 127 West Main St., Louisville, Ky.
TIERNEY, MYLES, 51 Newark St., Hoboken, N. J.
TROMBLY, HON. JOHN BRUNO, Altona, N. Y.
TROY, ROBERT P., 1776 Bush St., San Francisco, Cal.
    (Vice-President of the Society for California.)
WALSH, NICHOLAS F., 37 City Hall Pl, New York City.
WARD, J. V., Hollenden Hotel, Cleveland, Ohio.
WARNOCK, CATHERINE MURRAY, 6560 Harvard Ave., Chicago, Ill.

ANNUAL MEMBERS.

ADAMS, SAMUEL, 3rd and Westchester Ave., New York City.
ADAMS, T. ALBEUS, 525 West St., New York City.
ADAMS, THOMAS EVARTS, 25 West 57th St., New York City.
ADAMS, WILLIAM HERBERT, 489 Fifth Ave., New York City.
AHERN, LIEUT.-COL. GEORGE P., 1438 Belmont St., Washington, D. C.
AMBERG, JOHN H., 15 West Lake St., Chicago, Ill.
BAIRD, HENRY W., 66 Broadway, New York City.
BALDWIN, JAMES H., 18 Tremont St., Boston, Mass.
BALDWIN, JOHN E., 150th St. and Third Ave., New York City.
BANNON, HENRY G., 629 West 115th St., New York City.
BARRETT, ALFRED M., 165 Broadway, New York City.
    (Treasurer-General of the Society and Member of the Executive Coun-
    cil.)
BARRETT, ANTHONY J., 21 Convent Ave., New York City.
BARRETT, JOHN J., Hobart Bldg., San Francisco, Cal.
BARRY, HON. FRANK, Nogales, Ariz.
BARRY, JAMES H., 1122 Mission St., San Francisco, Cal.
BATTLE, HON. GEORGE GORDON, 37 Wall St., New York City.
BEALIN, JOHN J., 2334 Valentine Ave., New York City.
BERGEN, WALTER J., Wilmington, N. C.
BERGIN, PATRICK J., 81 Columbia Rd., Dorchester, Mass.
BIGHAM, DR. L T., 11 East 59th St., New York City.
BLACK, WILLIAM HARMON, 55 Liberty St., New York City.
BLAKE, JOHN J., 5 North 29th St., Richmond, Va.

BLAKE, MICHAEL, 149 Broadway, New York City.

BLISS, COL. ZENAS W., 171 Wesminster St., Providence, R. I.

BOHAN, OWEN W., 314 West 51st St., New York City.

BOLAND, W. I., Toronto, Canada.

BOUCHER, RICHARD P., M.D., 116 Academy Ave., Providence, R. I.

BOWE, AUGUSTINE J., R. 1239-127 N. Dearborn St., Chicago, Ill.

BOWES, EDWARD J., 1451 Broadway, New York City.

BOWLER, MICHAEL F., 4722 N. Talman Ave., Chicago, Ill.

BOYLE, HON. PATRICK J., Newport, R. I.

BOYLE, JNO, P., 6900 Sheriden Rd., Chicago, Ill.

BRADSHAW, SERGT RICHARD, Fort Pickens, Fla.

BRADY, DANIEL M., 95 Liberty St., New York City.

BRADY, JOHN EDSON, 165 Broadway, New York City.

BRADY, HON. JOSEPH P., 1634 West Grace St., Richmond, Va.

BRADY, OWEN J., 70 East 129th St., New York City.

BRANAGAN, WILLIAM I., Emmetsburg, Ia.

BRANSFIELD, MARK P., 1112 Chamber of Commerce Bldg., Chicago, Ill.

BREEN, HON. MATTHEW P., 115 Broadway, New York City.

BRENNAN, BERNARD G., 39th and Normal Aves., Chicago, Ill.

BRENNAN, REV. EDWARD J., Waterbury, Conn.

BRENNAN, HON. JAMES F., Peterborough, N. H.
   (Ex-Historiographer and Vice-President of the Society for New Hampshire.)

BRENNAN, JOHN J., 12 Elliot St., New Haven, Conn.

BRENNAN, JOSEPH P., 7 Plaza, Brooklyn, N. Y.

BRENNAN, REV. M. J., Henry, Ill.

BRENNAN, PATRICK, 4941 Drexel Blvd., Chicago, Ill.

BRENNAN, P. F., 34 Lincoln St., 34 Shamokin, Pa.

BRENNAN, P. J., 624 Madison Ave., New York City.

BRENNAN, THOMAS M., 215 East 39th St., New York City.

BRENNAN, REV. T. J., 418 Fifth Ave., San Rafael, Calif.

BRERETON, D. M., 121 Post St., San Francisco, Cal.

BRETT, FRANK P., 3 East Main St., Waterbury, Conn.

BRITT, PHILIP J., 27 William St., New York City.

BRITT, T. L. A., 271 Broadway, New York City.

BRODERICK, DAVID C., 51 Chambers St., New York City.

BRODERICK, J. JOYCE, 17 State St., New York City.

BRODERICK, WILLIAM J., 309 Bedford Pk. Boul., New York City.

BROPHY, HON. JOHN, Ridgefield, Conn.

BROPHY, WILLIAM H., Bisbee, Ariz.

BROSNAN, REV. JOHN, Cornwall-on-Hudson, N. Y.

BOURKE, RICHARD J., Peoples Bank Bldg., Scranton, Pa.

BROWN, HON. CALVIN L., Chief Justice Supreme Court of Minnesota, State Capitol, St. Paul, Minn.

BROWN, JOSHUA, Hermitage Club, Nashville, Tenn.
   (Vice-President of the Society for Tennessee.)

BUCKLEY, EDWARD, W. 230 5th Ave., New York City.

BUCKLEY, DR. E. W., 625 Lowry Bldg., St. Paul, Minn.

BUCKLEY, HOMER J., 605 South Clark St., Chicago, Ill.
BUCKLEY, JAMES R., 3521 Colnado Ave., Chicago, Ill.
BUCKLEY, JOHN J., 80 Maiden Lane, New York City.
BUCKLEY, JOHN, Elloam, Blaine Co., Mont.
BUCKLEY, PIERCE E., Public Library, Boston, Mass.
BURKE, REV. A., Battle Creek, Mich.
BURKE, EUGENE S., 20 Franklin St., Morristown, N. J.
BURKE, REV. EUGENE S., D.D., U. S. S. "Michigan" care of Postmaster, New York City.
BURKE, JAMES J., 12 W. 92d St., New York City.
BURKE, JOHN E., 418 Pembroke Ave., Norfolk, Va.
BURKE, DR. MARTIN, 147 Lexington Ave., New York City.
BURKE, ROBERT E., 1432 North LaSalle St., Chicago, Ill.
BURKE, THOMAS E., St. Charles, Ill.
BURKE, WALTER A., 19 Washington St., New York City.
BURKE, WILLIAM E., care of J. L. Carr, Esq., 1311 Rhode Island Ave., Washington, D. C.
BURKE, WILLIAM J., 271 Broadway, New York City.
BURNS, WILLIAM J., Woolworth Bldg., New York City.
BURR, WILLIAM P., 120 Broadway, New York City.
BUTLER, EDWARD J., 600 Pearl St., Elizabeth, N. J.
BUTLER, FRANCIS X., Office of Public Administrator, 148th St. and Third Ave., New York City.
BUTLER, PATRICK FRANCIS, M.D., 510 Commonwealth Ave., Boston, Mass.
BUTLER, WILLIAM, 55 John St., New York City.
BUTLER, WILLIAM E., 820 West 180th St., New York City.
BUTTIMER, THOMAS H., 18 Tremont St., Boston, Mass.
BYRNE, GERALD, Norfolk, Va.
BYRNE, JAMES L., 53 State St., Boston, Mass.
BYRNE, REV. JOSEPH, C. S. S. P., Ferndale, Darien, P. O., Conn.
BYRNE, THOMAS C., care of Byrne & Hammer Dry Goods Co., Omaha, Neb.
CAHILL, SANTIAGO P., 32 Nassau St., New York City.
  (Secretary-General of the Society and Member of the Executive Council.)
CAHILL, REV. WILLIAM F., St. Mary's Church, Riverside, Ill.
CALLAGHAN, HON. J. C., State Auditor, Phoenix, Ariz.
CALLAHAN, HON. CHRISTOPHER T., Judge of Superior Court, Holyoke, Mass.
CALLAHAN, D. J., Washington, D. C.
CALLAHAN, P. H., care of Louisville Varnish Co., Louisville, Ky.
CALLAN, JOSEPH P., 1010-12 First National Bk. Bldg., Milwaukee, Wis.
CAMPBELL, HON. RICHARD, 14 Wall St., New York City.
CANNON, THOMAS H., Stock Exchange Bldg., Chicago, Ill.
CAMPBELL, FRANCIS A., LL.D., 8 Beacon St., Boston, Mass.
CANTWELL, RT. REV. JOHN J., Los Angeles, Cal.
CAREY, PETER J., 97 Horatio St., New York City.
CAREY, THOMAS, Chamber of Commerce, Chicago, Ill.
CARMODY, MARTIN H., Grand Rapids, Mich.
CARMODY, T. F., 36 North Main St., Waterbury, Conn.
CARNEY, JOHN F., 118 East 235th St., New York City.

CARPENTER, MATT. H., 325 35th St., Milwaukee, Wis.
CARR, JAMES O., care of Rountree & Carr, Wilmington, N. C.
CARR, PATRICK R., 3508 South Western Ave., Chicago, Ill.
CARRIE, F. G., 41 West 62d St., New York City.
CARROLL, FRANCIS M., 68 Devonshire St., Boston, Mass.
CARROLL, JAMES T., 48 West Gay St., Columbus, Ohio.
CARROLL, MICHAEL, Gleason Bldg., Lawrence, Mass.
CARROLL, PIERRE G., 330 West 102d St., New York City.
CARRY, EDWARD F., 707 Railway Exchange, Chicago, Ill.
CARTY, JOHN J., Short Hills, N. J.
CASEY, HON. JAMES B., Lowell, Mass.
CARSON, JAMES T., 80 Broadway, New York City.
CASHIN, HON. MICHAEL P., Finance Department, St. Johns, Newfoundland.
CASHMAN, MICHAEL, Newburyport, Mass.
CASHMAN, MORRIS J., 53 State St., Boston, Mass.
CASHMAN, W. T., Guardian Bldg., Cleveland, Ohio.
CASSIDY, HARVEY B., 117 Market St., Syracuse, N. Y.
CASSIDY, JOHN J., 1610 West 14th St., Wilmington, Del.
    (Vice-President of the Society for Delaware.)
CASSIDY, GEN. PATRICK, M.D., Norwich, Conn.
    (Member of the Executive Council.)
CAVANAGH, HON. HOWARD W., 315 Ward Bldg., Battle Creek, Mich.
CAVANAUGH, F. J., 45 East 17th St., New York City.
CAVANAUGH, JAMES F., 20 Prospect St., Thompsonville, Conn.
CAVERLY, HON. JOHN R., 4336 Sheridan Rd., Chicago, Ill.
CHASE, H. FRANK, 241 West 101st St., New York City.
CHISHOLM, KENNETH O., The Wyoming, 55th St. and 7th Ave., New York
    City.
CHAMPION, D. J., 2490 Coventry Rd., Cleveland, Ohio.
CHRIMES, COMM. WALTER A. S., Sears Bldg., Boston, Mass.
CLAIR, FRANCIS R., 55 William St., New York City.
CLARE, WILLIAM F., 135 Broadway, Suite 916, New York City.
CLARK, EUGENE P., 1353 53d St., Brooklyn, N. Y.
CLARKE, JAMES, Aeolian Hall, New York City.
CLARKE, JOSEPH I. C., 159 West 95th St., New York City.
    (President-General of the Society and Member of the Executive Council.)
CLARKE, WILLIAM JOSEPH, 327 Central Pk. West, New York City.
CLARY, CHARLES H., Hallowell, Me.
CLINGEN, MRS. JULIA WARD, 329 N. Elmwood Ave., Oak Park, Ill.
CLUCAS, CHARLES, Fairfield, Conn.
COCHRAN, FRANK G., 110 Morningside Drive, New York City.
COFFEY, HON. JAMES, Internal Revenue Collector, Aberdeen, So. Dak.
COFFEY, JAMES C., 30 May St., Worcester, Mass.
COFFEY, JEREMIAH V., 2976 Washington St., San Francisco, Cal.
COGGINS, JEROME B., 1008 N. Saginaw St., Flint, Mich.
COGHLAN, REV. GERALD P., 2141 North Broad St., Philadelphia, Pa.
COHALAN, HON. DANIEL F., County Court House, Manhattan, New York City.
    (Member of the Executive Council.)

COHALAN, HON. JOHN P., 706 St. Nicholas Ave., New York City.
COKELEY, WILLIAM A., 3150 E. Tremont Ave., Bronx, New York City.
COLBY, BAINBRIDGE, 32 Nassau St., New York City.
COLLINS, WILLIAM, 1916 East 89th St., Cleveland, Ohio.
COMINSKEY, CHARLES H., 3816 Michigan Ave., Chicago, Ill.
CONATY, REV. B. S., 596 Cambridge St., Pittsfield, Mass.
CONBOY, MARTIN, 27 Pine St., New York City.
CONDON, P. JOSEPH, Binghamton, N. Y.
CONDON, T. J., 123½ South 5th St., Springfield, Ill.
CONDON, RICHARD F., 2835 Pine Grove Ave., Chicago, Ill.
CONEY, CAPTAIN PATRICK H., 316 Kansas Ave., Topeka, Kan.
    (Vice-President of the Society for Kansas.)
CONNELL, J. COTTER, 35 Nassau St., New York City.
CONNELL, W. F., 16 Court St., Brooklyn, N. Y.
CONNELLY, CORNELIUS E., 252 Court St., Binghamton, N. Y.
CONNELLY, JOHN M., 258 State St., Elmira, N. Y.
CONNELLY, L. J., Captain, U. S. Navy, U. S. Receiving Ship, Bay Ridge,
    Brooklyn, N. Y.
CONNERS, HON. WM. J., Buffalo, N. Y.
CONNERY, JOHN T., 1804 McCormick Bldg., Chicago, Ill.
CONNERY, JOSEPH F., 2028 Washington Boul., Chicago, Ill.
CONNERY, WILLIAM P., 506 Western Ave., Lynn, Mass.
CONNOLLY, REV. ARTHUR T., 365 Center St., Roxbury, Mass.
CONNOLLY, CAPT. GEORGE F., Presidio, San Francisco, Cal.
CONNOLLY, HON. JAMES C., 120 Broad St., Elizabeth, N. J.
CONNOLLY, REV. M. D., 221 Valley St., San Francisco, Cal.
CONNOLLY, THOMAS F. J., 126 N. Main St., Port Chester, N. Y.
CONNOR, HON. HENRY GROVES, Wilson, N. C.
CONROY, JAMES F. Flushing, N. Y.
CONROY, MICHAEL J., Boston City Library, Boston, Mass.
CONWAY, JAMES J., 117 East Washington St., Ottawa, Ill.
CONWAY, JAMES P., 296 East Third St., Brooklyn, N. Y.
CONWAY, PATRICK J., 1187 Lexington Ave., New York City.
CONWAY, HON. THOMAS F., 32 Nassau St., New York City.
CONWAY, WILLIAM H., Springfield, Ill.
CONWELL, JAMES, 511 Unity Bldg., Chicago, Ill.
COONEY, BRIG.-GEN. MICHAEL, U. S. A., 1326 Irving St., Washington, D. C.
COONEY, TERENCE, JR., Pittsfield, Mass.
COONEY, THOMAS F., 401 Grosvenor Bldg., Providence, R. I.
CORCORAN, CORNELIUS J., Lawrence, Mass.
    (Vice-President of the Society for Massachusetts.)
COTTER, JAMES E., 412 Sears Bldg., Boston, Mass.
CORR, COL. PETER H., Taunton, Mass.
CORR, JOHN J., 502 Atlantic St.. Bridgeport, Conn.
COSGROVE, JOHN J., 4 Weybosset St., Providence, R. I.
COUGHLIN, HON. JOHN T., Fall River, Mass.
COUGHLIN, MICHAEL J., 178 Bedford St., Fall River, Mass.
COWAN, HON. JOHN F., 62 East 130th St., New York City.

Cox, Hugh M., M.D., 285 St. Nicholas Ave., New York City.

Cox, Michael H., 4 Goden St., Belmont, Mass.

Cox, William T., 12 South 2d St., Elizabeth, N. J.

Coyle, Rev. James, Taunton, Mass.

Coyle, John G., M.D., 220 East 31st St., New York City.
    (Member of the Executive Council.)

Coyle, Miss May, 700 Columbia Rd., Dorchester, Mass.

Cranitch, William, 250 East 207th St., New York City.

Crew, John E., 1225 Euclid Ave., Cleveland, Ohio.

Crimmins, Capt. Martin L., Presidio of San Francisco, Cal.

Cronin, Cornelius, 320 Fifth St., East Liverpool, Ohio.

Cronin, Con P., Librarian, State Law & Legislative Reference Library,
    State House, Phoenix, Ariz.

Croston, J. F., M.D., 83 Emerson St., Haverhill, Mass.

Crowe, Bartholomew, Spring Valley, N. Y.

Crowford, Hon. Henry P., Greenwich, Conn.

Crowley, Harry T., 91 Essex Ave., Orange, N. J.

Crowley, J. B., 86 Third St., San Francisco, Cal.

Crowley, Patrick H., 301 Congress St., Boston, Mass.

Cruikshank, Alfred B., 43 Cedar St., New York City.

Culbert, Dr. Robert R., 373 S. Huntington Ave., Boston, Mass.

Cummins, Rev. John F., Roslindale, Mass.

Cunningham, Henry J., Cambridge, Mass.

Cunningham, Owen Augustine, 253 Devonshire St., Boston, Mass.

Curley, Hon. James M., Boston, Mass.

Curley, John J., 52 Winthrop St., Boston, Mass.

Curran, Philip A., Curran Dry Goods Company, Waterbury, Conn.

Curry, Francis A., 38 Park Row, New York City.

Curtin, Thomas Hayes, M.D., 391 East 149th St., New York City.

Cusack, Thomas, 6548 Washington Boul., Chicago, Ill.

Cushnahan, Rev. P. M., St. Joseph's Catholic Church, Ogden, Utah.

Dady, Col. M. J., Hotel St. George, Brooklyn, N. Y.

Dailey, James M., 549 West 31st St., Chicago, Ill.

Dailey, Miss Margaret F., 204 Columbia Hgts., Brooklyn, N. Y.

Daly, Charles T., 11 Monument St., West Medford, Mass.

Daly, Edward Hamilton, 52 Wall St., New York City.
    (Ex-Secretary-General and Member of the Executive Council.)

Daly, J. C., 3718 Clifton Ave., Chicago, Ill.

Daly, John J., 212 Lenox Ave., Westfield, N. J.

Daly, John S., 51 Chambers St., New York City.

Daly, T. A., *Catholic Standard and Times*, Washington Square, Philadelphia,
    Pa.

Daly, William J., 820 Tremont Bldg., Boston, Mass.

Danaher, Hon. Franklin M., Bensen Bldg., Albany, N. Y.

D'Arcy, James, Rome, Georgia.

Davies, J. Clarence, 3d Ave. and 149th St., Bronx, New York City.

Davitt, John B., 314 Page St., San Francisco, Cal.

Dawson, Thomas J., 945 Argyle St., Chicago, Ill.

DAY, ARTHUR, 99 John St., New York City.
DAYTON, CHARLES W., JR., 27 William St., New York City.
DEASY, HON. DANIEL C., Hall of Justice, San Francisco, Cal.
DEASY, JEREMIAH, 182 2nd St., San Francisco, Cal.
DELANEY, VERY REV. JOSEPH A., Rector Cathedral of Albany, 12 Madison
    Pl., Albany, N. Y.
DELANY, PATRICK BERNARD, E.E., Derrymore, Nantucket, Mass.
DELANY, VERY REV. WILLIAM, S.J., Saint Ignatius Hall, 35 Lower Leeson
    St., Dublin, Ireland.
DELEHANTY, HON. F. B., 32 Chambers St., New York City.
DEMPSEY, GEORGE C., Lowell, Mass.
DEMPSEY, WILLIAM P., care of Dempsey Bleach & Dye Co., Pawtucket, R. I.
DENNEN, REV. CHRISTOPHER, St. Thomas Church, Wilmington, N. C.
DEROO, REV. PETER, 1127 Corbett St., Portland, Ore.
DESMOND, HON. HUMPHREY J., 818–819 Wells Bldg., Milwaukee, Wis.
DESMOND, ROBERT EMMET, 11 Main St., San Francisco, Cal.
DEVLIN, JAMES H., JR., 11 Menlo St., Brighton, Mass.
DEVLIN, HON. JOSEPH, Alashiel House Mt. Royal, Bangor, Ireland.
DEVLIN, PATRICK J., Matawan, N. J.
DICKSON, ROBERT, Parker, Ariz.
DIGNAN, J. H., 76 Palm Ave., San Francisco, Cal.
DILLON, JAMES E., 510 East 87th St., New York City.
DILWORTH, PATRICK AUGUSTIN, Opt.D., 744 Lexington Ave., New York City.
DINNEEN, THOMAS, Ogdensburg, N. Y.
DIXON, GEORGE W., 425 S. Wells St., Chicago, Ill.
DIXON, HON. WARREN, 1 Montgomery St., Jersey City, N. J.
DOHERTY, DR. WILLIAM B., Louisville, Ky.
DOHERTY, HENRY A., 1 Washington St., Boston, Mass.
DOLAN, THOMAS S., 874 Broadway, New York City.
DONAHUE, DAN A., 178 Essex St., Salem, Mass.
DONAHUE, RT. REV. PATRICK JAMES, D.D., 13th and Bryon Sts., Wheeling,
    W. Va.
    (Vice-President of the Society for West Virginia.)
DONAHUE, R. J., Ogdensburg, N. Y.
    (Member of the Executive Council.)
DONELAN, DR. T. P., Springfield, Ill.
DONNELLY, GEORGE B., 917 Chestnut St., Philadelphia, Pa.
DONNELLY, JAMES F., 41 Park Row, N. Y.
DONNELLY, MATTHEW, 5134 North Broad St., Philadelphia, Pa.
DONNELLY, HON. THOMAS F., 51 Chambers St., New York City.
DONOVAN, CORNELIUS, 1160 Broadway, New York City.
DONOVAN, COL. HENRY F., 179 West Washington St., Chicago, Ill.
DONOVAN, HERBERT D. A., PH.D., 121 Decatur St., Brooklyn, N. Y.
DONOVAN, JAMES, Potsdam, N. Y.
DONOVAN, HON. JEREMIAH, South Norwalk, Conn.
DONOVAN, JOHN JOSEPH, 1210 Garden St., Bellingham, Wash.
DONOVAN, MRS. NELLIE McM., 219 Cole St., San Francisco, Cal.
DONOVAN, DR. S. E., 8 Wing St., New Bedford, Mass.

DONOVAN, THOMAS F., Young Bldg., Joliet, Ill.

DOOLEY, REV. JOHN, 535 West 121st St., New York City.

DOONER, THOMAS FRANCIS, Dooner's Hotel, Philadelphia, Pa.

DORAN, JAMES P., Masonic Bldg., New Bedford, Mass.

DORAN, PATRICK L., Symus Utah Grocer Company, Salt Lake City, Utah.

DOWER, REV. WILLIAM J., 89 Briggs Ave., Pittsfield, Mass.

DOUGHERTY, PATRICK, 1310 North Broad St., Philadelphia, Pa.

DOWLING, RT. REV. AUSTIN, 226 Summit Ave., St. Paul, Minn.

DOWLING, HON. VICTOR J., 25th St. and Madison Ave., New York City.

DOWNING, HON. BERNARD, 195 Monroe St., New York City.

DOWNING, D. P., care of National Biscuit Company, Cambridge, Mass.

DOYLE, ALFRED L., of John F. Doyle & Sons, 41 Pine St., New York City.

DOYLE, AUSTIN J., Schilles Bldg., Chicago, Ill.

DOYLE, JAMES G., *The Herald*, Chicago, Ill.

DOYLE, JOHN F., 41 Pine St., New York City.

DOYLE, JOSEPH, 18 Tremont St., Boston, Mass.

DOYLE, HON. LEO J., 1038 Loyola Ave., Chicago, Ill.

DOYLE, WILLIAM A., 3220 Washington Boul., Chicago, Ill.

DOYLE, WILLIAM F., 355 Hancock St., Brooklyn, N. Y.

DOYLE, HON. WILLIAM J., Katonah, N. Y.

DREW, FRANK C., 515 Balboa Bldg., San Francisco, Cal.

DRISCOLL, DENNIS F., 7 Pine St., New York City.

DRISCOLL, MICHAEL J., 271 Broadway, New York City.

DUFFICY, PETER J., 120 West 59th St., New York City.

DUFFY, HON. FRANK, Nogales, Ariz.

DUFFY, THOMAS J., 496 Linwood Ave., Columbus, Ohio.

DULIN, J. T., 111 South Hawk St., Albany, N. Y.

DUNNE, HON. EDWARD F., Conway Bldg., Chicago, Ill.

DUNNE, FINLEY PETER, 122 East 55th St., New York City.

DUNNE, F. L., 328 Washington St., Boston, Mass.

DUNNE, JAMES, 51 Chambers St., New York City.

DUNNE, JOHN P., Prescott, Ont., Can.

DUNNE, REV. JAMES K., 1316 Second Ave., Seattle, Wash.

DUNNE, MISS M. M., 2165 Mance St., Montreal, Can.

DUNN, J. PETER, 261 Broadway, New York City.

DURKIN, JOHN J., 401 West 59th St., New York City.

DUROSS, JAMES E., 100 Broadway, New York City.

DUSSAULT, DR. N. A., 28 Ursule St., Quebec, Can.

DUVAL, C. LOUIS, Pier 39 N. R., New York City.

DUVAL, G. HOWARD, Pier 80, N. R., New York City.

DWYER, W. D., 202 Despatch Bldg., St. Paul, Minn.

DWYER, REV. WILLIAM M., Cathedral Rectory, Syracuse, N. Y.

ELLIOTT, DR. GEORGE W., 116 Spring St., Portland, Me.

ELLIS, CAPT. W. T., Owensboro, Ky.

ELLISON, HON. WILLIAM B., 251 West 104th St., New York City.

EMMET, ROBERT, Moreton Paddox, Warwick, England.

ENNIS, MISS MARY G., 31 First Pl., Brooklyn, N. Y.

ENRIGHT, M. H., 3242 Warren Ave., Chicago, Ill.

ENRIGHT, PATRICK, 4530 North Albany Ave., Chicago, Ill.

ENRIGHT, THOMAS J., 412 Fletcher St., Lowell, Mass.

EUSTACE, MISS JENNIE A., Victoria Apartments, 97th St. and Riverside Drive, New York City.

EUSTACE, MARK S., Boonton, N. J.

FAHERTY, MICHAEL J., 2735 Pine Grove Ave., Chicago, Ill.

FAHY, THOMAS A., 1609 N. 10 St., Philadelphia, Pa.

FAHY, WALTER THOMAS, 607 Lincoln Bldg., Philadelphia, Pa.

FALAHEE, JOHN J., 120 West 59th St., New York City.

FARRELL, JOHN T., M.D., 1488 Westminster St., Olneyville Station, Providence, R. I.

FARLEY, RICHARD H., 9 Broadway, New York City.

FARRELLY, FRANK T., 25 Fort St., Springfield, Mass.

FARRELLY, T. CHARLES, 9 Park Pl., New York City.

FEELEY, WILLIAM J., 203 Eddy St., Providence, R. I.

FENLON, JOHN T., 55 Liberty St., New York City.

FENNESSY, RICHARD F., Postmaster, Danvers, Mass.

FINLEY, JAMES D., Board of Trade, Norfolk, Va.

FINN, REV. THOMAS J., St. Mary's Rectory, Norwalk, Conn.

FINN, RICHARD J., 1217 Ashland Block, Chicago, Ill.

FINNEGAN, P. J., 536 Rookery Bldg., Chicago, Ill.

FITZGERALD, DANIEL E., 2442 North Albany Ave., Chicago, Ill.

FITZGERALD, DESMOND, Brookline, Mass.

FITZGERALD, HON. JAMES, 149 East 79th St., New York City.

FITZGERALD, HON. JAMES REGAN, 163 East 83d St., New York City.

FITZGERALD, JOHN E., 7 Carroll St., Hammond, Ind.

FITZGERALD, MISS MARCELLA A., P. O. Box 52, Gilroy, Cal.

FITZGERALD, THOMAS B., Elmira, N. Y.

FITZGERALD, HON. WILLIAM T. A., Court House, Boston, Mass.

FITZGIBBON, JOHN C., 431 Fifth Ave., New York City.

FITZPATRICK, FREDERICK F., 30 Church St., New York City.

FITZPATRICK, JAMES C., 244 West Broad St., Tamaqua, Pa.

FITZPATRICK, JAY, 321 Bedford Pk. Boul., New York City.

FITZPATRICK, REV. MALLICK J., 375 Lafayette St., New York City.

FLAHERTY, JAMES A., 714 Hale Bldg., Philadelphia, Pa.

FLANAGAN, MICHAEL J., 41 Pacific St., Bridgeport, Conn.

FLANIGAN, JOHN, 3rd Ave. and 150th St., New York City.

FLEMING, COL. PHILIP B., R. 710, U. S. Army Bldg., Whitehall St., New York City.

FLEMING, JAMES W., Keenan Bldg., Troy, N. Y.

FLEMING, JOHN J., 415 Tama Bldg., Burlington, Ia.

FLEMING, JAMES D., 127 Ferry St., Troy, N. Y.

FLEMING, REV. T. RAYMOND, Harbor Beach, Mich.

FLETCHER, WILLIAM, Box 49, R. F. D., Canaan, N. Y.

FLYNN, STEPHEN, LL.D., 145 Moore St., Lowell, Mass.

FLYNN, THOMAS A., Phoenix, Ariz.

FLYNN, THOMAS P., 133 West Washington St., Chicago, Ill.

FOLEY, DANIEL, 108 North Delaware St., Indianapolis, Ind.

FOLEY, CAPT. DANIEL P., The Cairo, Washington, D. C.
FORD, MRS. M. H., 1837 Main St., Bridgeport, Conn.
FOX, WILLIAM E., Mercantile Library Bldg., Cincinnati, Ohio.
FRANKS, JACOB, 5052 Ellis Ave., Chicago, Ill.
FRAWLEY, HON. JAMES, 180 East 95th St., New York City.
FRAWLEY, MISS JOSEPHINE, 180 East 95th St., New York City.
GAFFNEY, HON. T. ST. JOHN, care of Michael Francis Doyle, Land Title
    Bldg., Philadelphia, Pa.
GALLAGHER, CHARLES H., 11 Riverdrive Ave., Trenton, N. J.
GALLAGHER, DANIEL P., 39 West 128th St., New York City.
GALLAGHER, JAMES, Cleveland, N. Y.
GALLAGHER, JAMES T., M.D., 20 Monument Sq., Charlestown, Mass.
GALLAGHER, T. F., 165 South Water St., Chicago, Ill.
GALLIGAN, JOHN JOSEPH, M.D., Cullen Hotel, Salt Lake City, Utah.
    (Vice-President of the Society for Utah.)
GALVIN, TIMOTHY P., Valparaiso, Ind.
GAMBLE, HON. ROBERT JACKSON, Yankton, South Dakota.
    (Vice-President of the Society for South Dakota.)
GANNON, FRANK S., 55 Liberty St., New York City.
GANNON, FRANK S., JR., 2 Rector St., New York City.
    (Member of the Executive Council.)
GARDE, JOSEPH A., 95 Hillside Ave., Waterbury, Conn.
GAREY, EUGENE F., 119 Forrest Ave., Rockford, Ill.
GAREY, EUGENE L., 208 South La Salle St., Chicago, Ill.
GARLAND, LOUIS P., Revenue Agent's Office, Boston, Mass.
GARRITY, HENRY, 425 Fifth Ave., New York City.
GARVAN, HON. FRANCIS P., 115 Broadway, New York City.
GARVEY, RICHARD, JR., 527 Riverside Drive, New York City.
GAVEGAN, HON. EDWARD J., 51 Chambers St., New York City.
GAVIN, JOSEPH E., Erie County Bank Bldg., Buffalo, N. Y.
GAVIN, RICHARD I., 127 North Dearborn St., Chicago, Ill.
GELSHENEN, WILLIAM H., 81 Fulton St., New York City.
GENTLEMEN'S SODALITY OF ST. IGNATIUS CHURCH, Hayes and Shrader Sts.,
    San Francisco, Cal.
GEOGHEGAN, CHARLES A., 537 West Broadway, New York City.
GIBBONS, MICHAEL, Cullen Hotel, Salt Lake City, Utah.
GIBLIN, JOHN A., 10 East Main St., Ilion, N. Y.
GILL, JAMES, 376 Twelfth St., Brooklyn, N. Y.
GILLERAN, HON. THOMAS, 49 Chambers St., New York City.
GILLESPIE, MRS. M. V., 15a Farwell Place, Cambridge, Mass.
GILMAN, JOHN E., 43 Hawkins St., Boston, Mass.
GILPATRIC, HON. WALTER J., Mayor of Saco, Me.
GLEASON, JOHN H., 25 North Pearl St., Albany, N. Y.
GLEASON, JOSEPH F., 105 Fulton St., New York City.
GLEESON, WILLIAM A., Torrington, Conn. ·
GLYNN, HON. MARTIN H., Albany, N. Y.
GODKIN, LAWRENCE, 26 Liberty St., New York City.
GOFF, HON. JOHN W., 319 West 104th St., New York City.

GORMAN, JAMES E., 4901 Sheridan Road, Chicago, Ill.
GORMAN, JOHN F., Stephen Girard Bldg., Philadelphia, Pa.
GORMAN, PATRICK F., Alexandria, Va.
GORMAN, PATRICK, 599 East 134th St., New York City.
GORMLEY, JAMES J., 916 St. Marks Ave., Brooklyn, N. Y.
GOURLEY, HON. WILLIAM B., Paterson, N. J.
GRACE, HON. JOHN P., Mayor of Charleston, S. C.
GRACE, JOSEPH P., 7 Hanover Square, New York City.
GRAHAM, HON. JAMES M., Springfield, Ill.
GRAHAM, WILLIAM J., 3232 South Park Ave., Chicago, Ill.
GRIFFIN, REV. E. J., Governor's Island, N. Y.
GRIFFIN, JOHN C., Skowhegan, Me.
GRIFFIN, STEPHEN D., 9335 West Adams St., Chicago, Ill.
GRIMES, RT. REV. JOHN, Syracuse, N. Y.
    (Vice-President of the Society for New York.)
GUERIN, HON. M. HENRY, County Bldg., Chicago, Ill.
GUERIN, HON. JAMES J., M.D. 4 Edgehill Ave., Montreal, Canada.
GUILFOILE, FRANCIS P., Waterbury, Conn.
GURRY, THOMAS F., care of Orinoko Mills, 215–219 Fourth Ave., New York
    City.
HAAREN, JOHN H., 284 Kingston Ave., Brooklyn, N. Y.
HACKETT, J. D., 2 East 23rd St., New York City.
HAGERTY, C. H., District Passenger Agt., Pa. Lines, Todd Bldg., Louisville,
    Ky.
HAGERTY, JAMES B., 517 Duboce Ave., San Francisco, Cal.
HAGGERTY, J. HENRY, 50 South St., New York City.
HALL, ROSS C., 309 South Scoville Ave., Oak Park, Ill.
HALLERAN, HON. JOHN J., 31 16th St., Browne Park, Flushing, N. Y.
HALLEY, CHARLES V., 756 East 175th St., New York City.
HALLEY, WILLIAM P. J., 139 North Clark St., Chicago, Ill.
HALLINAN, JAMES T., 35 Nassau St., New York City.
HALLORAN, JOHN H., 213 6th Ave., New York City.
HALLORAN, WILLIAM J., 309 Main St., Salt Lake City, Utah.
HALTIGAN, PATRICK J., Reading Clerk, House of Representatives, Washing-
    ton, D. C.
HAMILL, HON. JAMES A., 239 Washington St., Jersey City, N. J.
HANECY, HON. ELBRIDGE, 3116 Michigan Ave., Chicago, Ill.
HANLEY, MISS SARAH E., 27 East 72d St., New York City.
HANLON, P. J., 613 Paul-Jones Bldg., Louisville, Ky.
HANNA, MOST REV. EDWARD J., 1100 Franklin St., San Francisco, Cal.
HANNA, WILLIAM WILSON. Hotel Majestic, Philadelphia, Pa.
HANNAN, MISS FRANCES, 523 Stratford Pl., Chicago, Ill.
HANNAN, THOMAS F. J., Chappaqua, N. Y.
HANNIGAN, JOHN E., 206 Barrister's Hall, Boston, Mass.
HARDING, JOHN P., 19 North Clark St., Chicago, Ill.
HARKINS, RT. REV. MATTHEW, D.D., 30 Fenner St., Providence, R. I.
HARNEY, JOHN M., Item Bldg., Lynn, Mass.
HARRIGAN, JOHN F., 66 High St., Worcester, Mass.

HARRIGAN, DR. JOSEPH D., 114 Willett St., Jamaica, N. Y.
HARRIMAN, PATRICK H., M.D., Norwich, Conn.
HARRINGTON, DANIEL E., Postmaster, Saratoga Springs, N. Y.
HARRIS, HON. CHARLES M., 120 East 72d St., New York City.
HARRIS, WILLIAM L., M.D., 532 Broad St., Providence, R. I.
HART, LUKE E., 1201 La Salle Bldg., St. Louis, Mo.
HARTY, JOHN F., Savannah, Ga.
HASSETT, REV. PATRICK D., Watsonville, Cal.
HATTON, JOHN, 542 Winfield Ave., Philadelphia, Pa.
HAYDEN, J. EMMET, 1 Carl St., San Francisco, Cal.
HAYES, JOHN, 6421 University Ave., Chicago, Ill.
HAYES, HON. NICHOLAS J., 164 East 111th St., New York City.
HAYES, COL. PATRICK E., Pawtucket, R. I.
HAYES, MOST REV. PATRICK J., 452 Madison Ave., New York City.
HEALY, HON. EDMUND J., Bay View Ave., Far Rockaway, N. Y.
HEALY, JOHN F., Huntington, W. Va.
HEALY, JOHN J., 2728 Pine Grove Ave., Chicago, Ill.
HEALY, REV. PATRICK J., Catholic University, Washington, D. C.
    (Vice-President of the Society for District of Columbia.)
HEALY, RICHARD, 188 Institute Road, Worcester, Mass.
HEALY, THOMAS, Columbus Ave. and 66th St., New York City.
HEALY, THOMAS F., 66th St. and Broadway, New York City.
HEALY, THOMAS J., 1048 West Garfield Boul., Chicago, Ill.
HEELAN, REV. EDMOND, Sacred Heart Church, Fort Dodge, Ia.
HEFFERMAN, REV. DANIEL J., 327 Gorham St., Lowell, Mass.
HENNESSY, JOSEPH P., 642 Crotona Park So., Bronx, New York City.
HEPBURN, BARRY H., Franklin Bank Bldg., Philadelphia, Pa.
HEPBURN, W. HORACE, JR., Franklin Bank Bldg., Philadelphia, Pa.
HERBERT, VICTOR, 321 West 108th St., New York City.
HERNAN, J. J., Hotel del Coronado, Coronado Beach, Cal.
HICKEY, JOHN J., 8 East 129th St., New York City.
HIGGINS, JAMES J., 171st St., Elizabeth, N. J.
HIGGINS, J. FRANK, 1020 South Second St., Springfield, Ill.
HINES, EDWARD, 2431 South Lincoln St., Chicago, Ill.
HOBAN, RT. REV., M. J., D.D., Scranton, Pa.
HOEY, HON. JAMES J., 65 Central Park West, New York City.
HOFF, JOSEPH S., 56 Nassau Block, Princeton, N. J.
HOGAN, HON. JOHN J., 53 Central St., Lowell, Mass.
HOGAN, JOHN PHILIP, 17 East 11th St., N. Y.
HOGAN, M. E., Hogan Bank Co., Altamont, Ill.
HOGAN, MICHAEL S., 4903 13th Ave., Brooklyn, N. Y.
HOGAN, THOMAS F., Junction City, Kan.
HOGAN, WILLIAM A., 95 Stevens St., Lowell, Mass.
HOPKINS, GEORGE A., 27 William St., New York City.
HOPKINS, MISS J. A., 3236 Michigan Ave., Chicago, Ill.
HOPKINS, M. HOPKINS, 3150 South Michigan Ave., Chicago, Ill.
HOPKINS, MISS SARA M., 4340 Washington Boul., Garfield Park Station,
    Chicago, Ill.

HORIGAN, HON. CORNELIUS, 229–231 Main St., Biddeford, Me.
HOWLETT, JOHN, 49 Portland St., Boston, Mass.
HOYE, CHARLES T., 10 High St., Boston, Mass.
HUGHES, MARTIN, Hibbing, Minn.
HUGHES, PATRICK L., 454 West 14th St., New York City.
HUBBARD, H. WARREN, 47 West 34th St., New York City.
HUGHES, REV. WILLIAM F., D.D., 144 West 90th St., New York City.
HUNTER, FREDERICK C., 80 Maiden Lane, New York City.
HURLEY, JAMES H., 301 Union Trust Bldg., Providence, R. I.
HURLEY, JAMES F., 55–57 Franklin St., New York City.
HURLEY, HON. JOHN F., Salem, Mass.
HURLEY, TIMOTHY J., 3653 Grand Boul., Chicago, Ill.
HURST, WILLIAM H., 26 Beaver St., New York City.
HUSSEY, D. B., 815 Federal Reserve Bank Bldg., St. Louis, Mo.
HUSSEY, EDWARD J., Vice-President Commercial Bank, Albany, N. Y.
HYNES, THOMAS W., 1332 Pacific St., Brooklyn, N. Y.
IGOE, HON. MICHAEL L., 5434 Cornell Ave., Chicago, Ill.
IRVING, HON. JOHN J., Mayor, Binghamton, N. Y.
JACKSON, CHARLES A., Waterbury, Conn.
JAMES, JOHN W., JR., 603 Carlton Road, Westfield, N. J.
JENKINSON, RICHARD C., 289 Washington St., Newark, N. J.
JENNINGS, MICHAEL J., 753 Third Ave., New York City.
JENNINGS, THOMAS C., 1834 East 55th St., Cleveland, Ohio.
JOHNSON, ALFRED J., Room 1409, Hotel Plaza, New York City.
JOHNSON, MRS. MARY H., care of Humboldt State Bank, Humboldt, Ia.
JONES, PAUL, 38 Park Row, New York City.
JONES, HON. RICHARD J., Mayor, Sebring, Ohio.
JORDAN, MICHAEL J., 30 State St., Boston, Mass.
JOYCE, BERNARD J., 45 Grover Ave., Winthrop Highlands, Boston, Mass.
JOYCE, JOHN F., 20 Vesey St., New York City.
JUDGE, JOHN H., 261 Broadway, New York City.
JUDGE, PATRICK J., Holyoke, Mass.
JOYCE, MRS. MARY E., 718 St. Nicholas Ave., New York City.
KANE, MAURICE, 606 Michigan Ave., Chicago, Ill.
KAVANAGH, HON. MARCUS, County Bldg., Chicago, Ill.
KEARNS, BERNARD T., 68th St., and East River, New York City.
KEARNS, HON. HUGH J., 206 South Hamlin Ave., Chicago, Ill.
KEEFE, PATRICK H., M.D., 257 Benefit St., Providence, R. I.
KEEFE, REV. WILLIAM A., St. John's Church, Plainfield, Conn.
KEEGAN, DR. EDWARD, St. John's, Newfoundland.
KEELEY, JAMES, The Herald, Chicago, Ill.
KEENA, MISS MARY A., 48 West 84th St., New York City.
KEENAN, FRANK, 1911 Hillcrest Road, Hollywood, Cal.
KEENAN, JOHN J., P. O. Box 45, Boston, Mass.
KEENAN, THOMAS J., 709 Peoples Trust Co. Bldg., Binghamton, N. Y.
KEHOE, MICHAEL P., Law Bldg., Baltimore, Md.
    (Vice-President of the Society for Maryland.)
KEIGHER, EDWARD PATRICK, 126 North Austin Ave., Oak Park, Ill.

KELLEHER, DANIEL, 1116 Spring St., Seattle, Wash.

KELLER, JOSEPH W., 271 Broadway, New York City.

KELLEY, COMMANDER JAMES DOUGLASS JERROLD, 25 East 83d St., New York City.

KELLEY, JOHN E., 60 Broadway, New York City.

KELLY, DANIEL E., 62 Washington St., Valparaiso, Ind.

KELLY, DENNIS F., 1 North State St., Chicago, Ill.

KELLY, GERTRUDE B., M.D., 507 Madison Ave., New York City.

KELLY, HON. JOHN E., Register, U. S. Land Office, Pierre, South Dakota.

KELLY, JOSEPH THOMAS, 275 Lombard St., New Haven, Conn.

KELLY, P. J., Main St., Buffalo, N. Y.

KENAH, JOHN F., Elizabeth, N. J.

KENEDY, ARTHUR, 44 Barclay St., New York City.

KENNEDY, CHARLES F., Brewer, Me.

KENNEDY, DANIEL, Elmira, N. Y.

KENNEDY, JAMES F., 8 South Dearborn St., Chicago, Ill.

KENNEDY, JOHN J., 2925 Briggs Ave., New York City.

KENNEDY, HON. M. F., 32 Broad St.,Charleston, S. C.

KENNEDY, THOMAS F., Amsterdam, N. Y.

KENNEDY, WALTER G., M.D., 621 Dorchester St. W., Montreal, Canada.

KENNEDY, PATRICK H., 57 Broad St., Charleston, S. C.

KENNELLY, BRYAN L., 156 Broadway, New York City.

KENNEY, DAVID T., Plainfield, N. J.

KEOGAN, P. J., N. Y. Athletic Club, New York City.

KEOGH, THOMAS F., 233 Broadway, New York City.

KERBY, JOHN E., Tremont and Arthur Ave., New York City.

KERNEY, JAMES, 373 State St., Trenton, N. J.

KENNY, REV. MICHAEL, S.J., Loyola University, New Orleans, La.
(Vice-President of the Society for Louisiana.)

KERR, ROBERT BAGE, 74 Broadway, New York City.

KIERNAN, PATRICK, 200 West 72d St., New York City.

KIERNAN, PETER D., Arkay Bldg., Albany, N. Y.

KIGGEN, JOHN A., 125 West St., Hyde Park, Mass.

KILLEEN, HENRY W., 734 Richmond Ave., Buffalo, N. Y.

KILLION, BERNARD J., 18 Tremont St., Boston, Mass.

KILMARTIN, THOMAS J., M.D., Waterbury, Conn.

KILROE, EDWIN P., 51 East 42nd St., New York City.

KING, HON. JOHN T., 110 Waldemere Ave., Bridgeport, Conn.

KING, PERCY J., 52 Wall St., New York City.

KINSELA, JOHN F., 509 Gorham St., Lowell, Mass.

KINSELLA, REV. WILLIAM, 7200 Merriel Ave., Chicago, Ill.

KINSLEY, JOSEPH T., 140 Locust St., Philadelphia, Pa.

KIRBY, JOHN J., 32 Nassau St., New York City.

KIRCHNER, MISS ETTA, 87 State St., Brooklyn, N. Y.

KNOX, REV. P. B., St. Patrick's Church, Madison, Wis.

KYLE, DR. JAMES ORR, 167 West 71st St., New York City.

KYNE, PATRICK V., 228 West 42d St., New York City.

LAMB, NICHOLAS, JR., University City, St. Louis Co., Mo.

LANNON, JOSEPH F., 68 Main St., Susquehanna, Pa.
LARKIN, WILLIAM P., 461 4th Ave., New York City.
LARKIN, ROBERT E., Streator, Ill.
LAVERY, JAMES F., 99 Reade St., New York City.
LAWLER, JAMES G., St. Charles, Mo.
LAWLER, JOHN F., City Sergeant, Norfolk, Va.
LAWLER, THOMAS B., 70 Fifth Ave., New York City.
    (Ex-Librarian and Archivist of the Society.)
LAWLOR, JAMES, Manager St. James Hotel, Sapulpa, Okla.
LAWLOR, HON. WILLIAM P., Wells Fargo Bldg., San Francisco, Cal.
LAWRENCE, MRS. JOSEPHINE H., 936 Sunnyside Ave., Chicago, Ill.
LAWRENCE, JOSEPH W., 156 Broadway, New York City.
LEARY, JEREMIAH D., 246 Clark Pl., Elizabeth, N. J.
LEE, LAWRENCE P., Dept. Commerce and Labor, Ellis Island, N. Y.
LECHE, HON. PAUL, Donaldsonville, La.
LEGNER, WILLIAM G., 2950 Logan Boul., Chicago, Ill.
LENIHAN, RT. REV. M. C., Great Falls, Mont.
    (Vice-President of the Society for Montana.)
LENNOX, GEORGE W., Haverhill, Mass.
LESLIE, SHANE, "The Cedars," Port Washington, L. I.
LEWIS, ZAGORY J., M.D., 268 Westminster St., Providence, R. I.
LINEHAN, REV. T. P., Biddeford, Me.
LOFT, HON. GEORGE W., 400 Broome St., New York City.
LOGAN, JAMES F., 97 Alban St., Dorchester, Mass.
LONG, JAMES A., 227 West 60th St., Chicago, Ill.
LOUGHLIN, REV. JOHN J., 139 West 36th St., New York City.
LUCEY, HON. P. J., 928 Otis Bldg., Chicago, Ill.
LYMAN, W. H. Room 1520, 155 North Clark St., Chicago, Ill.
LYNCH, JEREMIAH JOSEPH, 127 Schermerhorn St., Brooklyn, N. Y.
LYNCH, MARTIN F., Lamartine Ave. and 5th St., Bayside, N. Y.
LYNCH, MISS MARY E., 8792 17th Ave., Brooklyn, N. Y.
LYNCH, MICHAEL LEHANE, 425 Hamilton Ave., Jackson, Miss.
LYON, JAMES B., Albany, N. Y.
LYONS, DAVID J., 333 Fifth Ave., New York City.
LYONS, JOHN, 10 Victoria St., Dorchester, Mass.
LYONS, REV. WILLIAM, 19 St. Mary's Ave., San Francisco, Cal.
MACDONALD, GEORGE, 315 West 90th St., New York City.
MACDWYER, PATRICK S., Municipal Bldg., New York City.
MACGUIRE, CONSTANTINE J., M.D., 120 East 60th St., New York City.
MCADOO, HON. WILLIAM, 300 Mulberry St., New York City.
    (Ex-President-General of the Society.)
MCALEENAN, ARTHUR, 390 West End Ave., New York City.
MCALEER, GEORGE, M.D., Worcester, Mass.
MCALEVY, JOHN F., 26 North Main St., Pawtucket, R. I.
MCALISTER, JOHN, 165 Meeting St., Charleston, S. C.
MCAULIFFE, DENNIS A., 1459 Lexington Ave., New York City.
MCBRIDE, D. H., 41 Park Row, New York City.
MCCABE, REV. F. X., 1010 Webster Ave., Chicago, Ill.

McCabe, Eugene, 159 East 60th St., New York City.
McCarthy, Col. Daniel E., 205 Peoples Bldg., Charleston, S. C.
McCarthy, Charles, Jr., Portland, Me.
  (Vice-President of the Society for Maine.)
McCarthy, Eugene, Casper, Wyoming.
  (Vice-President of the Society for Wyoming.)
McCarthy, George W., care of Dennett & McCarthy, Portsmouth, N. H.
McCarthy, James, 129 Howard St., Lawrence, Mass.
McCarthy, John F., Port Chester, N. Y.
McCarthy, John J., "The Quincy," Boston, Mass.
McCarthy, Maurice J., 27 William St., New York City.
McCarthy, M. R. F., P. O. Box 977, Binghamton, N. Y.
McCarthy, Hon. Patrick Joseph, 49 Westminster St., Providence, R. I.
McCarty, Rev. Thomas J., St. Joseph's Church, Carroll, Ia.
McCarty, T. J., 20 George St., Charleston, S. C.
McCaughan, Rev. John P., St. Paul's Church, Warren, Mass.
McClean, Rev. Peter H., Milford, Conn.
McCloud, Hon. Richard, Durango, Colo.
McCloud, William J., 114 Broad St., Elizabeth, N. J.
McCormack, J. L., 35 Broad St., New York City.
McCaughey, Miss Sadie, 5 East Ave., Pawtucket, R. I
McCormick, John F., 64 Fifth Ave., New York City.
McCormack, John, 511 5th Ave., New York City.
McCormack, John J., 163 Valley Road, Montclair, N. J.
McCormack, Rev. Peter J., 8 Allen St., Boston, Mass.
McCormick, John A., 7 West Madison St., Chicago, Ill.
McCormick, J. S., 1524 Masonic Ave., San Francisco, Cal.
McCormick, Hon. Medill, 1747 Conway Bldg., Chicago, Ill.
McCormick, Michael A., 137 Bellevue Ave., Newport, R. I.
McCoy, Eugene, 3083 16th St., San Francisco, Cal.
McCoy, Rev. John J., LL.D., St. Ann's Church, Worcester, Mass.
McCoy, William J., 8 and 9 Security Trust Bldg., Indianapolis, Ind.
McCullough, John, 38 South 6th St., New Bedford, Mass.
McDermott, James F., 117 Court House, Boston, Mass.
McDermott, Dr. John J., 30 North Michigan Blvd., Chicago, Ill.
McDermott, Mary E., 4841 Vincennes Ave., Chicago, Ill.
McDevitt, Edward, 2757 Devisadero St., San Francisco, Cal.
McDonald, Thomas C., 29 Broadway, New York City.
McDonnell, Robert E., 60 Broadway, New York City.
McDonough, Joseph P., 417 West 141st St., New York City.
McEnerney, Garrett W., Flood Bldg., San Francisco, Cal.
McFarland, Stephen, 59 West 87th St., New York City.
McFarland, Thomas F., 1112 Chamber of Commerce Bldg., Chicago, Ill.
McGann, James A., 326 Walnut St., Philadelphia, Pa.
McGann, Col. James H., 7 Kepler St., Providence, R. I.
McGann, Thomas F., 114 Portland St., Boston, Mass.
McGarry, John A., 5320 Wayne Ave., Chicago, Ill.
McGauran, Michael S., M.D., 258 Broadway, Lawrence, Mass.

McGILLEN, MISS ELIZABETH, 4541 North Paulina St., Chicago, Ill.
McGILLICUDDY, HON. D. J., Lewiston, Me.
McGINLEY, WILLIAM J., 420 Convent Ave., New York City.
McGINNEY, JOHN H., 766 McAllister St., San Francisco, Cal.
McGIVNEY, REV. P. J., 399 Ogden St., Bridgeport, Conn.
McGLYNN, THOMAS P., Montclair, N. J.
McGLYNN, DANIEL, 527 North 9th St., East St. Louis, Ill.
McGOLRICK, RT. REV. MGR. EDWARD J., 84 Herbert St., Brooklyn, N. Y.
McGOORTY, HON. JOHN P., Appellate Court, Boulevard Bldg., Chicago, Ill.
McGOVERN, M. H., Room 563, McCormick Bldg., Chicago, Ill.
McGOVERN, PATRICK, 50 East 42nd St., New York City.
McGRATH, ARTHUR R., 3749 Rokeby St., Chicago, Ill.
McGRATH, R. M., 26 East 11th St., New York City.
McGRATH, CAPT. THOMAS F., 375 29th St., San Francisco, Cal.
McGREAL, HON. LAWRENCE, 476 Bradford Ave., Milwaukee, Wis.
McGUIRE, HON. EDWARD J., 51 Chambers St., New York City.
    (Member of the Executive Council.)
McGUIRE, FRANK A., M.D., 73 East 85th St., New York City.
McGUIRE, JAMES K., 42 Elm St., New Rochelle, N. Y.
McGUIRE, JOHN C., Hotel St. George, Brooklyn, N. Y.
McGUIRE, CONSTANTINE E., Treasury Dept., Washington, D. C.
McGUIRE, DR. M. G., 4746 Ellis Ave., Chicago, Ill.
McGUIRE, P. H., 1267 Frick Building Annex, Pittsburgh, Pa.
McGURRIN, F. E., 32 Main St., Salt Lake City, Utah.
McGURRIN, JAMES, 1400 Grand Concourse, New York City.
McHALE, MARTIN, 55 Cedar St., New York City.
McINERNEY, JAMES S., 5033 Washington Boul., Chicago, Ill.
McISAAC, DANIEL V., 905 Barristers Hall, Boston, Mass.
McKENNA, JAMES A., 80 Maiden Lane, New York City.
McKENNA, JOHN J., 3837 Archer Ave., Chicago, Ill.
McKENNA, THOMAS P., 654 West End Ave., New York City.
McKIERNON, CHARLES F., 233 Union St., Jersey City, N. J.
McKINLEY, JOHN P., Room 712, Conway Bldg., Chicago, Ill.
McKINLEY, HON. L. M., 835 County Bldg., Chicago, Ill.
McLAUGHLIN, ALONZO G., of McLaughlin & Stern, 15 William St., New
    York City.
McLAUGHLIN, J. J., Hibernia Bank, New Orleans, La.
McLAUGHLIN, JOHN, 346 East 81st St., New York City.
McLAUGHLIN, HON. JOHN J., 29 South La Salle St., Chicago, Ill.
McLAUGHLIN, HON. JOSEPH, 1619 Chestnut St., Philadelphia, Pa.
McLOGLIN, REV. JOHN J., 9 Le Roy St., Binghamton, N. Y.
McMAHON, EDWARD, 100 Broadway, New York City.
McMAHON, REV. JOHN W., D.D., St. Mary's Church, Charlestown, Mass.
McMANUS, JAMES H., 105 West 28th St., New York City.
McMANUS, TERENCE J., 170 Broadway, New York City.
McNABOE, JAMES F., 144 West 92d St., New York City.
McNAMARA, THOMAS CHARLES, M.D., 613 Hudson St., Hoboken, N. J.
McNARY, HON. WILLIAM S., 268 Washington St., Boston, Mass.

McNamee, Rev. W. J., 718 West Adams St., Chicago, Ill.
McPartland, John E., 55 Park St., New Haven, Conn.
McPartland, Stephen J., 673 Eighth Ave., New York City.
McQuaid, William A., 165 West 10th St., New York City.
McShane, James C., 39 La Salle St., Chicago, Ill.
McQueeney, Miss Mary, 132 West 79th St., New York City.
McSweeney, Denis Florence, 511 Fifth Ave., New York City.
McTigue, John G., 346 Broadway, New York City.
McWalters, John P., 30 Church St., New York City.
McSweeney, Edward J., Framingham, Mass.
    (Member of the Executive Council.)
Madden, John, Wichita, Kan.
Maginnis, T. H., Jr., 5000 Baltimore Ave., Philadelphia, Pa.
    (Vice-President of the Society for Pennsylvania.)
Magner, Thomas, 87 North Prospect St., Burlington, Vt.
    (Vice-President of the Society for Vermont.)
Magner, Thomas J., 175 West Jackson Boul., Chicago, Ill.
Magrane, P. B., 133 Market St., Lynn, Mass.
Magrath, Dr. John F., 119 East 30th St., New York City.
Maguire, John F., 1520 West Market St., Bethlehem, Pa.
Maher, John L., 15 Kemble St., Utica, N. Y.
Maher, Michael E., 1420 Unity Bldg., Chicago, Ill.
Maher, Stephen J., M.D., 212 Orange St., New Haven, Conn.
Mahoney, Daniel Emmet, Keyport, Monmouth Co., N. J.
Mahoney, Daniel S., 277 Broadway, New York City.
Mahoney, E. S., Portsmouth, Va.
Mahoney, Jeremiah, Casper, Wyo.
Mahoney, John J., Principal State Normal School, Lowell, Mass.
Mahoney, John P. S., Lawrence, Mass.
Mahoney, Bernard J., Ashland Block, Chicago, Ill.
Mahoney, John J., 3942 West Jackson Boul., Chicago, Ill.
McSweeney, James E., 618 West 142nd St., New York City.
Mahoney, Joseph P., 69 West Washington St., Chicago, Ill.
Mahoney, Timothy, 840 Ogden St., Denver, Colo.
Malone, Hon. Dudley Field, 50 East 42nd St., New York City.
Malone, Hon. John F., 290 North St., Buffalo, N. Y.
Malone, John T., Louisville, Ky., care of Fidelity Trust Co.
Maloney, John H., 1619 Greene St., Harrisburg, Pa.
Manahan, Miss Mary G., 34 Jefferson Ave., Brooklyn, N. Y.
Manners, J. Hartley, Lotos Club, 110 West 57th St., New York City.
Manning, Joseph P., 66 Crawford St., Roxbury, Mass.
Mapother, W. L., Louisville, Ky.
Markey, Col. Eugene L., Duplex Printing Co., Battle Creek, Mich.
Marshall, Rev. George F., St. Peter's Church, North Walpole, N. H.
Marten, Frank, Box 75, Plattsburgh, N. Y.
Martin, J. F., Green Bay, Wis.
Martin, Patrick, 2496 E St., San Diego, Cal.
Martin, William J., 64 Wall St., New York City.

MASSARENE, WILLIAM G., 15 East 40th St., New York City.
MASSEY, JOHN, Pensacola, Fla.
MAYNES, MICHAEL, Jefferson House, Boston, Mass.
MEADE, RICHARD W., 1701 Dime Bank Bldg., Detroit, Mich.
MEAGHER, FREDERICK J., 222 Front St., Binghamton, N. Y.
MEAGHER, FRANCIS T., 306 Blue Hills Parkway, Mattapan, Mass.
MEDER, MRS. LEONORA, 139 North Clark St., Chicago, Ill.
MEE, HON. JOHN J., Woonsocket, R. I.
MEE, REV. PATRICK J., Holy Trinity Rectory, Mamaroneck, N. Y.
MELDRIM, HON. PETER W., 1007 National Bank Bldg., Savannah, Ga.
MEYERS, J. J., Carroll, Ia.
MINTURN, HON. JAMES, Associate Justice Supreme Court, N. J., Hoboken,
    N. J.
MITCHELL, GEORGE H. B., 142 West 72d St., New York City.
MITCHELL, WILLIAM L., 219 West 81st St., New York City.
MOLONEY, FRED G., 428 Peoples Gas Bldg., Chicago, Ill.
MOLONY, FRANK T., 207 West 131st St., New York City.
MOLONY, HENRY A., 112 Rut St., Charleston, S. C.
MONAHAN, FRANK D., 53 State St., Boston, Mass.
·MONAHAN, JOSEPH N., 58 Belmont St., Providence, R. I.
MONOHAN, EDWARD S., St. Matthews, Ky.
MOONEY, EDMUND L., 38 Pine St., New York City.
MOONEY, LOUIS M., M.D., 164 West 76th St., New York City.
MOONEY, MICHAEL P., 815 Society for Savings Bldg., Cleveland, Ohio.
MOONEY, WILLIAM J., 101 South Meridian St., Indianapolis, Ind.
MOORE, HON. ROBERT LEE, Statesboro, Ga.
MORAN, REV. GREGORY, Atlantic and California Aves., Atlantic City, N. J.
MORAN, JAMES T., 114 Court St., New Haven, Conn.
MORAN, JOSEPH F., 11-27 Imlay St., Brooklyn, N. Y.
MORIARTY, EDWARD T., 155-159 East 23d St., New York City.
MORIARTY, JOHN, Broadway, Waterbury, Conn.
MORONEY, PATRICK, 2 Cooke St., Providence, R. I.
MORRIS, SIR EDWARD P., London, England.
MORRISSEY, VERY REV. ANDREW, C.S.C., D.D., LL.D., University of Notre
    Dame, Notre Dame, Ind.
    (Vice-President of the Society for Indiana.)
MORRISSEY, LIEUT.-COL., W. J. 2141 North Gratz St., Philadelphia, Pa.
MORRISON, PAUL J., Department of Commerce and Labor, Ellis Island, N. Y.
MORRISON, ROBERT E., Prescott, Ariz.
MOYNAHAN, BARTHOLOMEW, 15 Park Row, New York City.
MOYNAHAN, DANIEL J., 250 Normandy St., Boston, Mass.
MULHERN, JOHN W., 1766 St. Clair St., St. Paul, Minn.
MULLANEY, BERNARD J., 122 South Michigan Ave., Chicago, Ill.
MULLEN, JOHN F., 309 Oxford St., Providence, R. I.
MULLIGAN, EDWARD HOWELL, Supt. So. California Edison Co., 55 East Col-
    orado St., Pasadena, Cal.
MULLIGAN, GEORGE F., 816 Ashland Block, Chicago, Ill.
MULLIGAN, JOSEPH T., 55 Liberty St., New York City.

MULLIGAN, WILLIAM J., 163 Pearl St., Thompsonville, Conn.
MULQUEEN, HON. JOSEPH F., 32 Franklin St., New York City.
MULQUEEN, MICHAEL J., 253 Broadway, New York City.
MULVEHILL, J. D., 417–19 First Ave., Spokane, Wash.
MUNHALL, WILLIAM D., 1208 Ashland Block, Chicago, Ill.
MURPHY, ANNA E., 5953 Magnolia Ave., Chicago, Ill.
MURPHY, HON. CHARLES F., 145 East 14th St., New York City.
MURPHY, EDWARD J., Fuller Bldg., Springfield, Mass.
MURPHY, EDWARD R., 130th St. and 12th Ave., New York City.
MURPHY, EDWARD S., 1205 Park Ave., New York City.
MURPHY, GEORGE, 57 East 9th St., New York City.
MURPHY, JAMES R., 31 Nassau St., New York City.
MURPHY, JAMES R., 1 Beacon St., Boston, Mass.
MURPHY, JEREMIAH B., 451 14th St., Brooklyn, N. Y.
MURPHY, JOHN H., 520 West 36th St., New York City.
MURPHY, HON. JOHN J., 70 West 11th St., New York City.
MURPHY, REV. MICHAEL, 526 Bush St., San Francisco, Cal.
MURPHY, M. W., 221 West Randolph St., Chicago, Ill.
MURPHY, T. M., 2896 Valentine Ave., New York City.
MURPHY, PHILIP H., 311 Greenbush St., Milwaukee, Wis.
MURPHY, MGR. WILLIAM G., 503 East 14th St., New York City.
MURRAY, CHARLES, 75 Broad St., New York City.
MURRAY, JOSEPH, 149 Broadway, New York City.
MURRAY, HON. LAWRENCE O., LL.D., Treasury Department, Washington, D. C.
MURRAY, DR. PETER, 159 West 71st St., New York City.
MURRAY, TIMOTHY, 141 Broadway, New York City.
MURRIN, JAMES B., Carbondale, Pa.
MYERS, JOHN CALDWELL, 14 Wall St., New York City.
MYLOD, JOHN J., Poughkeepsie, N. Y.
NASH, PATRICK A., 2946 Washington Boul., Chicago, Ill.
NALLY, EDWARD J., Marconi Telegraph & Cable Co., 233 Broadway, New York City.
NAGLE, GARRETT J., 69 East, 125th St., New York City.
NEACY, THOMAS J., Milwaukee, Wis.
NEAGLE, REV. RICHARD, 2 Fellsway East, Malden, Mass.
NEALON, HON. JAMES C., 960 Haight St., San Francisco, Cal.
NEE, P. J., 1341 Girard St., Washington, D. C.
NEWMAN, HARRY, 2457 Michigan Ave., Chicago, Ill.
NICKERSON, HENRY F., 524 Durfee St., Fall River, Mass.
NOLAN, DANIEL CARROLL, 55 Main St., Yonkers, N. Y.
NOLAN, JAMES C., 361 Orange St., Albany, N. Y.
NOLAN, LUKE J., 43 Exchange Pl., New York City.
NOLAN, W. J., care of Humler & Nolan, 137 South Fourth St., Louisville, Ky.
NOONAN, HON. THOMAS F., 314 West 54th St., New York City.
NOONAN, DANIEL M., 29 Davis Ave., New Rochelle, N. Y.
NOONAN, WILLIAM T., 155 Main St. W., Rochester, N. Y.
NORMOYLE, D. J., 139 North Clark St., Chicago, Ill.

NORTON, WILLIAM, 4401 South Troy St., Chicago, Ill.
NORTON, MICHAEL W., 450 Friendship St., Providence, R. I.
NUGENT, EDWARD, 20 Clinton St., Newark, N. J.
O'BRIEN, HON. C. D., Globe Bldg., St. Paul, Minn.
　(Vice-President of the Society for Minnesota.)
O'BRIEN, REV. DENIS J., L.B., 16, South Berwick, Me.
O'BRIEN, DENNIS F., 1482 Broadway, New York City.
O'BRIEN, REV. JAMES J., 179 Summer St., Somerville, Mass.
O'BRIEN, HON. JOHN F., City National Bank, Plattsburg, N. Y.
O'BRIEN, JOHN J., 4118 Washington Boul., Chicago, Ill.
O'BRIEN, JOHN A., 120 Market St., San Francisco, Cal.
O'BRIEN, REV. J. J., S.J., Loyola University, New Orleans, La.
O'BRIEN, J. P., Oregon Railroad & Navigation Company, Portland, Ore.
　(Vice-President of the Society for Oregon.)
O'BRIEN, JOHN P., Corporation Counsel's Office, New York City.
O'BRIEN, CAPT. LAURENCE, 70 Beach St., New Haven, Conn.
　(Vice-President of the Society for Connecticut.)
O'BRIEN, MARTIN J., 3845 Flournoy St., Chicago, Ill.
O'BRIEN, MICHAEL C., M.D., 161 West 122d St., New York City.
O'BRIEN, MICHAEL J., 230 Echo Pl., New York City.
　(Historiographer of the Society and Member of the Executive Council.)
O'BRIEN, HON. MORGAN J., LL.D., 120 Broadway, New York City.
O'BRIEN, HON. THOMAS J., B.L., LL.D., Grand Rapids, Mich.
O'BRIEN, THOMAS S., 13 Walter St., Albany, N. Y.
　(Member of the Executive Council.)
O'BRIEN, WILLIAM D., 12 Hamilton Ave., South Norwalk, Conn.
O'BRIEN, W. P., 1416 East 72d Pl., Chicago, Ill.
O'BYRNE, MICHAEL ALPHONSUS, Room 400, Germania Bank Bldg., Savannah, Ga.
　(Vice-President of the Society for Georgia.)
O'CALLAGHAN, CHARLES J., Spuyten Duyvil, N. Y.
O'CONNELL, RT. REV. DENNIS JOSEPH, S.T.D., 800 Cathedral Pl., Richmond, Va.
O'CONNELL, DANIEL, Dundalk, Ireland.
O'CONNELL, DANIEL J., 10–14 Grand St., New York City.
O'CONNELL, DANIEL T., 53 State St., Boston, Mass.
O'CONNELL, MISS GRACE, 1180 North Third St., Springfield, Ill.
O'CONNELL, JAMES, 424 West 43d St., New York City.
O'CONNELL, JEROME A., 1403 Whittier Ave., Springfield, Ill.
O'CONNELL, JOHN, 303 Fifth Ave., New York City.
O'CONNELL, HON. JOHN F., 495 River Ave., Providence, R. I.
O'CONNELL, JOHN J., 31 Nassau St., New York City.
O'CONNELL, HON. JOSEPH F., 53 State St., Boston, Mass.
　(Member of the Executive Council.)
O'CONNELL, P. A., 154 Tremont St., Boston, Mass.
O'CONNOR, FRANCIS P., 157 Tremont St., Boston, Mass.
O'CONNOR, DR. J. H., 175 21st Ave., San Francisco, Cal.
O'CONNOR, JOHN, 205 South State St., Chicago, Ill.

O'CONNOR, JOHN L., Ogdensburg, N. Y.

O'CONNOR, HON. JOHN M., 30 North Michigan Ave., Chicago, Ill.

O'CONNOR, MISS KATHLEEN REYNOLDS, 61 West 10th St., New York City.

O'CONNOR, P. J., Casper, Wyo.

O'CONNOR, THOMAS, 2454 South Park Ave., Chicago, Ill.

O'CONNOR, REV. TIMOTHY J., 55 Broadway, South Boston, Mass.

O'CONNOR, HON. W. A., Santa Cruz County, Nogales, Ariz.

O'CONNOR, WATSON B., 136 Grant St., Bangor, Me.

O'CONNOR, WILLIAM, Catholic Club, 120 Central Park South, New York City.

O'DOHERTY, HON. MATTHEW, Louisville, Ky.

O'DOHERTY, MOST REV. MICHAEL A., Archbishop of Manila, Philippine Islands.
> (Vice-President of the Society for the Philippine Islands.)

O'DONNELL, JAMES V., 420 Reaper Block, Chicago, Ill.

O'DONNELL, JOSEPH A., 3078 Palmer Sq., Chicago, Ill.

O'DONNELL, REV. PATRICK J., Tompkins Cove, Rockland Co., N. Y.

O'DONNELL, WILLIAM J., 115 Broadway, New York City.

O'DRISCOLL, DANIEL M., 22 Church St., Charleston, S. C.

O'DWYER, HON. EDWARD F., 32 Chambers St., New York City.

O'DWYER, GEO. F., 148 Midland St., Lowell, Mass.

O'DWYER, JOHN A., 623 Nicholas Bldg., Toledo, Ohio.

O'FARRELL, CHARLES, Bank of Commerce, 31 Nassau St., New York City.

O'FLAHERTY, DANIEL C., 1107 Mutual Bldg., Richmond, Va.
> (Vice-President of the Society for Virginia.)

O'FLAHERTY, JAMES, JR., 373 East 148th St., New York City.

O'FLYNN, J. J., 3249 Congress St., Chicago, Ill.

O'GALLAGHER, FRANCIS B., 5532 South Racine Ave., Chicago, Ill.

O'GARA, JOHN, 4726 North Winchester Ave., Chicago, Ill.

O'GORMAN, HON. JAMES A., 318 West 108th St., New York City.

O'HAGAN, WILLIAM J., Charleston, S. C.
> (Vice-President of the Society for South Carolina.)

O'HANLON, MICHAEL J., 583 Westfield Ave., El Mora, Elizabeth, N. J.

O'HANLON, PHILIP F., M.D., 121 West 95th St., New York City.

O'HEARN, WILLIAM, 298 Boylston St., Brookline, Mass.

O'KEEFE, JOHN A., 25 Exchange St., Lynn, Mass.

O'KEEFFE, JOHN G., care H. L. Horton & Co., 60 Broadway, New York City.
> (Member of the Executive Council.)

O'KEEFE, PATRICK JAMES, Kenwood Hotel, Chicago, Ill.

O'LEARY, FRAZIER, L., 52 Wells Ave., Dorchester, Mass.

O'LEARY, JEREMIAH A., 38 Park Row, New York City.

O'LEARY, JOHN J., 52 Broadway, New York City.

O'LEARY, COL. M. J., 122 Bay St. East, Savannah, Ga.

O'LOUGHLIN, PATRICK, 18 Tremont St., Boston, Mass.

OLSEN, MRS. M. O'C., 6698 Amboy Road, Richmond Valley, S. I.

O'MALLEY, CHARLES J., 184 Summer St., Boston, Mass.

O'MALLEY, EDWARD, Tueson, Arizona.

O'MEALEY, JOHN W., 53 State St., Boston, Mass.

O'NEIL, ARTHUR, 75 South St., New York City.

O'NEIL, HON. JOSEPH H., Federal Trust Co., Boston, Mass.
O'NEILL, REV. CLEMENT P., St. Mary of the Woods, Princeville, Ill.
O'NEILL, HON. CHARLES, Supreme Court, New Orleans, La.
O'NEILL, COL. C. T., 315 North 4th St., Allentown, Pa.
O'NEILL, REV. DANIEL H., 935 Main St., Worcester, Mass.
O'NEILL, CAPT. FRANCIS, 5448 Drexel Ave., Chicago, Ill.
O'NEILL, FRANCIS, 45 West 45th St., New York City.
O'NEILL, JAMES L., 220 Franklin St., Elizabeth, N. J.
    (Member of the Executive Council.)
O'NEIL, MISS MARY E., 259 Water St., Binghamton, N. Y.
O'NEILL, PATRICK J., 132 East 122nd St., New York City.
O'REILLY, THOMAS, 8 Mt. Morris Park W., New York City.
O'REILLY, THOMAS J., Broadway and 109th St., New York City.
O'REILLY, VINCENT F., 19 Forest St., Montclair, N. J.
    (Librarian and Archivist of the Society and Member of the Executive
    Council.)
O'REILLY, G. S., Irving National Bank, Woolworth Bldg., New York City.
O'REILLY, COMM. P. S., Crescent Club, Brooklyn, N. Y.
O'ROURKE, JOHN F., 17 Battery Pl., New York City.
O'RYAN, CAPT. JAMES EDMUND L., 720 Coster St., Bronx, New York City.
OSBORN, THOMAS I., 461 4th Ave., New York City.
OSBORN, WILLIAM N., 135 West 42d St., New York City.
O'SHAUGHNESSY, MAJ. EDWARD J., 912 St. Nicholas Ave., New York City.
O'SHAUGHNESSY, JAMES, Westminster Bldg., Chicago, Ill.
O'SHAUGHNESSY, JOHN P., 1252 Otis Bldg., Chicago, Ill.
O'SHAUGHNESSY, MICHAEL MAURICE, 2732 Vallejo St., San Francisco, Cal.
O'SHEA, D. G., Red Lodge, Carbon County, Mont.
O'SHEA, G. HARRY, 29 Broadway, New York City.
O'SHEE, JAMES A., 7837 Elm St., New Orleans, La.
O'SULLIVAN, DANIEL, 1360 Ellis St., San Francisco, Cal.
O'SULLIVAN, FRANK A., 110 Aberdeen St., Lowell, Mass.
O'SULLIVAN, P. T., 2500 East 74th St., Chicago, Ill.
O'SULLIVAN, HON. HUMPHREY, care of O'Sullivan Rubber Co., Lowell, Mass.
O'SULLIVAN, JAMES, Lowell, Mass.
O'SULLIVAN, JEREMIAH J., 38–39 Central Block, Lowell, Mass.
PAINE, WILLIAM E., 378 West 108th St., New York City.
PALLEN, DR. CONDÉ B., 197 Weyman Ave., New Rochelle, N. Y.
PATTERSON, RT. REV. GEORGE J., V.G., 267 Third St., South Boston, Mass.
PELLETIER, HON. JOSEPH C., Court House, Boston, Mass.
PHELAN, HON. JAMES D., Phelan Bldg., San Francisco, Cal.
PHELAN, JAMES J., 60 Congress St., Boston, Mass.
PHELAN, JOHN J., 16 Exchange Pl., New York City.
PHELAN, HON. JOHN J., 1836 Noble Ave., Bridgeport, Conn.
PHELAN, HON. MICHAEL F., Lynn, Mass.
PHELAN, REV. THOMAS P., LL.D., Brewster, N. Y.
PHELAN, TIMOTHY J., N. Y. Athletic Club, 58 West 59th St., New York City.
PHILBIN, PATRICK AMBROSE, Laurel St. Archbald, Pa.
    (Member of the Executive Council.)

PHILLIPS, JOHN, 47 Broadhurst Ave., New York City.
PIGGOTT, MICHAEL, 1634 Vermont St., Quincy, Ill.
PLATT, HON. WILLIAM POPHAM, Court House, White Plains, N. Y.
PLUNKETT, COUNT G. N., 26 Upper Fitzwilliam St. Dublin, Ireland.
PLUNKETT, JAMES, 423 West 120th St., New York City.
PLUNKETT, THOMAS, 326 6th St., East Liverpool, Ohio.
    (Vice-President of the Society for Ohio.)
POPE, ALEXANDER, D.D.S., 1305 Heyworth Bldg. 29 E. Madison St. Chicago, Ill.
POULTON, JOHN J., 7311 Oglesby Ave., Chicago, Ill.
POWER, RT. REV. MGR. JAMES W., 47 East 129th St., New York City.
POWER, NEAL, Mills Bldg., San Francisco, Cal.
PRESSINGER, ARNOTT M., 26 Broadway, New York City.
PRINDIVILLE, HON. JOHN K., Municipal Court, Chicago, Ill.
PULLEYN, JOHN J., 51 Chambers St., New York City.
QUIGLEY, WILLIAM F., 2426 University Ave., New York City.
QUIN, JEREMIAH, 178 Eleventh St., Milwaukee, Wis.
QUIN, JOSEPH F., M.D., 409 19th Ave., Milwaukee, Wis.
QUINN, R. A., M.D., P. O. Box 234, Vicksburg, Miss.
    (Vice-President of the Society for Mississippi.)
QUINN, FRANK J., Old Library Bldg., Peoria, Ill.
QUINN, COL. PATRICK HENRY, Turks Head Bldg., Providence, R. I.
QUINN, SAMUEL, 164 West Washington St., Chicago, Ill.
QUIRK, REV. M. A., Ottawa, Ill.
RAINEY, JOHN W., 3341 South Western Ave., Chicago, Ill.
RAMSAY, CLARENCE J., 132 West 12th St., New York City.
RAYENS, MICHAEL W., 26 Cortlandt St., New York City.
RAYMOND, HON. GEORGE G., New Rochelle, N. Y.
REARDON, WILLIAM J., Pekin, Ill.
REDDIN, JOHN H., 612 E. & C. Bldg., Denver, Colo.
REGAN, JOHN H., 320 Broadway, New York City.
REGAN, W. P., 296 Essex St., Lawrence, Mass.
REILLY, F. JAMES, 122 Centre St., New York City.
REILLY, JAMES OWEN, 212 Nun St., Wilmington, N. C.
REILLY, THOMAS F., Bryn Mawr, Philadelphia, Pa.
REILLY, THOMAS J., 560 West 26th St., New York City.
REILLY, HON. THOMAS L., Meriden, Conn.
REYNOLDS, REV. F. L., 1340 East 72d St., Chicago, Ill.
RIGNEY, JOSEPH, Port Royal, Va.
RILEY, A. J., 143 King St., Charleston, S. C.
RIORDAN, CHARLES F., Glenhill Farm, Sharon, Mass.
RIORDAN, JOHN, 197 High St., Boston, Mass.
RIORDAN, T. A., Flagstaff, Ariz.
    (Vice-President of the Society for Arizona.)
ROACH, REV. JOHN D., Church of the Holy Spirit, University Ave., New York City.
ROACH, WILLIAM J., 402 City Hall, Chicago, Ill.
ROCK, REV. P. M. J., 443 5th St., Louisville, Ky.

ROBINSON, PROF. FRED N., Longfellow Park, Cambridge, Mass.

ROCHE, MOST REV. EDWARD PATRICK, Archbishop of Newfoundland, St. John's, Newfoundland.

ROCHE, E. H., 1338 North Dearborn St., Lincoln Park Sta., Chicago, Ill.

ROGERS, JOHN J., 34 Chandler St., Worcester, Mass.

ROONEY, HENRY F., 251 Thames St., Newport, R. I.

ROONEY, HON. JOHN JEROME, 233 Broadway, New York City.

ROSSITER, W. S., care of Rumford Press, Concord, N. H.

RORKE, ALEXANDER I., Assistant District Attorney, New York County, 51 Chambers St., New York City.

ROURKE, THOMAS R., care of Crane Co., 490 Cherry St., New York City.

ROWAN, JOSEPH, 60 Wall St., New York City.

RYAN, CHARLES B., 112 Freemason St., Norfolk, Va.

RYAN, CHRISTOPHER S., Lexington, Mass.

RYAN, DANIEL C., 461 Fargo Ave., Buffalo, N. Y.

RYAN, FRANK J., 448 Riverside Drive, New York City.

RYAN, JAMES, 720 Coster St., New York City.

RYAN, JAMES J., 776 Carroll St., Brooklyn, N. Y.

RYAN, JOHN H., 806 Chamber of Commerce, Chicago, Ill.

RYAN, JOHN J., 25 Broad St., New York City.

RYAN, JOHN J., Haverhill Trust Bldg., Haverhill, Mass.

RYAN, JOSEPH T., 149 Broadway, New York City.

RYAN, LEO G., 545 Notre Dame St. West., Montreal, Canada.
(Vice-President of the Society for Canada.)

RYAN, HON. O'NEILL, 1811 3rd National Bank Bldg., St. Louis, Mo.
(Vice-President of the Society for Missouri.)

RYAN, HON. THOMAS, Litchfield, Conn.

RYAN, TIMOTHY M., M.D., Meara Block, Torrington, Conn.

RYAN, HON. WILLIAM, 375 Irving Ave., Port Chester, N. Y.

RYAN, WILLIAM F., 359 Fulton St., Jamaica, N. Y.

SADLIER, FRANK X., 37 Barclay St., New York City.

SCALLON, WILLIAM, Penwell Block, Helena, Mont.

SCANLAN, HON. CHARLES M., 307 Grand Ave., Milwaukee, Wis.
(Member of the Executive Committee.)

SCANLAN, MICHAEL, 613 West 40th St., New York City.

SCANLAN, M.D., LIEUT. PETER LAWRENCE, Prairie du Chien, Wis.

SCARLETT, WILLIAM, 35 Fairview Ave., North Plainfield, N. J.

SCOTT, JOSEPH, 1012 Black Bldg., Los Angeles, Cal.

SCULLY, REV. ALFRED E., Glassboro, N. J.

SCULLY, HON. P. JOSEPH, 4 Columbia St., New York City.

SCULLY, HON. THOMAS F., 1107 South Ashland Boul., Chicago, Ill.

SCULLY, HON. THOMAS J., South Amboy, N. J.

SEYMOUR, JOHN F., 52 Pierce St., San Francisco, Cal.

SHAHAN, RT. REV. THOMAS J., S.T.D., J.U.L., Catholic University, Washington, D. C.

SHANAHAN, DAVID E., 115 South Dearborn St., Chicago, Ill.

SHANAHAN, DENIS S., 1812 Clifton Park Ave., Chicago, Ill.

SHANAHAN, VERY REV. EDMUND T., PH.D., S.T.D., J.C.L., Catholic University, Washington, D. C.

SHANLEY, THOMAS J., 1491 Broadway, New York City.

SHANNON, REV. JAMES, 607 North Madison, Peoria, Ill.

SHANNON, M. M., 512 Davis St., Elmira, N. Y.

SHANNON, NEIL J., 30 North LaSalle St., Chicago, Ill.

SHANNON, DR. WILLIAM, 130 West 81st St., New York City.

SHAW, DAVID B., Penal Commissioner, Cedar St., Charleston, Mass.

SHEA, JAMES, 2415 Octavia St., San Francisco, Cal.

SHEA, JOHN E., Fort Dearborn Trust & Savings Bank, Chicago, Ill.

SHEAHAN, WILLIAM L., 73 Sherman Ave., New Haven, Conn.

SHEEDY, BRYAN DEF., M.D., 61 West 74th St., New York City.

SHEEHAN, DANIEL J., 2118 State St., Milwaukee, Wis.

SHEEHAN, JOHN LOUIS, LL.B., LL.M., LL.D., Boston University School of Law, Boston, Mass.

SHEEHAN, HON. JOSEPH A., Associate Justice Municipal Court, City of Boston, Court House, Boston, Mass.

SHEEHAN, WILLIAM S., 1170 Broadway, New York City.

SHEEHY, M. J., Foot of W. 132 St. N. R., New York City.

SHEPPARD, REV. J. HAVERGAL, D.D., Park Baptist Church, Port Richmond, N. Y.

SHERMAN, REV. ANDREW M., Morristown, N. J.

SHERMAN, HON. P. TECUMSEH, 15 William St., New York City.

SHIELDS, GEORGE C., Mansfield, Mass.

SHIELDS, HON. JOHN KNIGHT, Knoxville, Tenn.

SHINE, REV. M. A., Plattsmouth, Neb.
(Vice-President of the Society for Nebraska.)

SHORT, DR. WILLIAM B., Vanderbilt Concourse Bldg., 45th St. and Vanderbilt Ave., New York City.

SILO, JAMES P., 2020 Broadway, New York City.

SIMONS, THOMAS A., 241 Marshall St., Elizabeth, N. J.

SINNOTT, HON. PHILIP J., 795 St. Nicholas Ave., New York City.

SKELLY, REV. A. M., Holy Rosary Priory, 375 Clackamas St., Portland, Ore.

SKEFFINGTON, HARRY J., 7 Centennial Ave., Revere, Mass.

SLATTERY, JAMES M., 1522 Farwell Ave., Chicago, Ill.

SLAVIN, DENNIS J., Waterbury, Conn.

SLOANE, CHARLES W., 54 William St., New York City.

SMITH, HON. JAMES E., 122 West 103d St., New York City.

SMITH, REV. JAMES J., 397 Ferry St., New Haven, Conn.

SMITH, REV. JOSEPH, 328 West 14th St., New York City.

SMITH, REV. J. TALBOT, Dobb's Ferry, N. Y.

SMITH, THOMAS F., 60 Broadway, New York City.

SMYTH, SAMUEL, 41 Liberty St., New York City.

SMYTH, REV. THOMAS, Springfield, Mass.

SMITH, FRANK W., 606 West 116th St., New York City.

SMITH, LAURENCE J., 120 Central Park South, New York City.

SMYTH, THOMAS A., 2032 West Jackson Boul., Chicago, Ill.

SPELLACY, THOMAS J., 756 Main St., Hartford, Conn.

SPELLISSY, JOSEPH, M.D., 110 South 18th St., Philadelphia, Pa.

SPILLANE, J. B., 232 West 120th St., New York City.

STACK, MAURICE J., 1020 Hudson St., Hoboken, N. J.

STAFFORD, WILLIAM F., Flood Bldg., San Francisco, Cal.

STANTON, REV. JAMES F., 177 School St., Stoughton, Mass.

STAPLETON, HON. LUKE D., 294 Garfield Pl., Brooklyn, N. Y.

STAPLETON, HON. MATT., Rhinelander, Wis.

STROUSS, E. Washington, Congress Hotel, Chicago, Ill.

SULLIVAN, DANIEL, M.D., 43 East 25th St., New York City.

SULLIVAN, HON. DENIS E., 6009 Winthrop Ave., Chicago, Ill.

SULLIVAN, FRANCIS J., 1312 Rector Bldg., Chicago, Ill.

SULLIVAN, JAMES E., 254 Wayland Ave., Providence, R. I.

SULLIVAN, JAMES J., 818 Ernest and Cranmer Bldg., Denver, Col.
  (Vice-President of the Society for Colorado.)

SULLIVAN, JEREMIAH B., Board of General Appraisers, 641 Washington St.,
  New York City.
  (Vice-President of the Society for Iowa.)

SULLIVAN, J. J., Pensacola, Fla.
  (Vice-President of the Society for Florida.)

SULLIVAN, JOHN J., 203 Broadway, New York City.

SULLIVAN, JOHN J., 61–63 Faneuil Hall Market, Boston, Mass.

SULLIVAN, HON. MICHAEL F., M.D., Pine & Elm Sts., Lawrence, Mass.
  (Member of the Executive Council.)

SULLIVAN, MICHAEL W., Century Bldg., Washington, D. C.

SULLIVAN, MICHAEL X., PH.D., U. S. Public Health Service, Spartanburg,
  S. C.

SULLIVAN, OWEN, 211 South 6th St., Louisville, Ky.

SULLIVAN, THOMAS M., 4743 Washington Boul., Chicago, Ill.

SULLIVAN, WILLIAM B., Tremont Bldg., Boston, Mass.

SULLIVAN, DR. WILLIAM J., Lawrence, Mass.

SUPPLE, REV. JAMES N., St. Francis de Sales Church, Charlestown, Boston,
  Mass.

SUTTON, JOHN P., 134 North 18th St., Lincoln, Neb.

SWEENEY, ROBT. P., 141 Broadway, New York City.

SWEENY, REV. JOHN, St. Augustine's Church, Ocean City, N. J.

SWEENY, WILLIAM MONTGOMERY, 126 Franklin St., Astoria, L. I., N. Y.

SWEITZER, ROBT. M., 2958 West Jackson Boul., Chicago, Ill.

TAGGART, HON. THOMAS, French Lick Springs Hotel, French Lick., Ind.

TALLEY, HON. ALFRED J., 165 Broadway, New York City.
  (Member of the Executive Council.)

THOMPSON, COL. JAMES, 302 West Main St., Louisville, Ky.
  (Vice-President of the Society for Kentucky.)

THOMPSON, JOSEPH J., 1059 Loyola Ave., Chicago, Ill.

TIERNEY, EDWARD M., Ansonia Hotel, New York City.
  (Member of the Executive Council.)

TIERNEY, HENRY S., Arlington Hotel, Binghamton, N. Y.

TIMMINS, REV. JAMES, 2422 South 17th St., Philadelphia, Pa.

TOBIN, EDWARD J., 5607 Michigan Ave., Chicago, Ill.

TOBIN, E. J., 240 Montgomery St., San Francisco, Cal.

TOBIN, MISS MARY E., 2051 Jackson Boul., Chicago, Ill.

TOBIN, RICHARD M., Hibernia Bank, San Francisco, Cal.

TOOLAN, REV. FRANCIS J., 31 Walter St., Albany, N. Y.

TOOLEY, FRANK L., D.D.S., 157 East 79th St., New York City.

TOWLE, FELIX S., 332 Broadway, New York City.

TRAINOR, MRS. CHARLES J., 1314 East 72nd St., Chicago, Ill.

TRAINOR, CHARLES J., 1314 East 72nd St., Chicago, Ill.

TRAINOR, PATRICK S., 26 Broadway, New York City.

TUITE, GEORGE S., 612 South Flower St., Los Angeles, Cal.

TULLY, MICHAEL, 211 West 107th St., New York City.

TWOHY, JAMES F., Alaska Bldg., Seattle, Wash.

TWOMEY, D. RYAN, 4837 Forcetville Ave., Chicago, Ill.

TWOMEY, JOHN, 465 Washington St., Brighton, Mass.

TYMON, MICHAEL, 1061 Bedford Ave., Brooklyn, N. Y.

VREDENBURGH, WATSON, JR., 15 Broad St., New York City.

WALDRON, E. M., 207 Market St., Newark, N. J.

WALKER, DR. HUGH, Lowell, Mass.

WALL, RT. REV. MGR. FRANCIS H., 211 West 141st St., New York City.

WALLER, HON. THOMAS M., New London, Conn.

WALL, HON. JAMES M., Gwen Villa, Bound Brook, N. J.

WALSH, ANTHONY T., Wilkes-Barre, Pa.

WALSH, HON. DAVID I., Fitchburg, Mass.

WALSH, JAMES A., 103 Water St., N. Y.

WALSH, JAMES J., M.D., LL.D., 110 West 74th St., New York City.

WALSH, J. H., 8502 Hamilton Ave., Brooklyn, N. Y.

WALSH, JOHN J., 26 Beaver St., New York City.

WALSH, JOHN M., Westfield, N. J.

WALSH, L. J., Union Depot, Canal St., Chicago, Ill.

WALSH, PHILIP C., JR., 260 Washington St., Newark, N. J.

WALSH, P. J., 127 East 23d St., New York City.

WALSH, WILLIAM P., 247 Water St., Augusta, Me.

WARD, FRANCIS D., 469 West 57th St., New York City.

WELLS, JUDSON G., 1 Union Square, New York City.

WHALEN, JAMES M., 6457 Langley Ave., Chicago, Ill.

WHEELEHAN, MATTHEW J., 220 Broadway, New York City.

WHITE, JOHN B., 121 East 86th St., New York City.

WHITE, HON. JOHN J., Mayor, Holyoke, Mass.

WHITE, PATRICK, 3436 Indiana Ave., Chicago, Ill.

WILLIAMSON, BERNARDINE F., 162 Daniel Low Terrace, Tompkinsville, S. I.

WILLIS, JOHN, Postmaster, Manchester, N. H.

WILLS, ROBERT, Scranton, Pa.

WISE, JAMES F., 25 Welles Ave., Dorchester, Boston, Mass.

WITHROW, MRS. K. BUCKLEY, 435 West 51st St., New York City.

WOOD, RICHARD H., Refugio, Texas.

(Vice-President of the Society for Texas.)

Woods, John, 489 Broadway, South Boston, Mass.
Wynne, Rev. John J., S.J., 23 East 41st St., New York City.
Young, D. J., 507 Roscoe St., Chicago, Ill.

Honorary Members	5
Life Members	119
Annual Members	1,214
Total	1,338

INDEX